RECONSTRUCTING ͭͭͭ͞ NEW MODEL ARMY

Volume 1

Regimental Lists April 1645 to May 1649

Malcolm Wanklyn

'This is the Century of the Soldier', Falvio Testir, Poet, 1641

Helion & Company

Helion & Company Limited
26 Willow Road
Solihull
West Midlands
B91 1UE
England
Tel. 0121 705 3393
Fax 0121 711 4075
Email: info@helion.co.uk
Website: www.helion.co.uk
Twitter: @helionbooks
Visit our blog http://blog.helion.co.uk/

Designed and typeset by Farr out Publications, Wokingham, Berkshire
Cover designed by Paul Hewitt, Battlefield Design (www.battlefield-design.co.uk)
Printed by Henry Ling Limited, Dorchester, Dorset

Text © Malcolm Wanklyn 2015
Cover artwork by Peter Dennis © Helion & Company Ltd 2015

ISBN 978-1-910777-10-7

British Library Cataloguing-in-Publication Data.
A catalogue record for this book is available from the British Library.

All rights reserved. No part of this publication may be reproduced, stored in a
retrieval system, or transmitted, in any form, or by any means, electronic, mechanical, photocopying,
recording or otherwise, without the express written consent of Helion & Company Limited.

For details of other military history titles published by Helion & Company Limited contact the above
address, or visit our website: http://www.helion.co.uk.

We always welcome receiving book proposals from prospective authors.

Contents

Dedication

To my son Chris and daughter-in-law Melanie without whose hospitality I would have been unable to carry out much of the research for this volume.

Acknowledgements

My thanks to colleagues and friends who have helped me complete this volume: Professor Peter Gaunt, Dr. Stephen Roberts, Charles Singleton, Simon Marsh, and Alan Turton. I am also most grateful to the staff of The National Archives, the Bodleian Library and the British Library, but most particularly to Dr. Joanna Parker, Librarian of Worcester College, Oxford for lending me the library's microfilms of the Clarke Papers during the spring of 2013 when my wife's illness made it impossible for me to visit archives at any distance from Wolverhampton. Finally I thank the History Research Committee of my university for its generous support.

Part I

Introduction

1

Context

My interest in the offices of the New Model Army developed late in life but had a very long period of gestation. As a postgraduate student at the University of Manchester in the mid nineteen-sixties it was my ambition to compile a complete officer list of the regiments which fought in the king's armies in south and central England in the First Civil War. In this I collaborated with Brigadier Peter Young who lent me copious primary sources he had collected over the years, but our efforts fell far short of their objective. The problem was lack of evidence. Only in the case of a handful of regiments like the earl of Northampton's foot and Richard Bagot's horse did we manage to achieve anything approaching a complete listing of the troop and company commanders, but our efforts survive. They can be found amongst Young's manuscripts in the library of the National Army Museum.

For the next thirty-five years I worked as lecturer and head of department in what is now the University of Wolverhampton. My teaching was primarily on local and regional history whilst my research focused on various aspects of the economy of counties bordering Wales, most notably trade on the river Severn.[1] I continued to teach the English Civil War, but it was not until I retired from full-time employment in 2002 that I returned to research and publication. However, it was not long before the king's armies lost their attraction. From the nineteen-seventies onwards Roland Hutton, Peter Edwards and others had published very valuable work on the Royalist war effort, and there was little incentive to plough the same furrow once the strategic dimension had been thoroughly re-appraised in *A Military History of the English Civil War* (Pearson, 2004, with Frank Jones). By 2006 Parliament's armies had become my principal interest, but even so my preoccupations were much the same, generalship and the management of the war at the highest level.

However, whilst undertaking the research for *Warrior Generals* (Yale University Press, 2010), it became glaringly obvious that published material on the officers of the New Model Army was not as fit for purpose as it ought to be. Mistakes in identification had become set in stone through the process of creep by which one historian's speculation becomes another historian's fact. There were also major gaps which could now be filled. Documentary sources inaccessible in the past had been catalogued and some were accessible via the WWW. A full critique, however, had to wait until 'Choosing Officers for the New Model Army, February to April 1645' published in volume 92 of the *Journal of the Society for Army Historical Research* (2014).

Whilst unpicking the statistical constructs of others in 'Choosing Officers', I quickly came to the conclusion that what was missing from the early modern military historian's bookshelves was a listing of the officers who had served in the New Model Army, which was fully referenced and indexed, and which drew on a more extensive set of source materials. My first thoughts were that this should be the

---

1 The electronic database of trade on the river Severn 1565-1765 created by the Port Book Programme is stored in the ESRC data archive at the University of Essex. It is still being extensively used by research students and family historians.

work of a research team on similar lines to the one I had led during the nineteen eighties and nineties which produced the database of trade on the Severn, but the draft research proposal I sent to colleagues in other universities for their comments was too ambitious. Unsurprisingly it was not greeted with much enthusiasm. The fall-back position was a slimmed down version focusing on the captains and above which I might be able to complete on my own, but the prospect of working systematically through the Commonwealth Exchequer papers in the National Archives at seventy years of age was daunting in the extreme. However, the experience I had had of appraising and marshalling data on trade, agriculture and industry in the counties bordering Wales, and displaying it in tabular form, gave me the courage to start.

It goes without question that I was extremely fortunate in the work of my predecessor. My greatest debt is to Sir Charles Firth and Godfrey Davies for their two-volume regimental history of the New Model Army, unjustly disparaged in works published since.[2] Their principal source was the papers of William Clarke, the secretary first to Sir Thomas Fairfax, the commander of the New Model Army between 1645 and 1650, and then to successive army commanders in Scotland. These are extremely rich for the four and a half years from the lead-up to the first Army coup against Parliament in the spring of 1647 to the campaign which ended with the battle of Worcester in September 1651, but otherwise they are not that informative, They contain little material on the first two years of the army's existence, and for all but the last eighteen months of the sixteen-fifties they focus almost exclusively on the regiments quartered in Scotland. There is very little on those quartered in England post 1649 and nothing of any consequence on the army in Ireland. Firth and Davies were aware of the riches to be found in the Commonwealth Exchequer Papers in what was then the Public Record Office. They also knew that the material they contained would complement that in the Clarke Papers, but they faced problems of access and much of the archive was uncatalogued. They did, however, conduct sporadic forays into the SP28s returning with some valuable nuggets of information and some pointers to richer seams they were unable to exploit.[3]

My second debt is to the work of Lawrence Spring on the armies of the earl of Manchester and Sir William Waller, which gave me clues as to the early military careers of quite a number of the captains and above who served in the New Model Army.[4] Unlike Firth and Davies Spring has been through the SP28 and also the E121 series in the National Archives from end to end, but a serious deficiency in his published work is imprecise referencing. The series and box or volume number is frequently cited but never the piece or folio number. In addition Spring's observations on the New Model Army careers of officers who had served under Manchester and Waller are not to be relied upon. This does not, however, detract from the giant contribution he has made towards an understanding of the regimental histories of two of the New Model Army's predecessors.

There is no such coverage in print for the third army which supplied officers for the New Model, but Alan Turton's *The Chief Strength of the Army: Essex's Horse 1642-5* (Southend-on-Sea) has been a most useful source for the comparatively few cavalry officers who were commissioned by Essex and then went on to serve under Sir Thomas Fairfax. Peachey and Turton's less systematic account of Essex's infantry regiments is not so valuable for discovering who obtained a place in the New Model and who did not, but it does include a list of the company commanders for May 1644 compiled from pay warrants in SP28.[5] To complement their work I have compiled a listing of the earl's company and troop

2   Firth and Davies, *The Regimental History of Cromwell's Armies* (2 vols. Oxford, 1940). For disparaging comments, see R. Temple, 'The Original Officer List of the New Model Army', *Bulletin of the Institute of Historical Research* lix (1986), pp. 51, 52; M. Kishlansky, *The Rise of the New Model Army* (Cambridge, 1979), p. 336.

3   See, for example, their comments on the regiments of Phillip Skippon and Sir Arthur Haselrig which garrisoned Newcastle in the late 1640s. These draw on material in The National Archives (TNA), SP 28/133 pts. iii and iv.

4   L. Spring, *The Regiments of the Eastern Association* (Spring i) and *Waller's Army: The Regiments of Sir William Waller's Southern Association* (Spring ii). The first was published in Bristol in 1998, the second by the Pike and Shot Society in 2007.

5   S. Peachey and A. Turton, *Old Robin's Foot* (Southend-on-Sea, 1997).

commanders for early April 1645 just prior to his army being dismembered. This is to be found in in Appendix I.

Various studies have sought to update *The Regimental History*. Barry Denton's aim in *Cromwell's Soldiers: The Moulding of the New Model Army* (2005) was to provide regimental lists, but only for the first two years of the army's existence. His account of the company and troop commanders is the best that could have been achieved with the sources at his disposal and is a real advance on the work of Firth and Davies.

A narrower study still is Robert G.K. Temple's article 'The Original Officer List of the New Model Army', which transcribed two important documents in the House of Lords archives, the list of company and troop commanders for the New Model submitted by Fairfax to Parliament in late February 1645, and the changes to the document proposed by the House of Lords which were subsequently withdrawn. I have little criticism to make of his transcriptions.[6] However, he incorrectly identified quite a number of individual officers.[7] To make matters worse, the process he used to identify radical officers is logically flawed.[8] Sadly Ian Gentles relied heavily on Temple's article for information about the military careers of the officers serving in the New Model in the period 1645-7. This, however, is a minor blemish in what is otherwise an excellent corpus of work on the New Model Army which provided me with many leads in the early stages of my research.[9] Finally, I need to mention Mark Kishlansky. His study of the New Model is political rather than military history.[10] As a result my work overlaps only slightly with his, but I am very grateful for his critique of the extent of radicalism in the New Model before 1647 which I mistrusted at first but subsequently came to respect.

Having critiqued the work of others, I must make it very plain that my depiction of the officer corps of the New Model Army is neither comprehensive nor necessarily accurate in every detail. There are quite a number of gaps in knowledge. There are also some uncertainties regarding the timing of appointments and resignations/expulsions, but I hope that the footnotes provide sufficient information for readers to be able to distinguish between statements that are speculative and those that are based on first class documentary evidence. I do not doubt that, like my predecessors, I have made mistakes both in misinterpreting what I have read and in giving too much weight to sources which are in sufficiently robust. But I hope that the regimental listings will have lifted forever the obscurity surrounding the officer corps of the New Model Army in its first two year of existence remarked on by Gentles.[11] I also hope that in time this volume and its companion will provide a framework for the writing of complete life stories of the officers of the New Model Army on the lines of such multi-volumed works as the *Dictionary of Labour Biography*.

---

6   House of Lords Record Office (HLRO), Main Papers, 10 March 1645.

7   Temple, 'Original List', pp. 50-77.

8   M. Wanklyn, 'Choosing Officers for the New Model Army, February to May 1645', *Journal of the Society for Army Historical Research* 92 (2014), pp. 113-14, 124.

9   I. Gentles, *The New Model Army in England, Ireland and Scotland 1645-1653* (Oxford, 1992); I. Gentles, 'The Choosing of Officers for the New Model Army', *Bulletin of the Institute for Historical Research* 64 (1994); I. Gentles, 'The New Model Officer Corps in 1647: a Collective Portrait', *Social History* 22 (1997).

10 Kishlansky, *Rise of the New Model Army*.

11 ' The New Model Army Officer Corps', p. 131.

2

The Listings of the Commanders of Troops and Companies

Preamble and Scope

I began my work on the New Model Army with the focus firmly on the troop and company commanders who were in post between April 1645 and December 1646, my principal aim at the time being to investigate the overlap of the officer corps of New Model with those of the armies with which Parliament had fought the king during the first two years of the Civil War. My other concerns were to correct the errors in Temple's article and to supply the officers' names that were missing from *The Regimental History of Cromwell's Army*. However, subsequently I became as interested in the impact on the officer corps of the coups against Parliament carried out by the New Model in June/August 1647 and December 1648. I therefore decided to extend the coverage to June 1650, the date on which Sir Thomas Fairfax resigned as lord general. This coincided with a massive increase in the number of regiments as Oliver Cromwell, the army's new commander-in-chief, prepared an expeditionary force for a pre-emptive invasion of Scotland. His orders were to remove Charles Stuart, the son of the executed King Charles I, who the Scottish elites had proclaimed as their new king, and who made no secret of his intention of seizing the throne of England by force.

At the time I thought that there would be insufficient primary source material to continue listing company and troop commanders beyond June 1650. There had been a tailing off in the quantity of information in the Commonwealth Exchequer Papers as a new system of delivering pay to the cavalry regiments took hold from the end of 1647 onwards. This gap had been more than compensated for by volumes 67 and 69 of the Clarke Papers, which from 16 June 1647 provided a good record of commissions issued by General Fairfax for 23 of the 24 original New Model Army regiments, but entries came to an abrupt end on the very day of his resignation.[1]

It was not until I began to working on the troop and company commanders for the period between the second Army coup and Fairfax's departure that I began to see that continuing the regimental listings into the sixteen-fifties was not impossible. The tipping point was the wealth of documentary material relating to the army of occupation in Ireland to be found in the Commonwealth Exchequer papers. In August 1649 five old New Model Army infantry and three old New Model cavalry regiments had landed at Dublin. There they became the nucleus of a much larger army which conquered the country and then held its inhabitants down by force in the face of much guerrilla activity. I have no hesitation in describing it as an army of occupation which included horse and foot raised by the Protestant settlers in

---

1   These are mainly to be found in the library of Worcester College, Oxford but there are stray volumes elsewhere in the United Kingdom.

Ireland; regiments raised in England and shipped over in penny numbers from 1646 onwards; and yet more regiments which had arrived in Ireland since 1649. All came under the aegis of the New Model, and much to my surprise the practice by which successive commanders-in-chief in Ireland sent copies of the pay warrants they had issued to the Commonwealth government in London continued until 1654.

For the years1655 and 1656 a different type of documentary material would enable me to continue tracing the military careers of the company and troop commanders. The lessening of guerrilla activity made it possible for the government to disband many formations stationed there. Their pay arrears and the pay arrears of the regiments that continued in service were settled by the transfer into the officers' ownership of land confiscated from the Irish. The process yielded names in abundance which, combined with material concerning the army of occupation in Scotland amongst the Clarke Papers, would enable me to identify the many signatures appended to petitions and other documents dating from the period 1654-9. However, if regimental listings for the sixteen fifties were to be added to those of the sixteen-forties, the result would be a very large book indeed, but even so there did not seem to be quite enough material for one volume on 1649-1650 and another on 1650-1660.

What resolved the matter was the large amount of material concerning commissioned officers below the rank of captain in the E 121 series in particular which provided a good but not complete record of pay arrears due for the period up to the end of June 1649. Incorporating this into the regimental listings would have been a huge task given that in the New Model Army there were two junior commissioned officers per company of foot and three per troop of horse, but the value of putting something of this nature on record was obvious for an understanding of the make-up of the officer corps of the late sixteen-fifties. A pilot study of newcomers to the rank of captain in the purge of the army which followed the fall of the Protectorate in May 1659 had revealed quite a number of men who had been junior commissioned officers in the late sixteen-forties.

To have published as many listings of junior officers as troop and company commanders would have made for a very large publication, but the patchy nature of the source material for the sixteen-fifties meant that the number of listings of junior commissioned officers must necessarily be less numerous. The E 121 series contained little information later than the summer of 1649, whilst the weekly journals which dominate the Thomason Tracts after 1651 rarely give the names of junior officers. Even information concerning junior officers in the army in Ireland was meagre, as it was normally company and troop commanders who signed for their men's pay. In the event only three listings of junior officers by regiment were worth working on, two for the late sixteen forties to be published in this volume and one for 1659 a shortened version of which is to be published in volume two. In years to come when a much wider range of sources becomes available on line additional listings of junior officers which do not contain more gaps than facts may become practicable, but age alone will ensure that compiling them will be the work of others.

Structure

I knew from the start that presenting information about the military careers of the officers of the New Model in as user-friendly a manner as possible would not be served by hundreds of short biographies organised alphabetically. Instead the regiment must form the unit in which the data was displayed with the matrix being supplied by the army as established by Parliamentary ordinance in February 1645.[2]

The only previous attempt to reconstruct the officer corps of the New Model Army across the whole of its existence had been that made by Firth and Davies in the nineteen-thirties. The regiment also provided their basic unit of analysis with a chapter being devoted to every one of the 99 they chose to include. The result was a two volume work containing well over 700 pages of text. A publication organised in the same way eighty years later would be at least twice, if not three times as long. That was

---

2   LJ vii, p. 204.

something I had neither the wish nor indeed the stamina to undertake. What I had in mind was a work of reference, and for that continuous prose was not the most effective medium.

My approach in both volumes has been to condense the data into tables which can be likened to snapshots of the entire army. The term I will use throughout for such snapshots is listings. In the case of the company and troop commanders these depict the army at a specific point in time, but with the junior commissioned officers this is impossible for reasons outlined in Chapter Three.

It may seem bizarre that the six snapshots in the part of the volume devoted to troop and company commanders are not set out at regular intervals, but there is good reason. The dates were chosen either because they marked the end of a period during which a significant movement into and out of the army had taken place, or because a document or set of documents provided very full information about the composition of the officer corps at that point in time. However, should anybody wish to produce a snapshot of the officer corps at a different date, the listings on either side of it will provide sufficient information for the task to be easily accomplished.

The dates and my reasons for choosing them are as follows:

1. Early April 1645. This snapshot is essentially Fairfax's list of officers as presented to Parliament in late February, modified by the House of Commons and then approved by both Houses of Parliament. As such it was entered into the Lords Journal on 18 March,[3] but I have corrected some of the misspellings and removed Captain Chute who was discovered to be dead. The listing stops short of second week in April when there was a flood of withdrawals.

2. Early May 1645. Some but by no means all of the officers who refused to take up the positions they had been offered were Scots who were almost certainly acting on the instructions of their government which was unhappy at the whole selection process and with the religious complexion of the New Model Army officer corps. By the first week in May the new officers were very largely in place, though the process of re-ordering did not end until the departure of Colonel Bartholomew Vermuyden from the 6th regiment of horse a month later.

3. Early December 1646. *Anglia Rediviva,* the blow-by-blow account of the New Model Army's campaigns written by Joshua Sprigg, Fairfax's chaplain, and published in London early in 1647, is the principal source for the third listing. In an appendix he appeared to have noted down all the company and troop commanders in post in April 1645 and all the changes that had taken place since.[4] Firth and Davies were mistaken, however, in regarding it as a complete listing of the company and troop commanders for the first eighteen months of the New Model Army's existence.[5] Sprigg's listing is clearly incomplete as some of the infantry regiments have less than their full quota of company commanders.[6] Further investigation has also shown that quite a number of captains who took up their commissions in April 1645 but were not in the army for whatever reason by July of that year are missing, and also the names of some who took command of troops and companies during those three months but had left the army before December 1646.

4. 31 May 1647. Petitions from the army supporting or condemning agitation over soldiers' grievances provide valuable information about troop and company commanders and their junior officers for the period from late March to late May. The result is an almost complete record of the make-up of the commissioned officers in the New Model immediately before the first Army coup. The petitions also provide a useful guide to the ranks held by junior officers who were to be promoted as a result of the cataclysmic events of June and July.

5. 31 August 1647 All the commissioned officers who had sided with Parliament rather than with the army leadership during the first Army coup and been cashiered, or who had decided that

---

3   Journals of the House of Lords (LJ) vii, pp. 278-9.

4   I have assumed that a period of six weeks or so elapsed between the end of data collection and publication.

5   Firth and Davies, *Regimental History* (F. and D.), i, pp. 58,82, 102-3, 331, 348.

6   The 10th and the 12th regiments had only six captains each instead of seven and the regiments of Herbert and Rainborough only four.

they no longer wished to serve in the New Model, had been replaced by the end of August. The names of the new officers can be found in volume 67 of the Clarke Manuscripts, which purports to list all the commissions issued between 1647 and June 1650. This is not so. It does not provide a complete record of such commissions and the entries are not completely accurate. Also the so-called commissions' book provides few dates. As a result with most regiments it is impossible to determine when the commissions issued between June and August 1647 end and when those issued at a later date begin. Other sources also suggest that the clerk stopped making entries in the autumn of 1647 and did not take up his pen again until June 1649.[7] Moreover, the later entries are clearly not an official register updated on a daily or weekly basis. Instead the clerk seems to have relied on the memory of informants of whom Sir Thomas was probably the most important. Unsurprisingly he did not learn of all the appointments and promotions that had taken place, whilst jottings on the first page show that the volume is incomplete, as they are reminders of commissions that needed to be recorded in the main body of the work.

6. 10 May 1649. The final date is not tied to a particular source or indeed to a particular event,[8] but it is important to supply a record of the army as it was just before the great expansion that was to come about as the New Model Army's remit changed from fighting an English Civil War to fighting a war in and against Ireland and Scotland. Another consideration in choosing early May was that it enabled me to present the officer corps as it was before the army could react to the prospect of fighting in Ireland, which took the form of mutinies in the ranks and some officers deciding that they did not want to serve overseas. As a result an entire regiment of cavalry was disbanded, another comprehensively re-organised, whilst a third lost half its troop commanders. This was followed soon afterwards by a new procedure which was to become commonplace in the sixteen-fifties, namely units or levies from existing regiments being forced to provide cadres of experienced officers and men for regiments that had been newly commissioned.

Conventions Used in the Listings

Headings
For reasons of convenience I have adopted the numbers given to the regiments of horse and foot in the list that Sir Thomas Fairfax submitted to Parliament for its approval on 27 February 1645[9]. This has no real justification in a historical sense as the evidence that numbers were used at the time is very slim indeed, but it is a useful editorial device. For a discussion of numbering of regiments in the New Model Army, see chapter 7.

Column Two
In the spelling of officers' surnames a single form is used if there are many variants eg. Disbrowe, Haselrig, Rainborough. If there are only two spellings and they occur frequently, both are given when the officer is first mentioned but only one thereafter.

In the main body of the work officers' names are bolded if there is some doubt as to whether they were still in the regiment at the time of the listing. In Appendix I a different convention applies to the use of bolding. This is explained in the introductory paragraph.

When a question mark follows an officer's name, it indicates that he may not yet have attained such a rank in the regiment. A double question mark indicates that there is some doubt as to whether he served in the regiment at that rank or indeed at all.

---

7 Amongst the new cavalry officers whose commissions were not recorded were Captains Barker, Green and Peverill.
8 I had originally chosen February 1649 as it would provide a record of the resignations following the trial and execution of the king, but in terms of change in the New Model Army officer corps this was a non-event. Only Captain William Cecil, son of the earl of Salisbury, seems to have resigned between December 1648 and March 1649. For this, see below p. 96.
9 Journals of the House of Commons (CJ) iv, pp. 63-4.

A question mark in front of an officer's Christian name means that it may not be correct.

Officers named in the concluding lines of some regimental lists as probables are men known to have held captain's or field officer's rank in the regiment at a later date.

In the fourth listing the symbol * indicates an officer who signed the pledge of loyalty to Parliament dated by Thomason as 27 May. The symbol + indicates that the officer put his name to the Vindication of April 1647 challenging the criticisms Parliament had made of the way in which the army had presented its grievances.[10]

The symbol XXX used in both column two and column 3 indicates uncertainty ranging from 'nothing at all known' to 'there is a strong probability that'. The reader will be able to gauge the degree of uncertainty by looking at the accompanying footnote.

The vertical line is used at the end of each entry in column three and also to separate information concerning an officer's becoming a company or troop commander from that concerning his leaving.

Abbreviations used in the Listings[11]

1. Armies

E.A.	Eastern Association
L.G.	Lord General the Earl of Essex's
N.	Northern
N.M.	New Model
W.	Sir William Waller's

2. Officers

Capt.	Captain
Capt. Lt.	The lieutenant commanding the colonel's company or troop
c.	circa
co.	company
Col.	Full Colonel
Cor.	Cornet
D	Died
Dr.	Dragoons
Ens.	Ensign
F.	Foot
garr.	garrison
gov.	governor
H.	Horse
Lt. Col.	Lieutenant Colonel
Lt.	Lieutenant
prob.	probably
X	killed or mortally wounded.

Definitions

Battalion – this word was not in common use in the British Wars of the sixteen-forties and fifties, but it is a convenient descriptor for a regiment of foot which was divided in two for a long period of time. Several examples of divided regiments are to be found in volume two, but in this volume the term occurs only in footnotes.

Brigade – A term that was frequently applied to an assemblage of regiments of horse and foot amounting

---

10   British Library (BL), Thomason Tracts E 385 (19).

11   The only abbreviation I have used in the footnotes is a short hand form of dating when the month as well as the year is given. Thus September 1649 appears as 9/49.

in size to that of a small army. The term was also applied to what had earlier been described as a tertio – a number of infantry regiments brigaded together on the battlefield – and to *ad hoc* formations charged with besieging an enemy town or garrison.

Dragoons – These were soldiers who went on campaign on horseback but who usually fought on foot. The New Model Army regiment commanded by John Okey was made up of troops like a cavalry regiment but there were ten of these, not six. In the early 1650s a more flexible arrangement was introduced, which is not surprising as troops of dragoons often operated individually rather than as a regimental formation. In 1645 and later dragoons were armed with swords and short-barrelled firelock muskets.

Field Officer – a collective term for lieutenant colonels and majors.

Reformado – an officer whose regiment had been destroyed or disbanded but who chose to continue in service in another unit as a volunteer on a much reduced salary.

Regiment of foot – in the New Model Army an infantry regiment comprised ten companies of foot normally a hundred strong plus commissioned and non-commissioned officers. Seven of the companies would be commanded by captains, two by the field officers (major and lieutenant colonel) and one, the colonel's company, by a captain lieutenant. Despite what others have written, there is now no doubt whatsoever that foot soldiers were armed with muskets and pikes in the ratio of two to one.

Regiment of cavalry – in the New Model army a regiment comprised six troops, each a hundred strong plus officers. Four were commanded by captains, one by a major and one (the colonel's) by a captain lieutenant. All the New Model Army cavalry troopers were harquebusiers armed with a sword and a pair of long-barrelled pistols.

3

The Listings of Junior Commissioned Officers

Introduction

As explained above, the task of establishing the names and regiments of junior commissioned officers in the New Model Army is a necessary one for making sense of the military careers of company and troop commanders serving in the mid and late sixteen-fifties. The sources, however, are not identical to those used for constructing the listings of troop and company commanders.

In the case of junior officers in cavalry regiments, an important source for the period between the summer of 1645 and the summer of 1647 is Sir Arthur Haselrig's accounts for supplying horses to the army[1]. However, they have to be used with caution. Receipts for large numbers of animals were signed roughly equally by troop commanders and more junior officers, but on occasions there is little doubt that an officer from another troop was taking responsibility. Thus Lieutenant William Covell, who served under Major Disbrowe in Sir Thomas Fairfax's regiment and signed for horses for Disbrowe's troop, also signed for horses for Captain Evanson's troop in Colonel Whalley's regiment. Of a similar nature and covering almost the same period are the receipts for arms issued by the Ordnance Office.[2] Surprisingly the latter very rarely supply the names of junior officers in the infantry regiments.

More productive of names are the pay warrants in the Commonwealth Exchequer Papers, which in the case of the cavalry were issued to individual troops of horse rather than to whole regiments as was the practice with the infantry. However, it was the practice of many troop commanders to employ their clerk rather than a junior officer to sign on their behalf. Sadly the clerk's rank is rarely given, but there is not much doubt that quite a number were non-commissioned officers.[3]

A third important source is the claims for pay arrears for the period 1642 to mid 1649, which are to be found primarily in the E 121 series. These are most important for linking junior officers to regiments and to their troop and company commanders, but they give little help with dating. It is, however, normally possible to work out whether the arrears being claimed were for service in the New Model Army, in one of its predecessors, or in a provincial regiment. Much can also be learned about the length of a junior officer's time in the New Model by cross-referencing with the service record of his superior officers as most had served under more than one.

Finally, there is the commissions' book in the Clarke Papers. Some of the gaps in its coverage for the

---

1   TNA, SP 140/7.

2   Ibid, WO 55/1647; William Salt Library, Stafford (W. Salt Library), SMS 463.

3   Very occasionally responsibility for signinf for the pay was given to people with no connection with the regiment such as retired officers, officers from other units, and reformadoes.

period from late 1648 to June 1650 can be filled in the case of junior commissioned officers by reference to a companion volume.[4]

Scope and Structure

There are very few surviving comprehensive or near-comprehensive lists of the junior officers in a regiment by troop or company for the period 1645-50. However, a comparison between data in the National Archives sources mentioned above with the the signatures to petitions and declarations issued in the three months prior to the first Army coup of June/July 1647 make it possible to construct something close to a complete listing for March to May of that year. This has been brought together in the first snapshot.

Nothing so complete is possible until the very end of the sixteen-fifties when the House of Commons issued new commissions to army officers after the collapse of the Protectorate,[5] but volumes in the Clarke Papers at Worcester College, Oxford combined with the E 121 series in the National Archives and a number of petitions dating from the time of the second Army coup make it possible to identify many of the junior officers who were in service between June 1647 and June 1650. Nothing that ambitious can be achieved for the period April 1645 to May 1647. Maddeningly the copious lists of junior officers in the Commonwealth Exchequer papers for April 1645 only give the names of those who were discharged, not those who took service in the New Model Army. However, in Appendix V I have collected together the names of junior officers who served in the New Model but were no longer in post in the spring of 1647, the usual reason for their departure being promotion or death.

Conventions

These are very substantially the same as in the listings of company and troop commanders. The differences are as follows:

1. If the sole evidence of an officer's rank and company or troop is a claim for pay arrears which is not dated or for which the date cannot be inferred, his name has been bolded and only entered in one of the listings.
2. Junior officers have been entered into the regimental lists in the troops and companies in which they served, but troop or company commander often changed during the second time period.[6] In such circumstances several names may appear in the first column, but care has been taken to ensure that junior officers are associated with the man under whom they served, not with his predecessor or successor.
3. In the unplaced sections of the regimental lists, officers whose names appear in the same line did not necessarily serve in the same troop or company.
4. XXX is not used to draw the reader's attention to an absence of information about an officer's military career. This is indicated by a blank space. However, XXX is used where a first name is not known or where an officer's name is known to be missing.
5. References are not given if they have already been provided in the listings of troop and company commanders as, for example, in the case of captain lieutenants.

---

4   Worc. College, Clarke Mss 67 and 69. For a discussion of the gaps, see above p. 15.
5   CJ vii, pp. 529-727 passim; CSPD 1658-9, pp. 376-393, passim; ibid 1659-60, pp. 3-326, passim.
6   The reader is referred to the earlier part of the book for full information about such changes.

Part II

Some Observations on the Regimental Lists

4

The Army Origins of the Senior Commissioned Officers

It was the failure of the armies commanded by the earls of Essex and Manchester and Sir William Waller to win a decisive victory over the king's forces after over two years of fighting that caused Parliament to rethink the way in which the war was being conducted. The result was the New Model Army established by legislation passed between February and April 1645. It combined elements from the three armies into one, and it also obliged all three generals to hand in their commissions.[1]

Sir Thomas Fairfax, the new commander-in-chief, had been lieutenant general of cavalry to his father Lord Fairfax who commanded Parliament's Army of the North. The younger Fairfax had victories at Wakefield, Winceby, Nantwich and Selby to his credit and, although his wing was routed at the battle of Marston Moor, he had displayed remarkable personal bravery and resilience. Instead of quitting the battlefield, he bravely rode through the royalist ranks to join the Eastern Association and Scottish forces on the other wing which, having got the better of the formations facing them in the line of battle, were turning on the enemy centre and winning the battle. Young Fairfax and his father were also held in great respect for their Fabian grand tactics, which enabled them first to retain a presence in the north when the balance of resources was stacked against them, and then to seize much of Yorkshire and Lincolnshire when it tipped in their favour early in 1644 after the Scottish government had entered the war in support of Parliament.[2]

Fairfax's army according to the New Model, as authorised by an ordinance passed on 17 February 1645, was to contain far fewer units than its three predecessors combined, and they were to be more uniform. There were to be 24 regiments instead of at least 45. The regiments were also to be more uniform with 10 companies per infantry regiment and 6 troops per cavalry regiment, whilst the regiment of dragoons was to have 10 troops.[3]

Sir Thomas's first task on arriving in London the day after the ordinance became law was to produce the list of colonels, lieutenant colonels, majors and captains to serve in the new army, almost 200 names

---

1   By the so-called Self-Denying Ordinance MPs and peers were to give up their commands in the armed forces and were to return to the House of Lords in the case of Essex and Manchester and to the Commons in the case of Sir William Waller. All three were to play an active role in the Committee of Both Kingdoms, which acted as the war cabinet for the coalition fighting the king and as well as ensuring that the forces in the field were supplied with the means of conducting the war it determined strategy: M. Wanklyn and F. Jones, *A Military History of the English Civil War* (2004), pp. 231=2, 366-7, 239-40.

2   S. Carpenter, *Military Leadership in the British Civil Wars* (2005), pp. 60-89; A. Hopper, *Black Tom: Sir Thomas Fairfax and the English Revolution* (Manchester, 2007), pp. 41-8. Lord Fairfax's army was not remodelled until later in 1645, but as MP for Yorkshire he was to have resigned by the middle of May 1645 in accordance with the provisions of the Self-Denying Ordinance. However, he continued to run the army until the appointment of Colonel Sydenham Poyntz as his successor in June.

3   Manchester's army in comparison had had cavalry regiments consisting of between 4 and 14 troops and one infantry regiment with 19 companies: TNA, SP 28/28 pt iii, unfol.; F. and D. i, pp. 42-4; LJ vii, pp. 206-9.

in total, and this required the approval of the House of Commons and the House of Lords. Although the ordinance allowed him to pick and choose from all the armed forces in England, Fairfax confined himself for the moment to the armies of Essex, Manchester and Waller, but this was a monumental task in itself, as in the three southern armies alone the number of officers holding the rank of captain or above was almost twice as many as those required for the New Model. Nevertheless within less than ten days he had presented Parliament with the names of those he wished to re-employ and the regiments in which they were to serve.

The debates in the House of Commons were lengthy and contentious, but in the end the MPs made only five changes to Fairfax's nominees. The peers, however, deleted, demoted or otherwise reassigned about 30 per cent of them.[4] They also recommended replacements, but the Lower House was adamant. The new campaigning season was fast approaching. Any delay would allow the king's forces to capitalise on the strategic advantage they had gained in the autumn. Further debate was therefore potentially dangerous. The Lords therefore gave way.[5] The list of officers copied into the journal of the House of Lords amongst the entries for 18 March was thus substantially the same as the one that Fairfax had presented to Parliament three weeks earlier, but between mid-March and the start of the campaign season on 30 April the changes were substantial, as can be seen by comparing listings one and two.[6]

Most of the company and troop commanders chosen to serve in the New Model Army regiments had fought together in the same regiment in one or other of its predecessors, but the links between the old and the new cited by Firth and Davies require some modification. In the first place it is very clear that Fairfax's own regiment, the first regiment of foot, was much more closely identified with Manchester's army than with Essex's.[7] In the listing of 27 February 1645 eight of the nine company commanders had served in the former, whilst the ninth was almost certainly not serving under the old lord general in the winter and early spring of 1644-45.[8] The changes that took place during March and April did not change the overall pattern. Admittedly one of Essex's captains, Fulk Muskett, was granted the vacant tenth place, but neither of the officers who replaced two of Fairfax's original nominees can be linked to Essex's army. Thomas Highfield, who took over the company initially allocated to Captain Cooke, has yet to be identified, whilst Francis White, Robert Johnston's successor, had been his lieutenant in the army of the Eastern Association.[9]

Two of Manchester's infantry regiments joined the New Model as the 10th and the 12th regiments of foot with their company commanders almost unchanged, but the other two drew on number of sources. The 4th, which had been Major General Crawford's regiment, had had at least five Scottish company commanders.[10] These were not re-appointed but their replacements were all from the Eastern Association army, either captains from James Hobart's disbanded regiment, or else from Manchester's own regiment of foot. The 7th regiment of foot, on the other hand, was a complete dog's breakfast. Originally intended for Colonel Ayloffe of the Abingdon garrison, it was now commanded by Thomas Rainborough, a colonel in the Eastern Association but not in Manchester's field army. The 7th contained none of the company commanders of Rainborough's old regiment, which remained in the north Midlands under Colonel Henry Gray's command.[11] In May 1645 three of the company commanders were from Ayloffe's regiment, three from other regiments in Manchester's army, whilst two had served in Essex's army. The

---

4   CJ iv, pp. 64-6.

5   LJ vii, p. 277. I prefer the Lords' own reason for backing down stated here to Gentles's that they were forced to give way because the merchants of London threatened not to lend money for the war effort if the list was not approved in its entirety: *New Model Army*, p. 19. Like other reports by the agents of foreign powers this French source contained rumours that were both false and true.

6   The nature of these changes has been discussed at length elsewhere: Wanklyn, 'Choosing Officers', pp. 109-25.

7   *The Regimental History*, p. 317.The same is also true of the rank and file as shown by their claims for arrears of pay in the TNA, E 121 series, but this lies outside the compass of the present volume..

8   See p. 43 below.

9   Many of the statements that follow are unreferenced because the reference can be found in listings one and two.

10 Spring i, pp. 11-15; TNA, SP 28/27, fo. 262.; ibid, SP 28/35, fos. 367-8; .ibid, SP 28/145, fos. 420-9.

11 See below p. 46 and CJ iv, p. 109.

unit or units in which the lieutenant colonel and the captain lieutenant had previously served are not yet known.

The company commanders of both the regiments of foot whose roots lay in Waller's army have been seen as transferring *en bloc* into the New Model Army.[12] This is certainly true of Holbourne's, later the 3rd regiment of foot, but not necessarily of the Kentish regiment commanded by Ralph Weldon, which became the 8th. The names of his officers do not appear in either Fairfax's original army list or in the amended version printed in the Lords Journal. Instead they derive from the listing in Sprigg's *Anglia Rediviva* written well over a year later the shortcomings of which have been discussed above, and only seven can be found in the ledger recording payments to the Kentish regiment between March 1644 and January 1645. One of the three not named is known to have been a company commander by August 1645, but the other two whose antecedents cannot yet be traced could have been commissioned at any time between February 1645 and December 1646. Given the casualties in other regiments like Fortescue's and Ingoldsby's, which like Weldon's were involved in the defence of Taunton in May/June 1645 and in the storming of Bristol in September, there is a very good chance that one at least of the three captains had not been a company commander in April when the army set out on campaign.

Turning to the cavalry Sir Robert Pye's regiment of horse, described as being from Essex's army, was nothing of the sort. Pye had been a colonel of horse under Essex but he was a later insertion into the officer list. Fairfax had intended the regiment to be commanded by Nathaniel Rich, formerly major in the earl of Manchester's regiment of horse, but the House of Commons would have none of it. Pye it had to be, but all his troop commanders were from Manchester's army as were the men who fought under them. The junior officers and rank-and-file of Pye's own troop, however, were largely from Essex's army.[13]

An anomaly of a different kind is provided by William Bough who was commissioned as captain in the 7th regiment of horse under Colonel Algernon Sidney. Sidney had commanded Manchester's regiment of horse and five of his six troop commanders had served under him together with most of their men. . Firth and Davies left the antecedents of the sixth troop in the air, but it is now known that Bough had been captain lieutenant of Sir William Waller's troop of horse, and that he brought many of his junior officers and troopers with him into the New Model.[14]

With Sir Arthur Haselrig's regiment of horse, which became the 2nd regiment of horse in the New Model Army, it is a different story. This may have had as many as ten troops when it was in Waller's army.[15] It therefore would have lost at least four troop commanders in April 1645, but most were found places in other regiments. John Okey, Haselrig's major, became colonel of the New Model Army's regiment of dragoons, whilst Captains Pennyfather and Barry initially found places in the 11th regiment of horse whose first colonel was Sir Michael Livesey who had commanded it in Waller's army.[16] James Hopton chose to serve as major and then colonel of a regiment of horse, probably in the Welsh borders under Major General Massey's command, and then in the lifeguard of Lord Lisle, Lieutenant of Ireland. He entered the New Model in 1649 or thereabouts as adjutant general of horse.[17]

The regiment of dragoons was born out of a more complex coming together of disparate elements. Fairfax's initial list of February 1645 was an eclectic mix of officers some of whom had fought in cavalry regiments and some as dragoons. Four troop commanders were from Waller's army and three from Manchester's whilst John Farmer was a former cavalry captain in Essex's army whose troop was apparently disbanded early in 1644. The other two have yet to be certainly identified, but by the time the army set out on campaign there had been very considerable changes. Waller's regiment of dragoons

---

12 F. and D.

13 CJ vii, pp. 65, 66; TNA, E 121/1/1/unnumbered, entries 132-53.

14 Ibid, E 121/2/11/19, fos. 170-229.

15 This can be seen from Lawrence Spring's listing of Haselrig's captains in 1644 in *Waller's Army*, pp. 63-6.

16 See below p. 54

17 TNA, SP 28/289/17,entry 2; ibid, SP28/50, fo. 306; ibid, SP 28/73, fo. 63.

now provided six troop commanders and Manchester's three with Captain Farmer commanding the tenth troop.[18]

A more wide-ranging discussion of the degree of officer continuity in formations moved from the old armies to the New Model is to be found in my article published in volume 92 of the *Journal for Army Historical Research* (2014), but the fate of regiments of which Essex, Manchester and Waller had been colonels is worthy of additional comment. Eight out of eleven troop commanders in Manchester's regiment of horse found a place in either the 7th or the 8th regiment of horse in the New Model Army. However, to his disgust Waller's cavalry regiment was not chosen, Haselrig's and Livesey's being preferred.[19] Essex's regiment did not fare quite as badly. Like Waller's it did not form a discrete unit in Fairfax's army, but four of its eight troop commanders were found places as troop commanders in the New Model compared with only three out of ten or so in the case of Waller's.[20]

Waller's regiment of foot provided no company commanders for the New Model Army because it had to all intents and purposes ceased to exist in the autumn of 1644 some companies having been mounted and turned into dragoons whilst the rest were used to reinforce Parliament's garrisons in the south coast ports.[21] Essex's regiment certainly did exist, but it had had a chequered career during 1644 performing badly during the battle of Lostwithiel in early September but very well at the Second Battle of Newbury seven weeks later. Unlike several of the old lord general's regiments of foot it did not find its way into the New Model, but four of its company commanders did. Interestingly two, possibly three, had been commissioned after Lostwithiel.[22] Five captains from Manchester's regiment joined Fairfax's regiment of foot together with many of their men and two more found places elsewhere. This, however, gives a false impression of continuity as there were 18 companies in the regiment in January 1645.[23] The contrast with the experience of the former officers of Montagu's and Pickering's regiments mentioned above reinforces the point that Manchester's were under a cloud, possibly because of their loyalty to the earl, who had been the main scapegoat for the military failures of the latter half of 1644.

Finally do the first and second listings gives clues as to Fairfax's reasons for choosing one officer or regiment rather than another? The temptation is to see evidence of selections being made on political or connectional grounds rather than military ones, and it must be admitted that officers who had fought in Cromwell's or Haselrig's regiments of horse in 1643 and 1644 seem to have been favoured when it came to appointments in the New Model. For this see listing number one. However, the decision to prioritise officers from Manchester's cavalry regiments can be seen as being based on sound military considerations, namely that Essex's and Waller's had performed relatively poorly in the main battles of 1642-1644. Similarly the fact that the officers chosen for the New Model who had held commissions as captain and above in Essex's infantry regiments were more numerous in the February listing than those who had served in Manchester's is probably a reflection of what had happened on the battlefield at Second Newbury. Essex's regiments had totally routed the royalist foot facing them in the approaches to Speen village, whereas Manchester's had twice been repulsed in the fighting around Donnington Castle. Moreover, the trend of selecting company commanders from Essex's army rather than Manchester's

18 TNA, WO/1646, fos. 75, 112, 146. The future General George Monck, writing his treatise on military organisation and practice in the Tower of London in 1645-6, had probably seen how Okey's regiment had been armed and gave it his hearty approval: Monck, *Observations on Military and Political Affairs* (1671), p. 27.

19 BL, Harleian Ms 166, fo. 205.

20 For Waller's troop commanders, which included a lieutenant colonel as well as a major, see Spring, *Waller's Army*, pp. 146-9. For Essex's troop commanders, see Appendix IV below. Waller was incensed that his regiment had not been taken into the New Model in its entirety. In his last letter to the speaker of the House of Commons before giving up his command he stated that it was an outright insult to him and his men: BL, Harleian Ms 166, fo. 201.

21 How many musketeers Waller managed to convert into dragoons is not clear as horses were in very short supply, but he had no infantry with him by early October 1644 and 1500 dragoons as opposed to 150 in early September: CSPD 1644, pp. 489, 495, 521, 523; ibid 1644-5, p. 36; J. Adair, *Roundhead General: The Campaigns of Sir William Waller* (Stroud, 1997), p. 207. See also entries for John Gorges and Henry Scrimgeour below.

22 Rushworth, *Historical Collections* v, pp. 701-10

23 G. Davies, 'The Army of the Eastern Association', *English Historical Review* 46 (1921), p. 92.

continued. In April Fairfax chose four captains who had formerly served in Essex's infantry regiments as replacements for officers nominated in February who failed to take up their commissions. He took none from either Manchester's regiments or Waller's.

5

The New Model Army a National Army?

The regimental lists provide copious details of changes in the composition of the officer corps of the New Model between its setting out on campaign for the first time in late April 1645 and the summer of 1649. However, what the detail conceals is that the New Model Army four years down the line was much more of a national army than it had been in 1645.

The armies of Essex, Manchester and Waller were truly international armies with numerous Scottish officers and a sprinkling from the Netherlands and further afield. Mark Stoyle has made us very aware of the fact that the officer corps of the New Model was very different. Fairfax's proposal had been for four of the twenty-four colonels to be Scots, but the number of field officers and company and troop commanders from north of the border was to be very much reduced to possibly as low as two percent of the whole. Moreover nearly all the Scots Fairfax wished to retain refused to serve under him for reasons stated above. However, Stoyle misleads his readers when he describes the New Model Army without qualification as a national army.[1] It was in one sense as there were so few officers who were not English by nationality, but in another it was not. Even more clearly than its predecessors the New Model was an army of the south-east of England.[2]

Although the ordinance establishing the New Model had permitted Sir Thomas Fairfax to choose officers 'out of any forces under the command of Parliament',[3] he restricted himself almost without exception to the armies of Essex, Manchester and Waller insofar as troop and company commanders were concerned. In May 1645 there were no former officers of Parliament's Northern Army in the New Model. Even Fairfax's protégée John Lambert, a cavalry officer and seemingly Sir Thomas's second-in-command at Marston Moor, was passed over in the selection process.[4] There were, however, two exceptions both of whom were from the Midlands, and neither was his first choice. James Gray had been lieutenant colonel in a Warwickshire regiment. Not in the February, or indeed in the March listing, he did not receive his commission until mid-April and then only because of a vacancy in the 11th regiment of foot caused by the resignation of its colonel. The second was Captain Barton, who had belonged to Sir John Gell's Derbyshire regiment. He, and possibly his troop, joined the 10th regiment of horse at the end of April when one of its troops was removed to serve as a lifeguard for Sir Thomas Fairfax.

Fairfax's decision not to choose officers in the first instance from his former command was almost certainly based on a political consideration rather than a military one. Resentment amongst the officers and men from the three southern armies at the remodelling would have escalated had their new general shown any signs of showing favour to officers from his native Yorkshire or further north. However, once

---

1   M. Stoyle, *Soldiers and Strangers: An Ethnic History of the English Civil War* (2005), p. 131-2.
2   Waller's army in 1645 had included regiments officered by men from the central and western parts of southern England, though the rank and file recruited in Somerset and Gloucestershire had largely been lost at the Battle of Roundway Down in July 1643.
3   LJ vii, p. 209.
4   Kishlansky, *Rise of the New Model Army*, p. 63 citing BL, Thomason Tracts E 25 (18).

the new army had bedded down and won its first victories, appointing such men to vacant positions became much less of an issue.

The first major appointment came in September 1645 when John Lambert, despite having been a senior cavalry officer, was commissioned as colonel of the 10th regiment of foot on the resignation of Edward Montagu. What followed over the next two years was no more than a trickle. Walter Bethell, who had attached himself to the New Model Army in July, had to wait over six months before succeeding to a troop in the 2nd regiment of horse on the death of Captain Parry. Two Lilburnes from county Durham, cavalrymen by trade, entered the 8th regiment of foot as colonel and captain to the discomfort of the officers already in post who were very largely from Kent. A handful more entered other infantry regiments. To sum up by the time of the first Army coup in June 1647 two of the twelve infantry regiments and at most six companies of foot or troops of horse were commanded by officers from regiments who had served in the Army of the North.[5] Even with the addition of Sir Thomas Fairfax and the two Midlands' officers the company and troop commanders in the New Model who had not served in the armies of Essex, Manchester and Waller formed only six percent of the whole. Moreover, with the possible exception of Captain Barton, they had not brought their men with them.

The trickle of former officers of the army of the North into the existing New Model Army regiments continued after the first Army coup, but there were two developments of a more significant nature between June 1647 and the second coup eighteen months later which served to reduce the dominance of the south-east of England. First, whole regiments from other commands were incorporated into the New Model from the autumn of 1647 onwards, and there they remained until the army was disbanded after the restoration of the monarchy in 1660. The earliest was Colonel Francis Thornhaugh's Nottinghamshire regiment of horse, but it was soon joined by Francis Hacker's. Hacker had commanded the Leicestershire cavalry regiments in the First Civil War, but his captains were veterans who hailed from the counties close to the Scottish border. This fitted a pattern as most of the new regiments came directly or indirectly from the army of the North.

When the army that had been Lord Fairfax's was remodelled in the autumn of 1645 and again in the autumn of 1647, many units disappeared, but three regiments of foot commanded by Colonels Bright, Maleverer and Charles Fairfax and two regiments of horse sooner or later found their way onto the New Model Army pay roll. John Lambert and Robert Lilburne assumed command of the cavalry regiments not long after the first Army coup having given up their recently acquired infantry colonelcies. Lambert was replaced by the elderly Sir William Constable, who had also held regimental commands in the Lord Fairfax's army, and Lilburne by Sir Arthur Haselrig, not a Northerner but a former colonel of horse and foot in Waller's army. Moreover, when William Herbert left the 11th regiment of foot for service in Ireland he was replaced by Robert Overton, yet another Northern army colonel, on the recommendation of Oliver Cromwell.[6] As a result by the end of 1647, if Sir Thomas Fairfax is also included in the calculation, just under a quarter of the New Model Army regiments were commanded by officers who had served in the former Army of the North.

Second, new regiments raised in the far southwest of England, in Lancashire and Cheshire, in Northumberland and in South Wales also joined the army. Their duties from 1648 onwards were largely confined to maintaining order in their own localities, and most of them did not last for long. Once the war against Scotland ended in October 1651, they were surplus to requirements, as New Model Army regiments no longer needed in the north could act as replacements. Most were therefore disbanded, but their officers sometimes found their way back into military service by the back door. For example, entire companies belonging to Robert Duckenfield's Cheshire regiment were sent to Ireland where they

---

5   The officers were Lambert and Colonel Lilburne of the 8th regiment of foot and Captains Edward Salmon (3rd regiment of foot), Walter Bethell (2nd regiment of horse), Amor Stoddard (3rd regiment of foot), and Henry Lilburne and Abraham Holmes (8th regiment of foot) and possibly William Leigh (1st regiment of foot).

6   BL, Sloane Ms 1519, fo. 129.

brought Sir Hardress Waller's regiment up to strength.[7] Their commander Lieutenant Colonel Simon Finch was returning to his old stamping ground. Sent to England to fight for the king, he changed sides after being taken prisoner at the Battle of Nantwich in January 1644. He was then given command of a troop of dragoons in Sir William Brereton's regiment, which performed with distinction in operations in Cheshire from 1644 to 1646, before returning to the colours in 1648 or 1649.[8]

The third development, which widened the geographical composition of the New Model Army, took place during 1649 and early 1650 when war with Scotland was becoming increasingly likely. With seven regiments pinned down in Ireland, new ones were needed to reinforce the field army in England. Some were raised from scratch like Colonel William Daniel's, officered mainly by Cheshire veterans of the two Civil Wars and probably recruited in that county and in Lancashire, and Colonel George Gill's regiment of foot with Yorkshire officers and rank-and-file.[9] Another, Colonel James Hearne's, had as its nucleus the officers of a regiment raised in Dorset in 1643 to garrison Weymouth, whilst Sir Arthur Haselrig's newly commissioned regiment of cavalry drew its officers and rank-and-file from the four counties of the far north of England. For the moment it was based at Newcastle where Haslerig was governor.[10]

However, not all of the new units raised in 1650 were intended to serve in Scotland. For example Colonel Robert Bennett's regiment, which hailed from Cornwall and Devonshire, helped keep the far south-west of England secure as did Colonel Gibbon's the county of Kent.[11] Gibbon's also freed up older New Model Army units for service in the north, but subsequently it was to provide recruits for the army in Scotland as the campaign became bogged down in the Lowlands.[12] The regiments of Daniel Hearne (later Thomas Read's) and Gill's (later Matthew Alured's) were to form part of the army of occupation in Scotland, but both Bennett's and Gibbon's, like those regiments raised in 1648 mentioned above, were disbanded.[13] As a result the New Model Army of the mid and late sixteen-fifties was not only slimmer but also less of a national army than it had been in 1650 and 1651.

So far discussion of the development of a truly national army has focused on the troop and company commanders, but the composition of the rank-and-file is if anything more important in assessing how far the New Model had become a national army by 1650/51. The claims for arrears of pay in the TNA, E 121 series show that in the cavalry regiments in particular there remained a core of troopers alive in 1649 who had belonged to the pre-New Model Army regiments and would therefore have been very largely raised to the south and east of a line drawn from the Humber to Southampton. However, it is not possible to ascertain how many were still in active service. On the other hand the regiments which entered the army from the provincial command from 1647 onwards are most likely to have been full of soldiers from the parts of the country where they had been raised and had also campaigned.

Something can also be said about the geographical origins of those men who were impressed into the ranks of the original 24 New Model Army regiments in the last year of the First Civil War. The area of the country Parliament controlled in April 1645 meant that the 6,000 new soldiers required by the infantry could only be drawn from the south-east. Gentles discussed all four of the levies imposed on the country in the final year of the First Civil War his conclusion being that London was less important than it had been earlier in the war. Certainly the counties required to produce impressed men, limited at first to East Anglia and those close to the capital, expanded as Parliament conquered territory from the royalists. In the third levy of January 1646, for example, Somerset, Dorset, Wiltshire, Gloucestershire

7   F. and D., p. 446. However, Waller's regiment already had at least seven companies by the autumn of 1651. It is therefore likely that Duckenfield's former soldiers were condensed into three companies. For this, see the discussion of Waller's regiment in *Reconstructing the New Model Army*, vol. 2.

8   R. Dore, The Letter Books of Sir William Brereton, *Lancashire and Cheshire Record Society* 123 (2 vols., 1984, 1990) i, pp. 27, 34; ibid ii, pp. 194, 384, 511

9   CSPD 1650, pp. 138, 141, 142, 184, 539, 546, 548; F. and D., pp. 462-3.

10   Spring ii, p. 134: F. and D.

11   CSPD 1650, pp. 213, 298; ibid 1650-51, pp, 50-1, 311.

12   It was described as newly raised in 7/50: TNA, SP 28/67, fo. 131.

13   CJ vii, p. 24.

and Hampshire were required to produce 4,600 men as opposed to a slightly lower figure for London and the counties of the south east and East Anglia combined. In March the area in which men were to be impressed was extended still further into the far south-west and the Midlands, but I have found no clear evidence yet of impressment being extended any further west and north than a line drawn from the Humber to the Severn estuary. Moreover, as Gentles recognised, it is impossible to ascertain how many of the new recruits were actually delivered to their regiments or how long those who were remained in the army.[14]

The same caveat applies to the claims made at the time that the depleted ranks of the New Model were filled by royalists taken prisoner on the battlefield or in a captured town or lesser garrison, or simply at a loose end once fighting had ceased. Although it is known that 102 out of the prisoners taken at Naseby, about two percent of the total, immediately changed sides,[15] the size of the influx cannot be assessed with any degree of certainty as much of the other evidence is of a questionable nature. This is clearly the case with reports in the London newspapers, but how far did Sir Thomas Fairfax's natural courtesy cause him to inflate the quality, and by implication, number of ex-royalist soldiers in his army in June 1646 when making polite conversation with Sir Phillip Warwick, clerk of the signet to King Charles I, after the surrender of Oxford? And to what extent was the earl of Pembroke exaggerating for effect when he mentioned a figure of 4,000 as tensions between Parliament and the army escalated in the run-up to the first Army coup?[16]

Much work needs to be done on the changes in the rank and file after the end of impressment in the summer of 1646, but Gentles has shown that the army was kept up to strength by volunteers until the outbreak of heavy fighting in Scotland and Ireland from 1649 when impressment was briefly reintroduced. However, a major source of recruits was clearly provided by the reduction in the military establishment authorised by Parliament between the autumn of 1646 and the spring of 1648 during which time many thousands of officers and soldiers who were not part of the New Model Army were discharged. The biggest formation was Major General Massey's Western Brigade made up largely of regiments which had formerly belonged to Sir William Waller's army, but Massey's men were far outnumbered by those belonging to garrisons and to regiments raised for local defence purposes in all parts of England and Wales. Soldiers from such units who wished to continue their military career could seek service in Ireland or on the continent, but many found places in New Model Army regiments in a manner that was mainly haphazard but on occasions systematic, as is shown by their claims for pay arrears.

Research on this transference of military personnel is under way but by no means complete. For the moment two illustrations must suffice. In January 1648 the 10th regiment of foot took over garrison duties at Gloucester, Chepstow and Hereford. By 1650 when its officers and soldiers submitted their claims for pay arrears, the companies quartered in Gloucester were full of soldiers who had served in the regiment they replaced, Colonel Thomas Morgan's which had been disbanded soon after the 10th regiment arrived in Gloucestershire.[17] The new garrison regiment also included a supernumerary company taken directly from the old regiment and commanded by Captain Thomas Pury junior. It owed its survival almost certainly to the influence of Thomas Pury senior who was a prominent member of the Parliamentary committee responsible for paying and provisioning the New Model Army.

In the case of the 9th regiment of horse commanded by Colonel Edward Whalley filling up the ranks followed a completely different pattern. On Whalley's orders all the data concerning his men's

14 CSPD 1645-7, p. 319; Gentles, *New Model Army*, pp. 31-38.
15 TNA, SP 28/34, fo. 464.
16 Sir Phillip Warwick, *Memoirs*, p. 253; Gentles, *New Model Army*, p. 153.
17 For much of the First Civil War there had been two regiments in the Gloucester garrison. One had been raised for the earl of Essex's army in 1642. This became Massey's regiment a year or so later and joined his western brigade in 1645. The other was raised locally. It is clear from a comparison of the section discussing its commissioned officers in Lawrence Spring's study of Sir William Waller's army with claims for pay arrears in the E 121 series at the National Archives that this was the regiment that Morgan commanded.

arrears was copied into a bound volume and collated.[18] As a result it is possible to see at a glance when individual officers and soldiers entered the regiment. Large numbers had been with it from the birth of the New Model, and some had seen service in Manchester's army where its six troops had ridden in Oliver Cromwell's fourteen troop regiment of horse, but the troopers who joined it since April 1645 had come from all over the place. Some had fought in the Army of the North; others had been in the Gloucester garrison; yet others had fought under Colonel Mytton in Shropshire and North Wales and under Sir William Brereton in Cheshire; whilst a number had been in garrisons in the south at Farnham, at Windsor Castle, at Lyme in Dorset and at Plymouth. A small handful had even served in the 10th regiment of horse disbanded after the Leveller uprising of May 1649.

---

18   BL, Harleian MS 427.

6

Leaving the Army

Career patterns within the officer corps as a whole are clearly a topic of major importance, but one that is best placed in the introduction to the second volume as quite a number of commissioned officers in post in 1645 continued in service until well into the following decade. Nevertheless, there is a good argument for commenting here on how careers in the army came to an end between 1645 and 1649 as the circumstances were significantly different from what they were to be in the sixteen-fifties.

Between 1645 and 1650 the risks of physical mortality were much higher than later on in the life of the New Model Army. Troop and company commanders were killed in action, primarily on the battlefield or in storming enemy-held towns. They also died from disease or as a result of wounds sustained in the course of duty. Of the 198 company and troop commanders who took up commissions in the New Model Army in April 1645 at least 38 disappeared from the army under such circumstances, and to these can be added a dozen or so who were commissioned during the late sixteen-forties. After June 1650 deaths in service were much less common. Most of the casualties suffered by the New Model Army regiments serving in Ireland occurred during the first nine months, whilst in the Scottish campaigns of 1650/51 deaths as a result of enemy action were comparatively light, the sole exception being the storming of Dundee in September 1651. However, death from drowning as a result of shipwreck was a new hazard as the army became involved in military operations at a distance from the main island of Great Britain from the autumn of 1649 onwards. In addition death from disease was a most important killer in the campaigns in the Caribbean which began in 1654. The naval wars against the Dutch and the Spaniards caused casualties amongst the rank and file who went to sea as marines. However, so far I have only discovered a single army officer who lost his life. That was Major General Richard Deane, serving at the time as an admiral, whose career had begun in the artillery.

Expulsions also help to explain the rapid turnover of troop and company commanders in the late sixteen-forties. An officer could be cashiered or forced to resign for a range of offences from desertion to dissolute behaviour and from religious unorthodoxy to pocketing his soldiers' pay. Captain Richard Le Hunt, for example, accused of financial malpractice as the New Model set out on its first campaign, left the army very soon afterwards, but forged a most successful career in the army of occupation in Ireland where he rose to the rank of colonel. Captain Francis Freeman's offence was that he did not fit in with his colonel's view on religion. He lost his year-long attempt to keep his command just as the army was about to invade Scotland, but made his case known to the wider world in a ten thousand word pamphlet.[1] So far I have found no evidence that he resumed his military career at a later date.

However, most of those expelled from the New Model (some 46 or so) left their regiments in June 1647 at the time of the first Army coup. This exodus has been seen as a result of the coup itself with some of those who opposed it being driven away by their troops and others cashiered by General Fairfax.

---

1   TNA, SP 28/28, fo. 425; BL, Thomason Tracts, E 615 (7).

However, it is highly likely that some were allowed to resign as they went on to serve elsewhere. Into this category fell officers such as Colonel Richard Fortescue, the new governor of Pendennis Castle, Major George Sedacue, later adjutant general of horse, and Colonel Edward Rossiter and Captain Henry Markham of the 5th regiment of horse, who commanded formations in the East Midlands in the Second Civil War. Yet others like Richard Le Hunt took up commands in Ireland.[2]

In complete contrast the second Army coup of December 1648 to March 1649, which began with the expulsion of the army's opponents from the House of Commons and ended with the execution of the king and the abolition of the monarchy and the House of Lords, had very little impact on the New Model's company and troop commanders. Only a single captain, William Cecil, son of the earl of Salisbury, is known to have left the army at the time, but the circumstances are uncertain. A weekly journal printed in London early in 1649 informed its readers that he had refused to take part in the trial of the Duke of Hamilton, executed soon after the king, because he was Hamilton's cousin. However, it does not say if this was the reason for his leaving the army or his being expelled. Other possible reasons why his army career came to an end are that he heartily disapproved of the king's trial and execution and/or, given his father's peerage, the abolition of the House of Lords. Pay warrants for his troop might have shed further light on his motivation by giving a precise date for his leaving the army, but none survive that are dated between mid-December 1648 when he was still in command of his troop and April 1649 when he was not.[3]

Third, changes in the tempo or direction of the war must surely have been an inducement for officers to end his army career either by resignation or by doing enough to antagonise the high command, but both pieces of specific evidence I have found so far relate to the sixteen-fifties. John Hodgson, for example, resented serving in a regiment based in the London area and thought about giving up his army career, but changed his mind when offered a lieutenancy in a regiment which would normally be quartered close to his home in Yorkshire. Being tired of military life also explains the resignation of Captain Amor Stoddard in 1654.[4] However, the flood of resignations that might have been expected to follow the end of hostilities in the First Civil War did not materialise. The number of troop and company commanders who left the army in the late summer of 1646 was small, and it may have been a mere coincidence that an individual officer chose to do so at that point in time.

Having to serve abroad can be more easily identified as a reason for resignation. Sir Thomas Fairfax and Major John Barber refused to countenance invading Scotland in the summer of 1650 and left the army. It was also rumoured sometime after the event that three troop commanders in the 2nd regiment of horse were dismissed when they refused to go to Ireland with Oliver Cromwell a year earlier.[5] However, it cannot be proved that Major Lewis Audley and Captain George Hutchinson, who left the 7th regiment of foot and the 11th regiment of horse respectively in the second half of 1649, did so because they were unhappy about leaving England.[6] In the case of other officers like Major Carter and Captain Atkinson of the 12th regiment of foot the surviving documentation is too imprecise to show whether they refused to go to Ireland in August 1649, or went there and swiftly returned home. They were still connected with their respective regiments in early 1650, but may merely have been acting as

---

2 So far these are few in number but they include Captain Richard Pooley of the 5th regiment of foot and Major Nicholas Moore and Captain Harold Scrimgeour of the dragoons, but I do not doubt that more will come to light as research for the second volume progresses.

3 The same difficulty applies to Captain Francis Hawes of the 7th regiment of horse who may have resigned as a result of King Charles I's abduction from the Isle of Wight or been cashiered for speaking of it in the House of Commons' investigation. He appears to have been succeeded by his lieutenant before the outcome of the king's trial was known. For this see p. 107 below.

4 J. Hodgson, *Memoirs*, p. 30; ; J. Akerman ed. , *Letters of Roundhead Officers written from Scotland*, Bannatyne Club (Edinburgh 1856), pp. 171, 173.

5 Bulstrode Whitelock, *Memorials of the English Affairs* (1732), p. 466; BL, Thomason Tracts, The Moderate 21-28/11/1649. At least one was apparently hoping for a transfer to a regiment remaining in England, but if this was the case he failed.

6 Audley became major of a new regiment of infantry: CSPD 1650-1, p. 111.

its agents in London.[7]

Gentles has analysed the turnover of officers in the New Model Army but only between May 1645 and what must be July 1647.[8] He confidently asserts that during that period 57 per cent of the officers of the rank of captain lieutenant and above had left, namely 112 out of 196, but the sources he used were the listing in Joshua Sprigg's *Anglia Rediviva* and the data provided by pay warrants and the commission's book in the Clarke Manuscripts and both are defective for reasons given above[9] In fact at least twenty additional officers served as troop and company commanders at some time between the spring of 1645 and the spring of 1647. As a result if the listing of officers of the rank of captain lieutenant or above for late May 1645 is compared with that for late August 1647, the attrition rate turns out to be over 70 per cent. However, such a rapid turnover was not untypical for a period of two and a quarter years in the mid seventeenth century. Of the 80 or so company commanders in post in 1642 in the eight regiments still in the earl of Essex's army two years later less than 25 per cent were still in post in early April 1645.[10]

What is remarkable, however, about the captains and above who left the New Model between May 1645 and August 1647 is the contrast between those who had previously served in the army of the Eastern Association under the earl of Manchester and those who had served under Essex and Waller. Of the 64 from Manchester's army 49 remained; of the 57 from Essex's army only 21 were left; of the 33 from Waller's only 9. As those who were removed from the New Model Army during the first Army coup or who removed themselves are often viewed as moderates, such figures may look like a confirmation of the radicalism in the officer corps of Manchester's army compared with the two others claimed by Temple, but the losses have less to do with the crisis of June 1647 than with the experience of individual regiments in the previous two years.

Insofar as Essex's former troop and company commanders are concerned only 12 out of 36 left at the time of the first Army coup compared with 7 out of 15 of Manchester's. The departure of so many officers before June 1647 can, of course, be read in a number of different ways. However, there is a hint that infantry regiments whose officers had served in the army of the Eastern Association were for some reason or other not chosen to undertake tasks such as storming walled towns which often resulted in more deaths and serious injuries than did battles. Of the officers who were casualties between 6 May 1645 and late August 1646, eighteen had previously been in Essex's army, but only nine in Manchester's army of whom two, Major Richard Cromwell and Lieutenant Colonel Oliver Ingoldsby, were at the time of their deaths serving in the 5th and 6th regiments of foot the remainder of whose officers were formerly Essex's. None of Waller's former officers were wounded in the same period of time and only four are known to have died, but they constituted almost 25 percent of the New Model infantry officers known to have served in his army.[11]

Junior commissioned officers seem to have left the New Model Army in circumstances similar to those of company and troop commanders, but the limited documentation that survives makes it impossible in their case to do anything more than analyse the turnover which occurred as the time of the first Army coup. A document printed in London in June 1647 stated that 167 officers had left

---

7   Worc. College, Clarke Ms 67, fo. 44; TNA, SP 28/68, fo. 524.

8   Gentles, 'New Model Army Officer Corps', p. 130. He claims to be covering a period of two years but his inclusion of officers purged in June 1647 means that he must be covering a period of two years and three months.

9   See the critique of Sprigg on p. 14.

10 In compiling the officers' names in Essex's army in 1642 I have used lists in P. Young, *Edgehill* for the four of Essex's 1645 regiments which fought at that battle and Peachey and Turton, *Old Robin's Foot*, for the four regiments that began their life in the earl of Warwick's army, but which transferred to Essex's army in late 1642. For the cavalry I have used the list in E. Peacock, *Army Lists of the Roundheads and the Cavaliers* (1874) supplemented by Turton's *The Chief Strength of the Army*. The lists reproduced by Peacock and Young come from contemporary pamphlets, whilst those compiled by Peachey and Peachey and Turton are based on accurate readings of pay warrants and other documents in the Commonwealth Exchequer Papers.

11 Of the five regiments of infantry drawn mainly from Essex's army eleven company commanders had been killed and six wounded; of the four drawn mainly from Manchester's army five had been killed and only one wounded. If Rainborough's regiment is added to the calculations, the figure for Essex's army rises by one and Manchester's by two.

the army as a result.[12] As it is known that between 43 and 46 were captains or above, 120 or so must have been below that rank, almost exactly the same percentage of the whole as that of the more senior officers.[13] A level of attrition on such a scale seems feasible given the fact that 122 of the 165 signatures on a declaration of loyalty to Parliament printed a month earlier were those of lieutenants, ensigns, cornets and quartermasters. A count of over 150 new junior officers whose commissions were recorded in Worcester College, Clarke Ms 67, however, cannot be used as evidence that an even larger number of junior officers left the army during the first Army coup. Many of the men who became lieutenants in the horse and the foot and cornets in the horse were already ensigns and quartermasters in May 1647, and so adding up the number of individuals who were promoted runs the risk of double-counting.[14] However, even the smaller figure gave immense opportunities for sergeants of foot and corporals of horse to become commissioned officers with all that that meant in terms of pay and prestige. The like would not happen again until the very end of the sixteen-fifties.

---

12 BL, Thomason Tracts, E 394 (3).

13 Gentles presented a much lower percentage as he believed wrongly that the author of the pamphlet was enumerating all the officers who left the army in June 1647, that is both commissioned and non-commissioned.

14 If a lieutenant who left in early June was replaced by his troop's cornet and the cornet by the quartermaster, two officers' names would appear in the commissions' book in consequence of a single vacancy.

7

Numbering the Regiments

The list of New Model Army company and troop commanders presented to Parliament by Sir Thomas Fairfax on 27 February 1645 seems not to be of its own time as the regiments were numbered. This was the norm in the British army of the late eighteenth and the nineteenth centuries when the number allotted to a regiment was an indicator of seniority – the higher the number the earlier the date at which it was first raised. Before that time regiments were known by the name of their colonel.

	Foot		Horse
1	Sir Thomas Fairfax	1	Sir Thomas Fairfax
2	Phillip Skippon	2	John Middleton
3	James Holbourne	3	James Sheffield
4	Lawrence Crawford	4	Charles Fleetwood
5	Richard Fortescue	5	Edward Rossiter
6	Richard Ingoldsby	6	Bartholomew Vermuyden
7	Thomas Ayloffe	7	Algernon Sidney
8	Ralph Weldon	8	Nathaniel Rich
9	Harry Barclay	9	Edward Whalley
10	Edward Montagu	10	Richard Graves
11	Edward Aldridge	11	Sir Michael Livesey
12	John Pickering		John Okey[1]
1 Okey's regiment of dragoons was not given a number.			

Temple was of the opinion that, as Fairfax had placed his regiments in a certain order and used a system of numbering to endorse it, historians should follow suit. However, the fact that he chose to use that system of classifying them on that particular occasion seems insufficient justification. With no guidance from the preamble to the document itself as to why he placed the regiments in the order he did, it is necessary first to look for internal evidence for the sequence, and then to compare it with the sequences used in other lists of the New Model Army regiments. Only then can the question of whether to accept or to reject Temple's ruling be satisfactorily answered.

Clearly the regiments were not listed in alphabetical order. They were also not grouped together in accordance with their antecedents. Fairfax gave infantry regiments whose roots lay in Essex's army numbers 2, 5, 6, 9, and 11; those from Manchester's army numbers 1, 4, 7, 10 and 12; and those from Waller's numbers 3 and 8. Essex's former cavalry regiments are numbers 3 and 10, Waller's numbers 2 and 11, and Manchester's numbers 1, 5, 6, 7, 8 and 9.

Second, the order is not the same as that which appears in an earlier list, namely that of the colonels of the new army approved by the House of Commons on 21 January 1645.[1] All the names appear in Fairfax's list, but the two sequences bear no resemblance to one another from the second regiments of horse and foot onwards.

Third, in the case of the infantry regiments the order in which they appeared in Fairfax's list had nothing to do with the seniority of their colonels. For example, Edward Montagu and John Pickering (10th and 12th regiments) received their commissions some months before Richard Fortescue (5th regiment). The date at which the mother regiment was raised was also of no significance. The regiments originating in the earl of Essex's army (numbers 2,5,6,9 and 11) all predate those from the former Eastern Association army (numbers 1, 4, 7, 10 and 12).

All that can be said with any certainty with regard to the numbering of the foot, and then only in the case of the first few regiments, is that it appears to have been based on the rank held by the colonel immediately before the New Model Army came into being. Thus, Fairfax (colonel of regiment number 1) had been a lieutenant general, whilst Skippon, Holbourne and Crawford (colonels of regiments 2, 3 and 4) had been major generals in Essex's, Waller's and Manchester's armies respectively.[2]

There seems, however, to have been more of a rationale in the numbering of the cavalry regiments in the February 27 list. Sir Thomas Fairfax's was in the first place. It was followed by John Middleton's, which is logical as he had been Sir William Waller's lieutenant general of horse.[3] The third colonel, James Sheffield, had held a commission as colonel in Essex's army conferred early in 1644. There follows a run of four regiments commanded by officers from the Eastern Association army the first three of whom were already colonels of regiments – Fleetwood, Rossiter and Vermuyden. The fourth, Algernon Sidney, was a full colonel who had commanded the earl of Manchester's regiment of horse. The 8th and 9th regiments were intended for the most senior field officers in the Eastern Association army – Nathaniel Rich, lieutenant colonel of Manchester's regiment, and Edward Whalley, lieutenant colonel of Oliver Cromwell's. The 10th was commanded by Richard Graves who had held the same position as Sidney but in Essex's army and with the rank of lieutenant colonel rather than full colonel. The final regiment, however, bucks the trend. Its colonel was Sir Michael Livesey, a colonel of horse in Waller's army of almost two year's standing. He should therefore have come much higher in the sequence.[4]

It is now necessary to examine the order in which regiments appear in lists drawn up after 27 February 1645. The earliest is in an entry in the House of Lords Journal for 18 March, the day on which the listing of New Model Army officers passed both Houses. This did not number the regiments, but the sequence closely follows that of 27 February. 1-4 of the infantry regiments were in the same order. They were followed by regiments 9, 10, 11 and 12, and then by regiments 5, 6, 7, and 8, whilst the cavalry regiments were recorded exactly as in Fairfax's listing. The same order is also used in *Anglia Rediviva* compiled a year and a half later. However, like the clerk responsible for writing entries in Journal of the House of Lords, Sprigg did not number them.

The next contemporary source to display New Model Army regiments in sequence is the commissions' book in the Clarke Papers. Here the cavalry regiments appear in an order which bears no resemblance to the three earlier lists other than that General Fairfax's is first. One can understand why regiments number 6 and 11 were raised to second and third in the sequence, as they were commanded by Oliver Cromwell and Henry Ireton, general officers who had not been in post at the birth of the New Model.

---

1   CJ iv, p. 26.

2   Interestingly there is much more logic in the list of infantry colonels for the new army approved by the House of Commons on 21 January 1645. The commanders of regiments one to five had held commands in the old armies higher than the rank of colonel and the remaining seven were colonels in the armies of Essex (numbers six to eight), Manchester (numbers nine to eleven) and Waller (twelve). In the case of Essex's and Manchester's armies the colonels' names are given in order of precedence.

3   Oliver Cromwell and Phillip Stapleton, lieutenant generals in the armies of Manchester and Essex respectively, were ineligible for service in the New Model as they were MPs.

4   Livesey's commission had been issued in early 1644: Spring ii.

Thereafter, however, there seems no rhyme or reason to the order in which regiments were listed. Number 4 in the commissions' book had been number 10, number 5 number 4, number 6 number 9, and so on.

However, the compiler of the commissions' book does seem to have deferred to some extent to the earlier lists when recording changes in the infantry regiments. These appear in the order 1, 2, 3, 4, 10, 5, 7, 8, 11, 9, 6.[5] As the colonel of the 10th regiment was a major general, it probably moved up the sequence for the same reason as Cromwell's and Ireton's did in the section of the book concerned with the cavalry regiments. However, I can see no reason why the 6th regiment commanded by a colonel commissioned in 1644 was placed last or why the 9th and the 11th were in reverse order.

Thus there seems to be a measure of consistency in the order in which regiments were appeared in lists later than that of 27 February 1645, but nowhere to my knowledge other than in Fairfax's schedule are they given numbers. This, I think, is sufficient grounds for rejecting Temple's command that historians should henceforth apply an eighteenth-century system of classification to the regiments of the New Model Army. Nevertheless I have decided for purely practical reasons to use Fairfax's numbers throughout volume one and two, and indeed to extend it to regiments added to the army from 1647 onwards.[6] The text and the footnotes are shortened substantially if numbers are used instead of names. In addition the reader will find it easier to track a regiment over time as it will not be necessary to remember the names of its successive colonels.

5   A listing of the officers in Number 12 (Hewson's) appears elsewhere in the commissions' book amongst regiments intended for service in Ireland in 1649: Worc. College, Clarke Ms 67, fo. 44.
6   For the numbers allotted to the new regiments see Appendix Four.

Part III

The Regimental Listings: Company and Troop Commanders

Company and Troop Commanders in early April 1645

Infantry

1st Regiment	Name	Military career
Col.	Sir Thomas Fairfax	Col. and Lieutenant General H. N. army|
Lt. Col.	Thomas Jackson[1]	E.A. army|
Major	Richard Cooke[2]	E.A. army|
Captains	XXX Cooke junior[3]	XXX|Did not apparently serve in the N.M. army|
	Richard Beamont[4]	Capt. Manchester's regt. Dr. E.A. army|
	Samuel Gooday	Capt. Manchester's regt. F. E.A. army|
	Vincent Boyce	Capt. ditto|
	XXX Maneste	Capt. ditto|
	Robert Johnston[5]	Capt. ditto|Did not serve in the N.M. army|
	Fulk Muskett[6]	Capt. Essex's regt. F. L.G. army|
Capt. Lt.	William Fortescue[7]	XXX

1   Jackson was a captain in George Langham's regiment in Essex's army to 4/44 when it was disbanded. For the next year he was lieutenant colonel in a regiment in the Eastern Association army, probably Colonel Rainborough's or one of the garrison regiments: TNA, SP 28/267, fo. 83; ibid, SP 28/39, fo. 499; Spring i.

2   Temple identifies this officer as Gabriel Cooke, a captain in Richard Ingoldsby's regiment in Essex's army: 'Original Officer List', p. 55. This cannot be so. In March the House of Lords accepted the 1st regiment's company commanders in their entirety but attempted to put Gabriel Cooke into his old regiment, now the 6th, in place of Captain Francis Allen: House of Lords Manuscripts, Main Papers, 10/3/45. Moreover, warrants signed by Fairfax's major in 4/45 show that his first name was Richard: e.g. TNA SP 28/29, fo. 66. For evidence of Major Richard Cooke's association with the army of the Eastern Association in 1644-5 where he was probably a reformado, see C. Holmes, *The Eastern Association in the English Civil War* (Cambridge, 1974), p. 201-2, 286; TNA, SP 28/27, fo. 276.

3   Temple suggests for no apparent reason that this man's first name was Thomas: 'Original Officer List', p. 55. However, the fact that in the list of officers Fairfax gave to Parliament in late February 1645 the second Cooke is referred to as junior suggests that the major and the captain shared the same Christian name, this being the method used to distinguish between Colonel Richard Deane and his nephew Richard: see below p. 89. Otherwise the scribe would have given their first names, as he did in the case of the two Captains Clarke in the 2nd regiment of foot. Captain Richard Cooke was probably serving in the London garrison in early 1645: CSPD (Calendar of State Papers Domestic) 1625-49, p. 385.

4   This officer has been rightly identified with the captain who served in the regiment commanded by Lieutenant Colonel John Lilburne: F and D; Holmes, *Eastern Association*, p. 291; TNA, SP 28/29, fo. 330.

5   Temple claimed that this man must be Thomas Johnston, not the Robert Johnston who had served as a captain in Manchester's regiment in the Eastern Association army, citing Robert Johnston's accounts in TNA SP 28/255 as evidence: 'Original Officer List', p. 55. I do not see from an examination of the accounts how this conclusion can be sustained. Robert Johnston's service under Manchester came to an end on 5 April 1645, but so did that of other officers who went straight into posts in the New Model Army. Moreover, at least three of Johnston's fellow captains became company commanders in the 1st regiment of foot and are immediately above him in Fairfax's list. Finally, I have found no record of a Captain Thomas Johnston in either army.

6   There was a gap here in the officer list Fairfax presented to Parliament. Muskett's name was inserted by the House of Commons whilst the list was being discussed in the Lords: CJ iv, p. 79. He had been a lieutenant in Essex's own regiment of foot in 1642: E. Peacock, *Army Lists of the Roundheads and the Cavaliers (2nd ed., 1873)*, p. 26. There is confirmation that Muskett had risen to captain in Essex's regiment in Hugh Nevell's and Francis Robson's claim for arrears: TNA, E 121/1/1/37, entry 17; ibid, E 121/5/5/14, entry 6.

7   Fortescue was a settler in Barbados: ibid, SP 28/40, fo. 27.

2nd Regiment	Name	Military career
Colonel	Phillip Skippon	Col. and Major General F. L.G. army|
Lt. Col.	John Francis	Lt. Col. Skippon's regt. F. L.G. army|
Major	Richard Ashfield	Major ditto|
Captains	Samuel Clarke	Capt. ditto 22/11/42|
	Edward Streater	Capt. ditto 17/7/43|
	James Harrison	Capt. ditto 8/8/43|
	John Clarke	Capt. ditto 20/4/44|
	Maurice Bowen	Capt. ditto by 5/44|
	Devereux Gibbon[8]	XXX
	John Cobbett[9]	L.G. army|
Capt. Lt.	William Symonds	Capt. Lt. Skippon's regt. F. L.G. army|

8   Temple confirms Gibbon's identity, but the rest of his footnote is questionable: 'Original Officer List', p. 55. It cannot be argued that Gibbon was French because of his Christian name. Devereux was the family name of the earls of Essex, and in the 17th as in the 20th century it was not uncommon for parents to use a nobleman's surname as a Christian name for a male child. Gibbon had allegedly served in a regiment paid for by the county of Norfolk: Holmes, *Eastern Association*, p. 285. I have checked the reference, which covers expenditure in 1643, but cannot find him.

9   Cobbett had been a captain of foot in John Holmstead's regiment in Essex's army, but it had been disbanded in 4/44. Since then he had been serving as a reformado in the Lord General's regiment of horse in accordance with a provision made in the ordinance ordering the disbandment : TNA, E 121/4/5/64B, entry 7; ibid, E 121/3/5/103, entry 4; LJ vi, pp. 516-7.

3rd Regiment	Name	Military career
Colonel	James Holbourne[10]	Col. F. and Dr. Major General F. W. army |Resigned after 4/45|
Lt. Col.	Ralph Cottesworth	Lt. Col. Holbourne regt. F. W. army[11]|
Major	Thomas Smith	Major ditto|
Captains	Henry Cannon[12]	Capt. Holbourne regt. Dr. ditto|Capt. 9th regt. H. 6/45|
	Benjamin Holden[13]	Capt. Holbourne regt. F. W. army|
	John Wade	Capt. ditto|
	Richard Hill	Capt. ditto|
	John Blackmore[14]	Capt. ditto|Chose to serve in Massey's brigade|
	Thomas Gorges[15]	Capt. Holbourne's regt. Dr. W. army|Left N.M. Army c. 6/5/45|
	John Gorges[16]	Capt. ditto|
Capt. Lt.	XXX[17]	

10   In March 1645 Holbourne was apparently commanding the infantry regiment in Waller's army which had been raised by Sir Arthur Haselrig, and also a regiment of dragoons made up partly of companies formerly listed in Waller's infantry regiment: Spring ii; TNA, SP 28/35, fo. 635. Holbourne's New Model Army regiment included officers from both regiments. Like Colonels Crawford, Barclay and Middleton, he was a staunch Presbyterian. Holbourne therefore obeyed instructions from the Scottish government that he was not to serve in the New Model because of the radical religious beliefs of some of its English officers. News that they had refused to serve was widespread by 14/4/45: *The Letter Books of Sir Samuel Luke* (Luke, *Letter Books*) ed. H. Tibbutt (1963), p. 514.

11   Before that he had been major to Colonel Ceeley in the Lyme garrison: TNA, E121/3/4/48A, entries 19/20.

12   Temple suggests that this officer's name was Peter, but somewhat tentatively as Captain Peter Cannon was an artillery man: 'Original Officer List', p. 56. The settlement of the officer's arrears in 1652 shows very clearly that his first name was Henry, and that he had served under Haselrig and Holbourne in Waller's army and then under Sir Hardress Waller and Edward Whalley in the New Model: ibid, E 121/4/1/130, entries 1-3.

13   Not Richard Hodden as claimed by Temple, though a Richard Hodden commanded a company in this regiment in late 1640s: 'Original Officer List', p. 56. Spring shows that Captain Benjamin Holden was a company commander in Sir Arthur Haselrig's regiment in Sir William Waller's army in late 1644. He then transferred to the New Model Army as is shown by the fact that he signed a warrant in late May 1645 as captain in Sir Hardress's regiment:ibid, SP 28/30, fo. 339. The fact that Captain Hodden is the last name on Sprigg's list for this regiment suggests that Richard Hodden became company commander during 1646: J. Sprigg, *Anglia Rediviva* (1647), p. 329. A soldier claiming arrears on leaving the army in 4/48 claimed to have served for about two years in Richard Hodden's company: TNA, SP 28/54, fo. 559.

14   Blackmore failed to take up his command, but became major of Cromwell's regiment of horse in 6/48. In the meantime he served as lieutenant colonel in Colonel John Humphreys' regiment in Herefordshire, which was disbanded in early 1648: TNA, E 121/3/4/66, unnumbered; ibid, E 121/3/4/66, unnumbered. For this and his subsequent career, see note 585 below.

15   For his service in Waller's regiment, see ibid, E 121/1/6/63, entry 95; ibid, SP 28/43, fo. 829. A pay warrant issued in 5/45 mentions Gorges as transferring to Okey's dragoons but this was not so: ibid, SP 28/30, fo. 143. He persuaded Fairfax to allow him to take a troop of dragoons to accompany Colonel Weldon to the relief of Taunton, and then transferred to Edward Massey's brigade after the relief of Taunton: TNA, SP 28/253A/3, fo. 66.

16   Spring ii. John Gorges was seriously wounded in the leg, probably at Taunton in April, and was unable to assume command of his company until 8/7/45: ibid, SP 28/31, fo. 158.

17   The captain lieutenant was possibly James Knight who was captain lieutenant in 4/47.

4th Regiment	Name	Military career
Colonel	Lawrence Crawford[18]	Col. F. and Major General F. E.A. army| Refused commission|
Lt. Col.	Isaac Ewer	Major Manchester's regt. Dr. E.A. army|
Major	Robert Saunders[19]	Capt. Manchester's regt. E.A. army|
Captains	XXX Eaton[20]	Capt. Lawrence Crawford's regt. F. E.A. army|
	Israel Smith	Capt. ditto|
	Charles O'Hara	Capt. ditto|
	Richard Harby	Capt. James Hobart's regt. F. E.A. army| Gone by 6/45|
	William Disney[21]	Capt. ditto|
	John Boyce[22]	XXX
	John Puckle	Capt. James Hobart's regt. F. E.A. army|
Capt. Lt.	XXX	

18   Crawford like James Holbourne turned down the offer of a commission in the New Model Army. His successor Robert Hammond was in command of the regiment by mid-April.

19   This must be the Captain Saunders listed as company commander in Manchester's regiment of foot in 3/45: Davies, p. 92. Documents relating to the Eastern Association army rarely give officers' first names but they do in the case of the two Captain Saunders, Robert and Giles. For Robert serving in the army in early 1645 as captain, see TNA, SP 28/27, fo. 187.

20   This officer's first name may be Phillip who first served as a trooper in Captain Margery's troop in Oliver Cromwell's regiment of horse in Manchester's army: ibid, E 121/5/6/49C, entry 1. Another possibility is Simon, who was lieutenant colonel of Robert Tothill's regiment serving in Ireland in 1650. His predecessor as lieutenant colonel had been Captain Charles O'Hara, late of the 4th regiment of foot: ibid, SP 28/64, fo. 40.

21   Temple follows F. and D. in identifying this officer as Henry Disney, but neither gives a source. Evidence from 1647 indicates that Disney's first name was William. This places him in Hobart's regiment in the Eastern Association army in early 1645 when he gave evidence against officers promoting a petition in favour of the earl of Manchester's retaining his command: Worc. College, Clarke Ms 41, fo. 103; CSPD 1644-5, p. 254.

22   Boyce was probably the lieutenant of Captain Southcote's company in Manchester's regiment of foot in the Eastern Association army: Spring i. He was not the John Boyce whose governorship of Dover Castle was renewed in March 1646 as that man was already a major: CSPD 1644-5, p. 480; CJ vii, 13/3/47.

5th Regiment	Name	Military career
Colonel	Richard Fortescue	Col. F. L.G. army in succession to Col. Cunningham|
Lt. Col.	Thomas Bulstrode[23]	Lt. Col. Richard Fortescue's regt. F. L.G. army| Gone in 4/45|
Major	Jeffrey Richbell	Major ditto. Succeeded Bulstrode as lt. col.|
Captains	Severinus Dursey	Capt. ditto| Succeeded Richbell as major|
	Edward Gittins	Capt. ditto|
	John Fowne	Capt. ditto|
	Thomas Gimmins/Jennins[24]	Capt. or Capt. Lt. ditto|
	Arthur Young[25]	XXX
	Thomas Gollidge[26]	XXX
	Ralph Cobbett[27]	L.G. army|
Capt. Lt.	XXX	

23   Bulstrode left the regiment when appointed governor of Henley-on-Thames in 4/45: CSPD 1644-5, p. 386.

24   Temple was mistaken in thinking that this officer's first name was John: 'Original Officer List', p. 57. He was in fact the Captain Lieutenant Thomas Jennings who is named in Peacey and Turton's list of the infantry officers of Cunningham's regiment in Essex's

army in May 1644. On Richard Fortescue's promotion to colonel in late 1644 after the death of Colonel Cunningham Jennins probably became a company commander and in this capacity he signed the petition of Essex's infantry officers delivered to Parliament in 12/44: HLRO, Main Papers vol. 177, fo. 102: BL, Harleian Ms 166, fo. 174.

25 An ensign at Edgehill in Sir William Constable's regiment of foot, Young later became a company commander in the regiment but it was disbanded in 4/44. It is not known in which regiment he was serving immediately prior to the formation of the New Model Army, but he was probably a reformado like John and Ralph Cobbett: Peacock, *Army Lists*, p. 42; LJ vi, pp.516-17.

26 This was probably the man who in 8/43 was ensign to Captain Walter Lloyd, later colonel of the 11th regiment of foot, who was also killed at Taunton: TNA, SP 28/9, fo. 28. I am most grateful to Simon Marsh for this reference.

27 Cobbett had been successively ensign, lieutenant and captain in John Holmstead's regiment of foot in Essex's army until it was disbanded in 4/44. He then served as reformado in Essex's regiment of horse under Lieutenant Colonel Richard Graves: ibid, E 121/4/5/64B, entry 7; ibid, E 121/2/11/17B, entries 52-5.

6th Regiment	Name	Military career
Colonel	Richard Ingoldsby	Col. F. L.G. army|
Lt. Col.	Robert Farrington	Major Richard Ingoldsby's regt. F. L.G. army|
Major	Richard Cromwell[28]	XXX
Captains	Charles Duckett	Capt. Richard Ingoldsby's regt. F. L.G. army|
	Henry Ingoldsby	Capt. ditto|
	Job Gibson	Capt. ditto|
	Francis Allen[29]	XXX
	Andrew Ward	Capt. Essex's regt. F. L.G. army|
	John Mill	Capt. Lord Robartes'regt. F. L.G. army|
	Warwick Bamfield[30]	Capt. Essex's regt. F. L.G. army|
Capt. Lt.	William Duckett[31]	

28 This officer was identified by F. and D. and Temple as Philip, son of Sir Phillip Cromwell and a cousin of the Ingoldsbys: 'Original Officer List', p. 58. However, warrants he signed in the spring of 1645 show that his first name was Richard: e.g. TNA SP 28/29, fos. 26, 72. He had probably been captain in John Pickering's regiment in the Eastern Association army: G. Davies ed., *Eastern Association*, p. 95.

29 Allen was a lieutenant to Captain Samuel Clarke in Skippon's regiment of foot in Essex's army until c. 5/44. He then resigned to become captain in Colonel Bowen's regiment being raised for service in Wales but he did not serve. Allen was recommended by Skippon for a command at Newport Pagnell in 11/44 but he was arrested instead. He was probably a reformado in 3/45: Luke, *Letter Books*, pp. 192-3, 384.

30 At this point there was a gap in the list of officers for this regiment that Fairfax sent to Parliament on 27/2/45. Bamfield was appointed company commander by the Commons on 15 March: CJ iv, p. 79. He was without doubt the Captain Warwick Bamfield who was serving in the earl of Essex's regiment of foot in 1644 and early 1645: TNA, SP 28/28, fo. 281; ibid, E 121/1/6/117, entry 220.

31 Duckett was lieutenant in Ingoldsby's own company in Essex's army but was not discharged in 4/45: ibid, SP, 28/29, fo. 283. It is therefore highly probable that he continued to serve as captain lieutenant in the New Model Army regiment.

7th Regiment	Name	Military career
Colonel	Thomas Rainborough[32]	Col. F. E.A. army|
Lt. Col.	Henry Bowen[33]	XXX
Major	John Done	Capt. Lawrence Crawford's regt. F. E.A. army|
Captains	John Horsey	Capt. Essex's regt. F. L.G. army|
	Francis Weston[34]	XXX|Did not serve in N.M. army|
	XXX Barber[35]	XXX|Did not serve in N.M. army|
	Thomas Crosse	Capt. Francis Russell's regt. F. E.A. army|
	John Edwards	Capt. ditto|
	Lionel? Lingwood[36]	Capt. ditto|Did not take up his commission|
	XXX Snelling	Capt. ditto|Ditto|
Capt. Lt.	XXX Fleming[37]	XXX

32 Thomas Ayloffe, colonel of an Eastern Association regiment in the Abingdon garrison, was named as colonel of this regiment in 1/45, but the House of Commons had second thoughts a month later. Fairfax was asked to think again, and the Commons approved Rainborough as his replacement on 1/3/45: CJ iv, p. 27, 64-5.

33 Bowen was probably the man who failed to raise a regiment for service in Wales in the summer of 1644. For this see note 29 above.

34 Weston was almost certainly the Francis Weston who commanded a company in Ayloffe's regiment at Abingdon: TNA, E 121/3/4/ unnumbered, entries 164, 204; Spring ii.

35 There are two possible identifications. A Captain John Barber was associated with the Abingdon garrison. He had originally been in Sir John Whittewronge's Hertfordshire regiment, which merged with Ayloffe's in late 1644. In 5/45 he was serving as a major in Colonel Alban Cox's Hertfordshire regiment of foot: Thomson, *Impact of the Civil War on Hertfordshire*, pp. 24, 106; TNA, E 121/4/8/72, entry 1; CSPD 1644, p.326; Spring ii, p. 16. Another Captain Barber served in Manchester's regiment of foot but had left by 3/45: Spring i; Davies, Eastern Association, p. 92. The former seems the more likely candidate given that Ayloffe was nominated as the first colonel of the 7th regiment of foot, and that three captains from Ayloffe's regiment were chosen as company commanders in the regiment between 2 and 5/45. There is, however, the possibility that the two Barbers were the same man.

36 If this man was the Lionel Lingwood who was commissioned as captain in the 2nd regiment of foot in 1650 he chose instead to serve in Sir Thomas Fairfax's lifeguard: TNA, E 121/2/3/32, entry 9; Worc. College, Clarke Ms 67, fo. 3.

37 See below p. 57.

8th Regiment[38]	Name	Military career
Colonel	Ralph Weldon	Col. F. W. Army|
Lt. Col.	Nicholas Kempson	Lt. Col. Weldon's regt. F. W. army|
Major	William Masters[39]	Major ditto|
Captains	Christopher Peckham	Capt. ditto|
	Nicholas Fenton[40]	Capt. ditto|
	John Francklin	Capt. ditto|
	Francis Dormer	Capt. ditto|
	Jeremiah Tolhurst?	XXX
	John Munday/Munden?[41]	XXX
	Stephen Caine/Kaine?[42]	XXX
Capt. Lt.	XXX	

38 The first seven company commanders were captains in the regiment in Waller's army by 31/1/45: TNA, SP/130, fos. 140-53. Temple asserts that all ten were commissioned into Weldon's New Model Army regiment, but the entry in the Lords Journal does not list them by name. It merely states that the House was convinced that the Kent county committee would recommend very good and able officers to Sir Thomas Fairfax for the regiment they had raised and financed: 'Original Officer List', p. 59; LJ vii, p. 265. The earliest listing of the 8th regiment of foot is in Sprigg's *Anglia Rediviva*. Sprigg is sound on officers who were in place from 7/45 onwards, but not infrequently he fails to mention troop and company commanders who were appointed in 4/45 but left during the first three months of the New Model Army's existence: see note 137 below. Tolhurst, Munday and Caine may thus have been appointed at a later date. The first mention of Caine and Munday as company commanders was after 6/45, which makes it possible that they were replacements for officers killed in operations around Taunton where the regiment was trapped between mid- May and early July.

39 Originally a captain in the regiment, Masters succeeded Major Thomas Womwell in 12/44: TNA, SP/130, fo. 141.

40 Not James Fenton as stated by Temple and F. and D. The officer was Lieutenant Nicholas Fenton who took over Cornelius Lamb's company in Weldon's regiment in 8/44 and was still serving in 4/45: Spring ii.

41 Munden occurs in TNA, SP 28/48, fo. 38. Shreeve Parker, his lieutenant, was commissioned in 7/45: ibid, SP 28/48, fo. 244.

42 For Caine's first name, see ibid, SP 28/44, fo. 198. The first mention of him as a captain in the regiment is in a warrant issued in 7/47: ibid, SP 28/31, fo. 170.

9th Regiment	Name	Military career
Colonel	Harry Barclay[43]	Col. F. L.G. army|Did not serve in the N.M. army|
Lt. Col.	John Innes[44]	Lt. Col. ditto|Did not serve in the N.M. army|
Major	William Cowell	Capt. ditto|
Captains	William Goffe[45]	Capt. ditto|
	George Gregson	Capt. ditto|
	George Ramsey[46]	Capt. ditto|Did not serve in the N.M. army|
	George Sampson[47]	Capt. ditto|

9th Regiment	Name	Military career
	William Leete[48]	Capt. ditto| Resigned 4/45|
	Vincent Goddard[49]	Capt. F. Abingdon garrison|Did not serve in the N. M. army. Reassigned to Abingdon 4/45|
	John Blagrave[50]	Capt. F. in ditto| Ditto|
Capt. Lt.	XXX	

43 Like many other Scottish officers Barclay refused the offer of a commission in the New Model Army.

44 This man was also probably a Scot.

45 I have kept to Firth and Davies's convention of spelling this officer's name as Goffe rather than Gough so as to distinguish him from Captain William Gough who became a company commander in Robert Overton's regiment in the late 1640s.

46 Ramsey was also probably a Scot.

47 This officer signed the petition of the earl of Essex's company commanders in 12/44: HLRO, Main Papers vol. 177, fo. 102; TNA, SP 28/301, fo. 612. F. and D. were wrong to claim that he was Captain Latimer Simpson, who had no connection with the 9th regiment of foot or its predecessor. Instead he served in General Skippon's Bristol garrison regiment: TNA, E 121/2/44B, entry 23.

48 The date of Leete's resignation appears on his request for pay arrears in 1646: TNA, SP 28/265, fos. 206-14.

49 Goddard's first name is given in ibid, SP 28/28, pt. 1. His and Blagrave's companies had been taken into Barclay's regiment in 2/45: ibid, SP 28/28, fo. 384. Their reassignment in mid-April is noted in CJ iv, p. 98.

50 Blagrave was a major in the Reading garrison by 1647 and a captain in the Berkshire militia in 1650: TNA, E 121/10/49, entry 479; CSPD 1650, p. 510.

10th Regiment	Name	Military career
Colonel	Edward Montagu	Col. F. E.A. army|
Lt. Col.	Mark Grime	Lt. Col. Montagu's regt. F. E.A. army|
Major	Thomas Kelsey[51]	Garr. officer. E.A. army|
Captains	Wroth Rogers	Capt. Montagu's regt. F. E.A. army|
	John Biscoe[52]	Capt. ditto|
	Francis Blethin	Capt. ditto|
	Lawrence Nunney/Nonney	Capt. ditto|
	William Wilkes	Capt. ditto|
	Giles Saunders	Lt. to Capt. Pritchard's co. in ditto and then capt.[53]|
	Thomas Disney[54]	XXX
Capt. Lt.	XXX	

51 Kelsey had served in the garrisons of Norwich and Boston: Google search; Spring i.

52 Temple gave this man's name as Butler, but the correct reading is Bisser (rightly Biscoe): Original Army List', p. 61. He had served as captain in Richard Ingoldsby's regiment of foot in Essex's army before transferring to Montagu's: TNA, E 121/3/3/115, entries 66, 70. There is no mention of him in the list of the Eastern Association company commanders in early 1645: ibid, SP 28/27, fo. 262. He was, however, at Henley in 2/45: CSPD 1644-5, p. 314.

53 TNA, E 121/5/7/unnumbered, entries 149, 164.

54 Not a captain in Montagu's regiment in the Eastern Association army in 1/3/45, Disney seems to have taken over Captain Weedon's company of which he may have been the lieutenant. Weedon's lieutenant's name does not appear in the listing of the regiment in Spring i.

11th Regiment	Name	Military career
Colonel	Edward Aldridge[55]	Col. F. L.G. army| Resigned 4/45|
Lt. Col.	Walter Lloyd	Lt. Col. Aldridge's regt. F. L.G. army. Succeeded as col. 4/45|
Major	Thomas Read[56]	Capt. William Davies's regt. F. L.G. army|
Captains	William Wilkes[57]	Capt. Aldridge's regt. L.G. army|
	John Melvin	Capt. Lord Robartes' regt. F. L.G. army|
	John Spooner	Capt. ditto|
	XXX Smith[58]	XXX|Did not serve in the N.M. army|

11th Regiment	Name	Military career
	Benjamin Wigfall/Wingfield	Capt. William Davies's regt. F. L.G. army|
	Phillip Gittins[59]	Capt. Aldridge's regt. F. L.G. army	
	Richard Lundy	Capt. ditto|
Capt. Lt.	Thomas Cooper[60]	Capt. Lt. ditto|

55 Aldridge, unsatisfied with the officers he had been allotted, wrote a letter of resignation on 28/3, but Fairfax asked him to stay for a few more days. He was still in post on 5/4/45: Bodleian Library, Oxford (Bodleian), Tanner Ms 60, fos. 30, 34; TNA, SP 28/34, fo. 2.

56 Ibid, SP 28/301, fo. 613. For his service in Essex's army, see ibid, E 121/1/7/unnumbered, entry 62.

57 William Wilkes succeeded Captain Luke Meakin: Ibid, E 121/1/5, entries 3, 4, 12. He signed the petition of Essex's infantry officers delivered to Parliament in 12/44 and was not discharged from the regiment in 4/45: BL, Harleian Ms 166, fo. 174: TNA, SP 28/29, fo. 323. It can be asserted with confidence that the officer's first name was not Timothy Wilkes as claimed by Temple: 'Original Army List', p. 61. For this see F. and D., p. 572.

58 This officer may be Francis Smith who was a captain in Lord Robartes' regiment in 5/44: Peachey and Turton, p. 61. He was succeeded by Nathaniel Short.

59 According to pay warrants of Essex's army examined by Peachey and Turton, Gittins was a company commander in Aldridge's regiment in 5/44: Peachey and Turton, *Old Robin's Foot*, p. 61. His career in that army has left no further trace, but as Gittins was not one of the company commanders who was dismissed in 4/45 he almost certainly moved straight into the New Model Army: TNA, SP 28/29, fo. 323.

60 Cooper had been Aldridge's captain lieutenant in Essex's army. He was not dismissed in 4/45: Peachey and Turton, Old Robin's Foot, p. 61; BL, Harleian Ms 166, fo. 174; TNA, SP 28/29, fo. 323.

12th Regiment	Name	Military career
Colonel	John Pickering	Col. F. E.A. army|
Lt. Col.	John Hewson	Lt. Col. Pickering's regt. F. E.A. army|
Major	John Jubbs	Major ditto|
Captains	Daniel Axtell	Capt. ditto|
	Azariah Husbands[61]	Capt. ditto|
	John Jenkins[62]	Capt. ditto| X at Faringdon c. 1/5/45|
	John Silverwood	Capt. ditto|
	John Carter	Capt. ditto|
	Reynold Gayle[63]	Capt. Lt. ditto|
	Thomas Price[64]	XXX
Capt. Lt.	Alexander Brayfield[65]	

61 Temple suggests that this officer's first name was James. Spring asserts that it was Azariah, who subsequently became a captain in the 7th regiment of horse, and he is right: 'Original Officer List', p. 62; TNA, E 121/11/19, entries 107-8.

62 Jenkins's first name was George according to Temple, but it was in fact it was John who was killed at Faringdon. George, who later commanded a company in the regiment, was probably ensign at the time. He signed the Vindication of the army's conduct in 4/47 as a lieutenant: 'Original Officer List', p. 61; BL, Thomason Tracts E 385 (19). See also pp. 104 and 119 below.

63 Gayle had been captain lieutenant in the last few months of Manchester's army's existence: TNA, SP 28/27, fo. 262.

64 Price's previous rank is not known, but the almost complete list of commissioned officers for Pickering's regiment for 1/45, Price being the most junior captain in 4/45, and the strong suggestion in the row over the regiment's composition in Parliament in 3/45 that Fairfax intended Pickering's officers to be transferred *en masse* from Manchester's army to the new army, make it highly likely that he was lieutenant to Captain Carter. The claim of Sergeant Thomas Chapman for pay arrears suggests that Price took over Captain Richard Cromwell's company, Cromwell having been chosen as major of the 4th regiment of foot: ibid, SP 28/27, fo. 262; Temple, 'Original Army List', pp. 71, 75; TNA, E 121/4/7/50, entries 88-9.

65 Brayfield was lieutenant to Captain Beaman in the earl of Manchester's regiment of dragoons in the Eastern Association army and then a lieutenant in Pickering's regiment in that army: Spring i.

Dragoons

Regiment	Name	Military career
Colonel	John Okey	Major Sir Arthur Haselrig's regt. H. W. army|
Major	William Gwilliam[66]	Capt. Waller's regt. H. W. army[67]| Transferred to 11th regt. H. N.M. army as capt. before 2/5/45|
Captains	John Farmer[68]	XXX
	XXX Butler[69]	XXX|Did not serve in the N.M. army|
	Christopher Mercer[70]	Capt. Manchester's regt. Dr. E.A. army|
	Daniel Abbott	Capt. ditto|
	XXX Larken[71]	XXX|Did not serve in the N.M. army|
	Ralph Farr[72]	Lt. to Major Okey in Haselrig's regt. H. W. army|
	XXX Bulkham[73]	XXX|Did not serve in N.M. army|
	Tobias Bridge[74]	Capt. Manchester's regt. Dr. E.A. army|
Capt. Lt.	William Hext?[75]	Corp. Okey's troop. Haselrig's regt. H. W. Army|

66 Temple suggested that this man's first name was Ralph or Robert but did not provide any evidence: 'Original Army List', p. 69. In fact it was William: TNA, SP 28/30, fo. 335.

67 Spring ii.

68 Farmer had served as a captain in Sir William Balfour's regiment of horse in the Lord General's army from mid-1643 to c. 6/44, but he was not a troop commander when the regiment was in Cornwall in August: Turton, *Chief Strength*, p. 31; Richard Symonds, Diaries of the Marches of the Royal Army during the Great Civil War, C. Long ed., *Camden Society* LXXIV (1859), p. 73.

69 This man was probably Nathaniel Butler who was captain of a company of Kentish dragoons under Waller's command in the latter half of 1644: CSPD 1644, pp. 375, 469. Temple identifies him as William Boteler who was active in putting down Colonel Penruddock's uprising in 1655 and who later became one of Cromwell's infamous major generals: 'Original Officer List', p. 69. However, that Captain Butler spent the mid-1640s in the Northampton garrison in Lionel Lytcott's regiment of horse: Luke, *Letter Books*, p. 500.

70 Mercer habitually signed his name Ch. Mercer. The fact that his first name was Christopher, not Charles, is apparent from a warrant made out in 5/45: TNA, SP 28/30, fo. 316.

71 According to Temple this officer was Lawrence Larkin, an Irishman who preferred to fight in Ireland and therefore did not take up his commission: 'Original Officer List', p. 69. This seems improbable. More likely candidates are to be found amongst the infantry officers in the Eastern Association army, such as the Captain Larken in Colonel Valentine Walton's regiment of foot: Spring i, p. 105.

72 TNA, E 121/2/3/43A, entry 1.

73 Possibly this was Captain Burket of Manchester's regiment of dragoons who was in service in 2/45. Less likely is Herbert Birkham who was John Lilburne's cornet in 11/44: Spring i. However, Bulkham was not a clerk's error for Henry Fulcher as Temple suggests: 'Original Officer List', p.69. Fulcher did not gain a captaincy in this regiment soon after the formation of the New Model Army but in 6/47: F. and D.

74 Spring i.

75 Hext received pay for Okey's troop in the New Model dragoon regiment in 7/45 at which time he held the rank of lieutenant: Spring ii; TNA, SP 28/31, fo. 293.

Cavalry

1st Regiment	Name	Military career
Colonel	Sir Thomas Fairfax	Col. and Lieutenant General H. N. army|
Major	John Disbrowe[76]	Major Oliver Cromwell's regt. H. E.A. army|
Captains	John Browne	Capt. ditto|
	Adam Lawrence	Capt. ditto|
	James Berry	Capt. ditto|
	Robert Swallow	Capt. ditto|
Capt. Lt.	John Gladman	Capt. Lt. Oliver Cromwell's regt. H. E.A. army|

76 See F. and D., pp. 1-41 for the composition of Cromwell's regiment in the Eastern Association army.

2nd Regiment	Name	Military career
Colonel	John Middleton[77]	Lieutenant General H. W. army|Did not serve in the N.M. army|
Major	Thomas Horton	Capt. Lt. in Sir Arthur Haselrig's regt. H. W. army|
Captains	John Butler	Adjutant General W. army and Capt. in Haselrig's regt. H.|
	Edward Foley	Capt. ditto|
	Samuel Gardiner	Capt. ditto|
	Walter Parry/Perry[78]	Capt. ditto|
Capt. Lt.	XXX	

77 A Scotsman, he returned home in 5/45. After many ups and downs he became and an earl and Charles II's representative in Scotland in the early sixteen-sixties.

78 Not James as Temple would have it but Walter: 'Original Officer List', p. 63; A.J. Adair, *Cheriton: the Campaign and the Battle* (Kineton, 1971), p. 218; TNA, SP 28/29, fo. 103. Parry was wounded at Naseby but returned to his command in mid-July: ibid, SP 28/31, fo. 120.

3rd Regiment	Name	Military career
Colonel	James Sheffield[79]	Col. H. L.G. army| Withdrew in 5/45|
Major	Thomas Sheffield	Capt. James Sheffield's regt. H. L.G. army. Succeeded his brother James as col.|
Captains	Arthur Evelyn[80]	Capt. ditto L.G.army|
	William Rainborough	Capt. Sir Arthur Balfour's regt. H. ditto|
	Gabriel Martin[81]	Capt. or lt. Essex's regt. H. ditto|
	Robert Robotham	Capt. Sheffield's regt. H. ditto|
Capt. Lt.	Thomas Jewkes?	Lt. to Col. Sheffield in Essex's army[82]|

79 Colonel of horse from 17 July 1643, Sheffield was paid as such until 5 May 1645. His troop was then reduced into another troop in the regiment: TNA, SP 28/140/15.

80 According to Turton this officer's troop in Essex's army lost its independent existence in August 1643 when it was absorbed into Captain Thomas Wogan's troop: Turton, *Chief Strength*, p. 30. Spring believes Evelyn's troop lived on, having been detached from Essex's army. His grounds are that in 7/44 it was serving in the Thames valley with Major-General Browne. In fact the reference is to 7/45: CSPD 1645-7, p. 28. Evelyn may therefore have been a reformado, but it is possible that his troop was detached from Essex's army to assist in the establishment of the garrisons at Taunton and Weymouth in 7/44, and that this explains why Evelyn does not appear in the list of Essex's troop commanders operating in Cornwall in 8/44: Symonds, Marches of the Royal Armies, p. 73. Alternatively Evelyn served under Browne in both 1644 and 1645. There is a hint of this in the claims of one of his troopers for pay arrears. This man had fought under Evelyn as a captain in Essex's army and then as captain and major in Colonel Henry Marten's regiment in Browne's brigade: TNA, E 121/4/8/57B, entry 4.

81 Martin had been lieutenant in Captain Lionel Copley's troop. Early in 1645 he may have succeeded Copley, who was in trouble with the House of Commons: ibid, SP 28/29, fo. 356; Turton, *Chief Strength*, p. 26; CJ iii, pp. 613-14, 708. However, he may still have been lieutenant in 4/45: TNA, SP 28/29, fos. 92, 356.

82 W. S. Library, SMS 463, unfol. 12/4/45; Turton, *Chief Strength*, p. 61.

4th Regiment	Name	Military career
Colonel	Charles Fleetwood	Col. H. E.A. army|
Major	Thomas Harrison	Major in Charles Fleetwood's regt. H. E.A. army|
Captains	Richard Fincher	Capt. Waller's regt. H. W. army| Major 3rd regt. H. N.M. army in 5/45|
	Richard Le Hunt	Capt. Fleetwood's regt. E.A. army|
	William Coleman[83]	Capt. Lt. ditto|
	John Selby[84]	Capt. ditto|
Capt. Lt.	Joseph Blisset?[85]	Cor. to Fleetwood's troop E.A. army|

83 Coleman was not an officer in Oliver Cromwell's regiment as Temple claimed: 'Original Officer List', p. 64. In Manchester's army he was captain lieutenant in Colonel Fleetwood's regiment: ibid, E 121/5/6/49B, entries 2-3.

84 Not Thomas Selby and not an officer in Cromwell's regiment of horse as Temple claimed: 'Original Officer List', p. 64. He had probably served as lieutenant of Colonel Francis Russell's troop in the army of the Eastern Association: ibid, SP 28/27, fo. 288.

85 Ibid, E 121/5/7/12, entry 31. Blissett was captain lieutenant at Naseby where at least eight of his men were wounded: ibid, SP 28/173/1, fo. 12. An abbreviated list of all the casualties is printed in G. Foard, *Naseby the Decisive Campaign* (Whitstable, 1995), p. 408-13, but I have cited the original as Foard's list contains aome serious errors in the transcription of officers' names.

5th Regiment	Name	Military career
Colonel	Edward Rossiter	Col. H. E.A. army|
Major	Phillip Twistleton	Major Rossiter's regt. H. E. A. army|
Captains	Anthony Markham	Capt. ditto|
	John Nelthorpe	Capt. ditto|
	Christopher Bushy[86]	Capt. ditto|
	Original Peart	Capt. ditto|
Capt. Lt.	XXX	

86 TNA, E 121/3/3/113B, entry 119.

6th Regiment	Name	Military career
Colonel	Bartholomew Vermuyden	Col. H. E.A.army|
Major	Robert Huntington	Capt. Vermuyden's regt. H. E. A. army|
Captains	John Jenkins	Capt. ditto|
	Thomas Bush[87]	Capt. ditto|
	John Reynolds[88]	XXX
	Henry Middleton[89]	Capt. Sir John Norwich's regt. H. E. A. army|
Capt. Lt.	Richard Curzon[90]	XXX|

87 For Bush's first name, which is not given in Spring i, see TNA, SP 28/29, fo. 48. Bush was in trouble in 4/45, seemingly for his maltreatment of civilians in Buckinghamshire: Luke, *Letter Books*, p. 196: CJ iv, p. 117. However, in the Journal his name is given as Bushy. If the clerk in the Commons misheard the name of the regiment, this would explain Captain Christopher Bushy's leaving the 5th regiment of horse not long afterwards.

88 Captain Reynolds was related to Oliver Cromwell by marriage: M. Noble, *Memoirs of the Protectorate House of Cromwell* (1784), p. 419. He was probably an officer in the Plymouth garrison regiment of horse who had attracted attention by his bravery during the Lostwithiel campaign: F. and D., p. 605.

89 There were several Captain Middletons in Parliament's armies in 1644, but the fact that Edward Sharpe was Henry Middleton's lieutenant in the Eastern Association army and was wounded at Naseby, also as Middleton's lieutenant, makes the identification certain: Spring i; TNA, SP 28/173/1, fo. 11.

90 Spring knew Curzon's rank but not his regiment. It seems very likely that he was captain lieutenant to Vermuyden in Manchester's army as well as in the New Model: Spring i, p. 115; TNA, SP 28/173/1, fo. 11.

7th Regiment	Name	Military career
Colonel	Algernon Sidney	Col. Manchester's regt. H. E.A. army|
Major	John Alford	Major ditto|
Captains	Edward Dendy[91]	Capt. ditto|
	Thomas Neville[92]	Capt. ditto|
	Thomas Ireton	Capt. Oliver Cromwell's regt. H. in ditto|
	William Bough[93]	Capt. Lt. Waller's regt. H. W army|
Capt. Lt.	Roger Hopkins XXX [94]	

91 Dendy appears to have been captain lieutenant to the earl of Manchester: ibid, E 121/4/1/10, entry 1.

92 This officer was incorrectly described as Jonas Neville by F. and D. and Temple. Jonas does appear once against Captain Neville's name in a contemporary transcription of a document but it was a clerical error.

93 Bough was formerly captain lieutenant in Waller's regiment of horse. He was not the Lieutenant Bough who had served previously in the Warwickshire militia as Temple claimed: 'Original Officer List', p. 66. George Elsmore, who was Bough's cornet in the New Model and who took over the troop on his departure, had served under Bough as quartermaster in Waller's army, whilst Caleb Lee, a corporal in his troop in Waller's army, was his quartermaster in the New Model. However, what clinches the matter is the fact that in 1650 when Elsmore was captain at least 33 of his soldiers claimed arrears for their service in Waller's regiment: Spring ii; TNA, E 121/2/11/19, entries 170-229. Bough's first name is given as William in ibid, E 121/2/9/31, entries 25-6.

94 W.S. Library, SMS 463, unfol. 12/4/45. He transferred to Alford's troop, presumably after his colonel resigned. For this, see note 261 below.

8th Regiment	Name	Military career
Colonel	Sir Robert Pye[95]	Col. H. L.G. army|
Major	Nathaniel Rich	Lt. Col. Manchester's regt. H. E.A. army|
Captains	Matthew Tomlinson[96]	Capt. ditto|
	Ralph Knight[97]	Capt. ditto|
	Henry Ireton[98]	Capt. Oliver Cromwell's regt. H. E.A. army| Col. 11th regt. H. by 5/45. Capt. Barry 11th regt. H. succeeded him|
	Ralph Margery	Capt. ditto|
Capt. Lt.	Edward/Edmund Hamden[99]	

95 Fairfax's intention was for Nathaniel Rich, lieutenant colonel of the earl of Manchester's regiment of horse, to command the 8th regiment of horse, but the House of Commons decided he should be its major instead: CJ iv, p. 66. For a convincing narrative of the events surrounding Rich's loss of rank in March 1645, see Temple, Original Army List, p. 65.

96 Tomlinson was intended by Fairfax to serve as major but this was not approved by the House of Commons who preferred Nathaniel Rich. Tomlinson held the rank of captain as late as 20/5/45 when he was described as such by Oliver Cromwell: Luke, *Letter Books*, p. 542.

97 Knight had been lieutenant to Captain John Okey and then commander of the troop in the earl of Manchester's regiment that was often described as Manchester's lifeguard: TNA, E 121/4/2/ 73, entry 179.

98 Ireton had also been Commissary General of Horse in the Eastern Association Army.

99 W.S. Library, SMS 463, unfol. 26/6/45. Hamden had served as lieutenant in Pye's troop in Essex's army: ibid, E 121/2/11/33, entry 397.

9th Regiment	Name	Military career
Colonel	Edward Whalley	Lt. Col. Oliver Cromwell's regt. H. E.A. army|
Major	Christopher Bethell	Capt. ditto|
Captains	Samuel Porter[100]	Capt. ditto|
	John Grove	Capt. ditto|
	XXX Horseman[101]	XXX
	William Packer	Capt. Oliver Cromwell's regt. H. ditto|
Capt. Lt.	William Evanson[102]	Lt. to Whalley's troop E.A. army|

100 Despite Temple's comment that Porter did not take up his commission, he was in command of the troop when it fought at Naseby: 'Original Army List', p. 67. TNA, SP 28/30, fo. 560 (warrant dated 24/6/45). Evanson had replaced him by 10/7/45: F. and D.

101 This officer is either Edward who had been a captain in Cromwell's regiment in the Eastern Association Army or Robert who was a commander in the garrison of Rockingham Castle: Luke, *Letter Books*, p. 345; Spring i. Temple believed that there was a single Captain Horseman – Robert – but Edward certainly existed as is shown by the war record of soldiers who had served under him: Temple, 'Original Officer List', p. 67; BL, Harleian MS 427, fo. 122; TNA, E 121/4/1/92, fo. 16. In 1650 Edward was major of the militia horse for Northamptonshire: CSPD 1650, p. 504. However, the uncertainty as to which Captain Horseman was nominated by Fairfax is of little significance as his successor was in command of the troop by the time of the battle of Naseby: TNA, SP 28/173/1, fo. 18.

102 BL, Harleian Ms 427, fo. 88.

10th Regiment	Name	Military career
Colonel	Richard Graves	Lt. Col. Essex's regt. H. L.G. army|
Major	Adrian Scroop	Capt. Sir Robert Pye's regt. H. L.G. army|
Captains	Nicholas Bragg[103]	Capt. Lt. Phillip Skippon's troop. Essex's regt. H. L.G. army|
	Charles Doyley[104]	Capt. Lifeguard H. L.G. army| Capt. Fairfax's lifeguard N.M. army by 25/4/45[105]. Succeeded by Capt. Nathaniel Barton|
	Christopher Fleming	Capt. Hans Behre's regt. H. L.G. army|
	William, Lord Caulfield[106]	XXX
Capt. Lt.	Charles Holcroft	Capt. Lt. Essex's regt. H. L.G. army|

103 TNA, E 315/5, fo. 7; W.S. Library, SMS 463, unfol. 28/4/45. The troop continued to be described as Skippon's troop until 3/49.

104 This officer is clearly Charles Doyley, not Edward, as claimed by Temple. This is proved by a pay warrant for Fairfax's lifeguard dated 24/6/45: ibid, SP 28/30, fo. 538.

105 CJ iv, p. 122.

106 Fairfax had nominated Captain Chute of the earl of Essex's regiment of horse as commander of this troop, but he died during March. The House of Commons named Lord Caulfield in his stead. A refugee from Ireland, where his brother and predecessor as Lord Caulfield had been killed by the Catholic insurgents, he had been captured at the Second Battle of Newbury in 10/44: CJ iv, pp. 98-9; F. and D. At the time he was serving in Essex's lifeguard: F. and D.; TNA, SP28/20, fo. 57. I am most grateful to Simon Marsh for the information about Caulfield serving in Essex's lifeguard.

11th Regiment	Name	Military career
Colonel	Sir Michael Livesey[107]	Col. H. W. army|Cashiered for disobedience 4/45| Succeeded by Henry Ireton of the 8th regt. H.|
Major	George Sedascue[108]	Major Sir Michael Livesey's regt. H. W. army|
Captains	Robert Gibbon	Capt. ditto|
	John Hoskins	Capt. ditto|
	Thomas Pennyfather	Capt. Sir Arthur Haselrig's regt. H. W. army| Moved to 2nd regt. H. by 15/4/45.[109] Succeeded by Capt. William Gwilliam, initially major Dr. N.M. army|
	Samuel Barry[110]	Capt. Haselrig's regt. H. W. army|Transferred to 8th regt. H. N.M. army late 4/45.
Capt. Lt.	William Cecil?[111]	XXX

107 For the reasons for Livesey's dismissal, see F. and D.

108 This man may have been the Lieutenant Sedeskins in Livesey's troop in Waller's army who was accused of plundering the inhabitants of Kent early in the Civil War: TNA, SP 28/43, fo. 568.

109 W.S. Library, SMS 463, unfol.

110 According to Temple this officer was the Samuel Barry who later served as a colonel in the West Indies and he is almost certainly right: 'Original Officer List', p. 69. When Henry Ireton was promoted to colonel of the 11th regiment of horse Barry replaced him in the 8th regiment. It seems most likely that this involved their respective troops of horse also being transferred from one regiment to the other: see note 182 below.

111 A pay warrant dated 25/6/45 shows that William Cecil commanded Livesey's former troop: TNA, SP 28/30, fo. 569.

Lifeguard[112]		

112 The Lifeguard of Horse was not established until the end of April 1645: CJ iv, p. 122.

Company and Troop Commanders in early May 1645

Infantry

1st Regiment	Name	Military career
Colonel	Sir Thomas Fairfax	
Lt. Col.	Thomas Jackson	
Major	Richard Cooke	X at Bristol in 9/45[113]
Captains	Samuel Gooday	Succeeded Cooke as major
	XXX Maneste[114]	D c. 9/45. Succeeded by Thomas Wolfe
	Vincent Boyce	
	Richard Beamont[115]	Left in early 6/45. Succeeded by Michael Bland
	Fulk Muskett	
	Francis White[116]	Succeeded Capt. Johnston
	Thomas Highfield[117]	XXX Succeeded Capt. Cooke
Capt. Lt.	William Fortescue[118]	

113 Sprigg, *Anglia Rediviva*, p. 329.
114 Wolfe had been Maneste's lieutenant in the Eastern Association army: Spring i. For the date at which he became captain, see p. 65 below.
115 Beamont took delivery of the 1st regiment of foot's ten colours in late April and remained in the army until early June: TNA, SP 28/29, fo. 247; Luke, *Letter Books*, pp. 322-3, 328, 582. For Bland, see TNA, SP 28/44, fo. 218. A Captain Richard Beamont was apothecary extraordinary to the army in Scotland in 10/50: ibid, SP 28/71, fo. 259.
116 White had been Johnston's lieutenant. He took over the company when his captain turned down the offer of a commission in the New Model Army: ibid, SP 28/265, fo. 126.
117 The first sign of Highfield as a company commander is a pay warrant dated 3/5/45: ibid, SP 28/30, fo. 151. He must therefore have taken Captain Cooke's place. Less than two months earlier he had been prisoner of war with the rank of captain: CJ iv, p. 81.
118 Fortescue left the regiment in 12/45: TNA, SP 28/38, fo. 438.

2nd Regiment	Name	Military career
Colonel	Phillip Skippon	
Lt. Col.	John Francis	X at Naseby in 6/45[119]
Major	Richard Ashfield	Succeeded Francis as lt. col.
Captains	Samuel Clarke	Succeeded Ashfield as major
	Edward Streater	
	James Harrison	
	John Clarke	
	Maurice Bowen	
	Devereux Gibbon	
	John Cobbett	
Capt. Lt.	William Symonds	

119 Sprigg, *Anglia Rediviva*, p. 329.

3rd Regiment	Name	Military career
Colonel	Sir Hardress Waller	Col. F. W. army. Succeeded James Holbourne
Lt. Col.	Robert Cottesworth	X at siege of Oxford c. 5/46.[120] Succeeded by Major Edward Salmon
Major	Thomas Smith	
Captains	John Gorges	

	Benjamin Holden	Fought at Naseby but not in the army in 6/46[121]	
	John Wade[122]	
	Richard Hill	X at storming of Bristol 9/45	
	William Howard[123]	Reformado. Capt. in John Weare's regt. F. L.G. army 12/43-10/44	
	John Clarke[124]	Capt. Holbourne's regt. Dr. W. army	
	Daniel Thomas	Capt. ditto	
Capt. Lt.	XXX	

120 For the deaths of Cottesworth and Hill, see ibid, p. 329.

121 TNA, SP 28/173/1, fos. 8-9; ibid, SP28/56, fo. 407.

122 Wade had transferred to the 11th regiment as major by 9/46: TNA, SP 28/40, fo. 270. He replaced Major Thomas Read who became lieutenant colonel soon after James Gray's departure in 7/46: ibid, SP 28/265, fos. 254-65.

123 Ibid, SP 28/265, fo. 445.

124 Both Clarke and Thomas were officers surplus to the needs of the New Model Army and were discharged at Wokingham on 25/4/45: ibid, SP 28/35, fo. 635. Within days they had been found places in the 3rd regiment of foot to replace some of the company commanders approved by Parliament in March, who had either refused to serve or been transferred to another regiment. Clarke had been quartered at Wareham in 11/44 with Ralph Wilson, later captain lieutenant in the regiment, as his lieutenant: ibid, SP 28/121A, fo. 685.

4th Regiment	Name	Military career
Colonel	Robert Hammond[125]	Major of Major General Edward Massey's regt. H. Gloucester command. Succeeded Crawford|
Lt. Col.	Isaac Ewer	
Major	Robert Saunders	
Captains	XXX Eaton[126]	Succeeded by Edmund Rolfe, lt. to Capt. Adam Lawrence, 1st regt. H. c. 8/45|
	Israel Smith	
	Charles O'Hara	
	William Disney	
	John Boyce	
	John Puckle	
	William Stratton	Lt. to Capt. Harby. Succeeded him before Naseby|
Capt. Lt.	XXX Hammond??[127]	

125 Hammond had killed a fellow-officer in the Gloucester garrison in a duel in 8/44 but had been acquitted at a court martial held three months later. His promotion from major to colonel is remarkable, but he had powerful family connections as both cousin of Oliver Cromwell and nephew of Thomas Hammond, General of Artillery in the Eastern Association and the New Model Armies: F. and D.

126 Eaton left the regiment between 14/7/45 and 11/8/45: TNA, SP 28/38, fo. 181. For Rolfe, see ibid, E 121/2/2/16, entry 9. Having served with Lawrence Crawford, he was apparently very briefly a lieutenant in Hammond's regiment: ibid, E 121/2/2/16, entry 10.

127 Cuthbert Faunsby claimed for arrears of pay having served under 'Captain Hammond in Colonel Hammond's now Ewer's regiment': ibid, E 121/3/4/4, unnumbered. If this was true, Hammond would have been the captain lieutenant, but I have found no other evidence of his existence.

5th Regiment	Name	Military career
Colonel	Richard Fortescue	
Lt. Col.	Jeffrey Richbell	X at Taunton in spring 45.[128] Succeeded by Dursey, who was succeeded in his turn by Oliver Ingoldsby|
Major	Severinus Dursey	X as lt. col. at Bristol in 9/45. His co. passed to John Denison|
Captains	Oliver Ingoldsby?[129]	Major Sir John Norwich's regt. H. E.A. army| X at Pendennis Castle 3/46|
	Edward Gittins[130]	Left the regt. on or just after 20/8/46|
	John Fowne	X at Tiverton in 11/45|

	Thomas Jennins (Gimmins)	Major when Cobbett succeeded Ingoldsby as lt. col.
	Arthur Young	
	Thomas Gollidge	X at Taunton|
	Ralph Cobbett	Major when Dursey became lt. col., and lt. col. on the death of Ingoldsby|
Capt. Lt.	XXX	

128 For the deaths of Richbell, Dursey, Ingoldsby, Fowne and Gollidge, see Sprigg, *Anglia Rediviva*, p. 330.

129 For Ingoldsby's career in Manchester's army, see Spring i. His troop was reduced into Colonel Fleetwoood's regiment in 4/45: CSPD 1625-49, p. 679. It is possible that he was brought into the 6th regiment after the death of Dursey because none of the captains was thought worthy of promotion. For Ingoldsby's rank in Norwich's regiment see TNA, E 121/5/1/13B, entry 2.

130 Ibid, SP 28/265, fo. 427.

6th Regiment	Name	Military career
Colonel	Richard Ingoldsby	
Lt. Col.	Robert Farrington[131]	Cashiered in 12/45|
Major	Richard Cromwell	X at the storming of Bristol in 9/45.[132] His co. seemingly passed to Capt. John Grime|
Captains	Charles Duckett	Succeeded Richard Cromwell as major|
	Henry Ingoldsby	
	Job Gibson[133]	Left by 12/46. Succeeded by Capt. Stephens|
	Francis Allen	
	Andrew Ward	X at Bristol. Succeeded by Capt. Williams|
	John Mill	
	Warwick Bamfield	Left by 12/46. Succeeded by Capt. Wagstaffe|
Capt. Lt.	William Duckett	

131 A petition relating to Ensign Thomas Johns shows that Farrington was not in post on 22/12/45 as on that date Johns became lieutenant to Lieutenant Colonel Kelsey: ibid, SP 28/51, fo. 6.

132 For the deaths of Cromwell and Ward, see Sprigg, *Anglia Rediviva*, p. 330.

133 Gibson may have left the regiment as early as 7/45. I have not encountered his name subsequently. He was a captain of foot in the Buckinghamshire militia in 1650: ibid, SP 28/301, fo. 775; CSPD 1649-50, p. 521.

7th Regiment	Name	Military career
Colonel	Thomas Rainborough	
Lt. Col.	Henry Bowen	
Major	John Done	X at the siege of Sherborne in 8/45[134]	
Captains	John Horsey	X at Sherborne|
	Thomas Crosse	X at Sherborne as major|
	John Edwards	
	George Drury[135]	Capt. in Thomas Ayloffe's regt. F. E.A. army|
	Thomas Dancer	Capt. ditto|
	Thomas Creamer[136]	Capt. in John Weare's regt. F. L.G. army|
	Edward Sterne	Capt. in Ayloffe's regt. F. E.A. army| X at Bristol|
Capt. Lt.	XXX Fleming[137]	X at Sherborne|

134 For the deaths of Done, Horsey, and Crosse at Sherborne and Sterne at Bristol, see Sprigg, *Anglia Rediviva*, p. 330. However he writes Horsey as Crosse.

135 All four of the new captains had joined the regiment by the end of May: TNA, SP 28/29, fos. 130, 476. A Captain Sanford also had soldiers wounded at Naseby: ibid, SP 28/173/1, fo. 7. He presumably commanded a company attached to the regiment on a temporary basis. For this practice see note 159 below.

136 Ibid, E 121/2/5/59C, entry 7. Creamer's company was disbanded by Essex on 12/10/44 and so he was probably a reformado in 4/45: ibid, E 315/5, fo. 37; ibid, SP 28/265, fo. 445. See also note 381 above.

137 For Fleming's death see Historical Manuscripts Commission (HMC), First Appendix to the 13th Report: Duke of Portland Mss i, p. 242.

8th Regiment	Name	Military career
Colonel	Ralph Weldon[138]	Gone by 7/46. Succeeded by Col. Robert Lilburne|
Lt. Col.	Nicholas Kempson	
Major	William Masters	
Captains	Christopher Peckham	
	Nicholas Fenton	
	John Francklin[139]	X at the siege of Exeter. Succeeded by Capt. Abraham Holmes|
	Francis Dormer	
	Jeremiah Tolhurst	
	John Munday[140]	X at Bradninch in Devon. Succeeded by Capt. George Weldon|
	Stephen Caine	
Capt. Lt.	XXX	

138 Weldon became governor of Plymouth in 12/45 but retained his New Model Army colonelcy until the summer of 1646: TNA, SP 28/39, fos. 30-1.

139 For Francklin's death see Sprigg, Anglia Rediviva, p. 330.

140 Ibid; TNA, SP 28/54, fos. 741-3.

9th Regiment	Name	Military career
Colonel	Edward Harley	Col. F. in Major General Massey's brigade in1644|
Lt. Col.	Thomas Pride[141]	Major in Harry Barclay's regt. F. L.G. army|
Major	William Cowell	
Captains	William Goffe	
	George Gregson	
	George Sampson	
	William Hinder	Capt. Lt. Lord Robartes' regt. F. L.G. army|
	John Ferguson	Capt. William Davies's regt. F. L.G. army|
	John Mason[142]	Lt. to Major Pride in Harry Barclay's regt. F. L.G. army|
	Waldine Lagoe[143]	Lt. to Capt. Cowell in ditto|
Capt. Lt.	XXX	

141 Fairfax's original intention was that Pride should not hold a command in the New Model Army as he was discharged from the army at Reading in 4/45 together with William Arnold, Barclay's captain lieutenant: ibid, SP 29/28, fo. 327.

142 For Mason's rank and regiment in Essex's army, see ibid, E 121/4/8/40B, entry 583.

143 For ditto, see ibid, E 121/4/8/40B, entry 588.

10th Regiment	Name	Military career
Colonel	Edward Montagu[144]	Resigned. Succeeded by Col. John Lambert	
Lt. Col.	Mark Grime	
Major	Thomas Kelsey[145]	Transfer to 6th regt. F. as lt. col. in late 12/45|
Captains	Wroth Rogers[146]	Succeeded Kelsey as major by 4/46|
	John Biscoe	
	Francis Blethin	
	Lawrence Nunney	
	William Wilkes	X at Basing 10/45. Succeeded by Capt. Cadwell[147]|
	Giles Saunders	

10th Regiment	Name	Military career
	Thomas Disney	
Capt. Lt.	XXX	

144 Montagu resigned on 27/10/45: ibid, SP 28/37, fo. 373.
145 See note 131 above for the date. Kelsey was still apparently major in the 10th regiment earlier in the month: ibid, SP 28/33, fo. 612. However, it is possible that, as the regiment was campaigning in Devonshire at the time, the Committee for the Army meeting in London had not yet been informed of his transfer and promotion.
146 For Rogers's promotion see HMC, Duke of Portland Mss i, p. 390; TNA, SP 28/37, fo, 612.
147 Sprigg, *Anglia Rediviva*, p. 329.

11th Regiment	Name	Military career
Colonel	Walter Lloyd[148]	Lt. Col. Edward Aldridge's regt. F. L.G. army| X at Taunton. Succeeded by Col. William Herbert|
Lt. Col.	James Gray[149]	Lt. Col. Godfrey Bosseville's Warwickshire regt. F.| Gone by 8/46|
Major	Thomas Read	
Captains	William Wilkes[150]	X at Taunton|
	John Melvin[151]	
	John Spooner	
	Benjamin Wigfall[152]	X at the siege of Berkeley Castle in 9/45|
	Phillip Gittins	D in Gloucestershire[153]|
	Richard Lundy	
	Nathaniel Short[154]	Capt. Lord Robartes's regt. F. in L.G. army.[155] Succeeded Capt. Smith|
Capt. Lt.	Thomas Cooper[156]	Co. commander in 1645, he must have succeeded Capt. Wilkes X at Taunton, but he himself was X in 9/45 at the storming of Bristol[157] His successor as capt. lt. was Robert Read[158]|

148 Ibid, p. 329. In case of this regiment as with Fortescue's and Rainborough's, Sprigg does not give the names of the men who succeeded to the captaincies of officers who had died.
149 TNA, SP 28/265, fo. 454.
150 Sprigg, *Anglia Rediviva*, p. 329.
151 Melvin was one of the few Scotsman to take up a commission in the New Model: CSPD 1644-5, p. 246.
152 Sprigg, *Anglia Rediviva*, p. 329.
153 Sprigg gives the location but not the date: ibid, p. 329.
154 Short was captain in the regiment by 28/4/45: TNA, SP 28/29, fo. 95.
155 Short's commission in Lord Robartes's regiment was dated 3/2/45: ibid, SP 28/40, fo. 16.
156 Cooper had been captain lieutenant to Colonel Aldridge in Essex's army and almost certainly became a full captain on Aldridge's resignation: ibid, SP 28/47, fo. 370; ibid, SP 28/49, fo. 505
157 Ibid, SP 28/49, fo. 505.
158 Ibid, E 121/5/7/unnumbered, entry 32.

12th Regiment[159]	Name	Military career
Colonel	John Pickering[160]	D at Ottery St. Mary 24/11/45. Succeeded by Lt. Col. Hewson|
Lt. Col.	John Hewson	Col. c. 6/46[161]|
Major	John Jubbs	Replaced Hewson as lt. col.
Captains	Daniel Axtell	Replaced Jubbs as major|
	Azariah Husbands[162]	Moved to 7th regt. H. by 5/46. Prob. succeeded by Capt. Samuel Grime|
	John Silverwood	
	John Carter	
	Reynold Gayle	X at the storming of Bristol|

12th Regiment[159]	Name	Military career
	Thomas Price	
	Peter Tomkins[163]	Lt. to Capt. Daniel Axtell in the E.A. army. He succeeded Capt. Jenkins but was X at Naseby. Prob. succeeded as capt. by Lt. Toppendene|
Capt. Lt.	Alexander Brayfield[164]	

159 At Naseby the regiment appears to have had nine full captains, the seven listed above and two others, Captains Davie and Margerum: ibid, SP 28/173/1, fo. 3. It is possible that one or both were temporary additions, but they do not appear to have been captains whose companies were raised too late to take part in the relief of Taunton. Davie may have been acting captain on the death of Captain Peter Tomkins. For further discussion, see notes 246 and 247.

160 For the deaths of Pickering, Gayle and Tomkins, see Sprigg, *Anglia Rediviva*, pp. 329-30.

161 The colonelcy remained unfilled for some months. In 5/46 the regiment was still being described as the late Colonel Pickering's: TNA, SP 28/38, fo. 138.

162 The petition of John Gillingham wounded at Maidstone in 6/48, shows that Husbands had left by 5/46: ibid, SP 28/56, fo. 385.

163 Tomkins was lieutenant to Captain Axtell in Manchester's army in early 1645: ibid, SP 28/27, fo. 262. Henry Davies had been John Jenkins's lieutenant in the Eastern Association army but Tomkins was preferred as captain on Jenkins's death. Davies was probably acting captain immediately after Tomkins's death at Naseby, but he was superseded by John Toppendene, Hewson's lieutenant. However, Davies was a full captain by 4/47 at the very latest, but possibly before the end of 1645: BL, Thomason Tracts E 385 (19). A confident identification of Peter as Tomkins's first name can be made from a claim for pay arrears submitted by one of his soldiers, though the man claimed that Tomkins served in Hewson's regiment: TNA, E 121/4/7/42, entries 2-3.

164 Having been commissioned as captain lieutenant to Colonel Pickering, he apparently lost that position on Pickering's death and became instead lieutenant to Captain Toppendene: ibid, E 121/2/1/18, entry 12.

Dragoons

Regiment	Name	Military career
Colonel	John Okey	
Major	Nicholas Moore[165]	Capt. Waller's regt. Dr. Succeeded Major Gwilliam|
Captains	John Farmer	XXX
	Christopher Mercer	
	Daniel Abbott	
	Ralph Farr	
	Tobias Bridge	
	Harold Scrimgeour[166]	Capt. Waller's regt. F. W. army|
	Thomas Gorges??[167]	Listed as capt. 3rd regt. F. N.M. army|Capt. William Turpin was in command of the troop in early 7/45[168]|
	Edward Wogan[169]	Capt. Waller regt. Dr. W. army|
Capt. Lt.	William Hext?	

165 Moore and Wogan were in the regiment by 2/5/45: ibid, SP 29/30, fo. 143-5.

166 Scrimgeour was a troop commander in the regiment by 13/5/45 at the latest: ibid, SP 28/30, fo. 199.

167 On 2/5/45 Thomas Gorges, listed initially as captain in the 3rd regiment of foot, was seemingly in command of a troop in Okey's regiment: TNA, SP 28/29, fo. 143. Later Gorges transferred to Colonel Edward Cooke's regiment in Major General Massey's brigade: ibid, E 121/2/2/unnumbered, entry 146; ibid, SP 28/43, fo. 829. In his claim for pay arrears Gorges denied having served in the New Model, but he had been sent westwards by Fairfax on 6/5/45 with a troop of dragoons to accompany the relief expedition to Taunton: ibid, SP 28/253A/3, fo. 66.

168 Ibid, SP 28/31, fo. 26.

169 Wogan had apparently received his commission just before Waller's army was disaggregated in mid to late 4/45: ibid, E 121/1/4/56, entry 69.

Cavalry

1st Regiment	Name	Military career
Colonel	Thomas Fairfax	
Major	John Disbrowe	
Captains	John Browne	
	Adam Lawrence	
	James Berry	
	Robert Swallow	Transferred to 9th regt. H. as capt. 6/45. Succeeded by Capt. William Packer[170]
Capt. Lt.	John Gladman	

170 The list of officers and men wounded at Naseby gives Grove instead of Packer in this regiment, but Grove was serving in the 9th regiment of horse: ibid, SP 28/173/1, fo. 18. This confusion suggests that Packer took over the troop just before the battle.

2nd Regiment	Name	Military career
Colonel	John Butler	Capt. 2nd regt. H. N.M. army|
Major	Thomas Horton	
Captains	Edward Foley	
	Samuel Gardiner	
	Walter Parry[171]	Dead by 2/46. Succeeded by Capt. Walter Bethell|
	Thomas Pennyfather	Capt. 11th regt. H. N.M. army|
Capt. Lt.	Josias Mullineaux[172]	Lt. to Col. Butler|

171 Walter Bethell, Parry's successor, was in command of the troop by 2/46 at the latest: ibid, SP 28/36, fo. 114. The last mention of Parry's troop is in 12/45: ibid, SP 28/33, fo. 537.
172 For Mullineaux's career in Waller's army and his first name, see ibid, E 315/5, fo. 35.

3rd Regiment	Name	Military career
Colonel	Thomas Sheffield	Major 3rd regt. H. N.M. army|
Major	Richard Fincher	Capt. 4th regt. H. ditto|
Captains	Arthur Evelyn	
	William Rainborough	
	Gabriel Martin	
	Robert Robotham	
Capt. Lt.	Thomas Jewkes	

4th Regiment	Name	Military career
Colonel	Charles Fleetwood	
Major	Thomas Harrison	
Captain	Richard Le Hunt[173]	Succeeded by his lt. Richard Zanchy|
	William Coleman	
	John Selby	X at Naseby|
	Hon. Thomas Howard[174]	XXX
Capt. Lt.	Joseph Blissett	XXX

173 Sprigg has Zanchy as the first commander of the troop: *Anglia Rediviva*, p. 331. This is incorrect. Two soldiers wounded at Naseby claimed Le Hunt was their commanding officer and pay warrants were issued for Le Hunt's troop throughout May and early June 1645. Zanchy succeeded Le Hunt on 16/6 immediately after the battle: TNA, SP 28/173/1, fos. 12-13; ibid, SP 28/38, fo. 77. This was probably because Fairfax had been convinced by the accusation of peculation levelled against Le Hunt, which Zanchy had

orchestrated: ibid, SP 28/28, fo. 425; ibid, SP 28/29, fo. 593. Nevertheless Le Hunt was to have a distinguished military career subsequently in Wales and in Ireland: F. and D.

174 Sprigg's list gives Howard as the first captain of a troop in this regiment: *Anglia Rediviva*, p, 331. However, there is no doubt that he took over Richard Fincher's troop when Fincher was promoted to major in Sheffield's regiment in 4/45. The first pay warrant to name Howard as troop commander is dated 19/5/45: TNA, SP 28/30, fo. 232. Firth and Davies suggested that he was the Phillip Howard who was captain of the lifeguard of horse in February 1660. Kishlansky converted this into fact, but he was incorrect to do so: *Rise of the New Model Army*, p. 336. One of Howard's former soldiers gave his first captain's name as Thomas, whilst a Captain Thomas Howard received arms for a troop of horse from the ordnance officers in 9/45 and again in 2/46: ibid, E 121/ 4/5/81, entry 1; ibid, WO 55/1646, fo. 222 and unfol. A document in the muster rolls shows without any shadow of doubt that the officer in Fleetwood's regiment was the Honourable Thomas Howard, who was either the brother of the Earl of Suffolk or the son of Lord Howard of Escrick: ibid, SP 28/121A, fo. 562. The former seems the most likely. Howard left the regiment in June 1647 at the time of the first Army coup as befitting the brother of one of the leading Presbyterian peers.

5th Regiment	Name	Military career
Colonel	Edward Rossiter	
Major	Phillip Twistleton	
Captains	Anthony Markham	
	John Nelthorpe	
	Original Peart	
	Christopher Bushy[175]	Left the regt. after 27/5/45. Succeeded by Henry Markham|
Capt. Lt.	XXX	

175 Bushy may have been in trouble in late April for insolent language about members of the House of Commons. For this see BL, Harleian Ms 166, fo. 202; CJ iv, p. 117. It is interesting that Sir Simon D'Ewes also gives the name Bushy rather than Bush.

6th Regiment	Name	Military career
Colonel	Bartholomew Vermuyden	
Major	Robert Huntington	
Captains	John Jenkins	
	Thomas Bush	X at Naseby. Succeeded by Capt. John Blackwell|
	John Reynolds	
	Henry Middleton	
Capt. Lt.	Richard Curzon[176]	Succeeded by Lt. Joseph Wallington|

176 Curzon fought at Naseby but appears to have been moved to another regiment after the battle, as his pay arrears for serving under Cromwell as opposed to Vermuyden were tiny: ibid, E 121/2/11/unnumbered, entries 307-8. Possibly Cromwell did not find him congenial. Curzon's new regiment is not known but Rossiter's seems the most likely. He was still in post in 5/47: ibid, SP 28/173/1, fo. 11; BL, Thomason Tracts, 669 f11 (15).

7th Regiment	Name	Military career
Colonel	Algernon Sidney[177]	Resigned in 5/45. Replaced by Nathaniel Rich|
Major	John Alford	
Captains	Edward Dendy[178]	Resigned in early 46. Capt. Azariah Husbands of the 12th regt. F. succeeded him|
	Thomas Neville	
	Thomas Ireton	
	William Bough[179]	Left in 5/46|
Capt. Lt.	Roger Hopkins[180]	Succeeded by Francis Hawes|

177 Sidney resigned the colonelcy on 14/5/45 because he had not recovered from wounds suffered at the battle of Marston Moor. He became governor of Chichester instead: BL, Sloane Ms 1519, fo. 112; CSPD 1644-5, p. 60.

178 Dendy was commander of the troop in 12/45: TNA, SP 28/33, fo. 623. In 2/46 his successor Azariah Husbands received its pay warrant in Dendy's name but not as troop commander. However, he had taken over from Dendy by the end of 5/46: TNA, SP 28/36, fo. 608; ibid, SP 28/38, fo. 171. Dendy's duties at Westminster as sergeant of arms to Parliament probably explain his retirement. Nevertheless he commanded a troop of horse to protect the Council of State, England's executive body, long after leaving the New Model Army: CSPD 1653-4, p. 5.

179 Bough's troop is mentioned in a pay warrant issued in early 5/46, but he had left his command by 11/5/46 His replacement was Francis Hawes, previously captain lieutenant: TNA SP 28/38, fos. 18, 167.

180 See above p. 52. When Rich became colonel, his lieutenant Francis Hawes became captain lieutenant of the regiment: ibid, SP28/31, fo. 67.

8th Regiment	Name	Military career
Colonel	Sir Robert Pye	
Major	Nathaniel Rich	Col. 7th regt. H. in 5/45|
Captains	Matthew Tomlinson[181]	Succeeded Rich as major|
	Ralph Knight	
	Ralph Margery	
	Samuel Barry[182]	Transfer from 11th regt. H. to replace Henry Ireton|
Capt. Lt.	Edward Hamden	

181 Tomlinson was commissioned as major by mid- June 1645: ibid, SP 28/173/1, fo. 10.

182 Barry had been lieutenant to Captain James Hopton in Haselrig's regiment and then captain when Hopton left in 12/44. He was named as captain in the 11th regiment of horse, which is not surprising as he had fought in the other cavalry regiment belonging to Waller's army which entered the New Model. His transfer to the 8th regiment occurred before the end of April: Spring ii; TNA, E 121/4/8/57B, entries 1-2; ibid, SP28/29, fo. 105. He probably brought his troop with him, see note 187 below.

9th Regiment	Name	Military career
Colonel	Edward Whalley	
Major	Christopher Bethell	X at the storming of Bristol. Succeeded by John Pitchford his lt.|
Captains	Samuel Porter[183]	Gone by 7/45. Succeeded by Capt. Lt. Evanson|
	John Grove	
	XXX Horseman[184]	Succeeded by Capt. Robert Swallow of the 1st regt. H. 6/45|
	William Packer	Capt. 1st regt. H. by 6/45. Succeeded by Capt. Henry Cannon[185]|
Capt. Lt.	William Evanson	Succeeded by Daniel Dale|

183 Evanson was in command of the troop at the battle of Langport where it took part in Major Bethell's rout of the royalist horse at the crossing of the Wagg Rhyne: F. and D.

184 Horseman left his command before the battle of Naseby but after the beginning of June: Naseby: TNA, SP 28/29, fo. 419.

185 By 6/45 Capt. Henry Cannon was in charge of the troop initially commanded by Captain Packer. Cannon had been captured at Faringdon in 5/45 whilst fighting in Sir Hardress Waller's regiment of foot: W.C. Abbott, *The Writings and Speeches of Oliver Cromwell* (Harvard, 1937, 4 vols.) i, p. 345. He then escaped or was exchanged, and was serving in Whalley's regiment at Naseby: TNA, E 121/4/1/103, entries 1-3.

10th Regiment	Name	Military career
Colonel	Richard Graves	
Major	Adrian Scroop	
Captains	Nicholas Bragg	
	Christopher Fleming	
	William, Lord Caulfield	
	Nathaniel Barton[186]	Ex capt. Sir John Gell's regt. Derbyshire H|
Capt. Lt.	Charles Holcroft	

186 For Barton's earlier military career, see Dore, Brereton Letter Books i, p. 524. Captain Barton had no predecessor according to Sprigg, but he had succeeded Charles Doyley when Doyley took command of General Fairfax's lifeguard in late April: *Anglia Rediviva*, p. 331; F. and D.

11th Regiment	Name	Military career
Colonel	Henry Ireton[187]	Capt. 8th regt. H. N.M. army|
Major	George Sedascue	
Captains	Robert Gibbon	
	John Hoskins	X at Naseby. Succeeded by Capt. John Bury[188]|
	William Gwilliam[189]	Major Okey's regt. Dr. N.M. army. Succeeded Capt. Pennyfather| X at Bristol 9/45|
	William Cecil[190]	
Capt. Lt.	Robert Kirkby[191]	Lt. in the regt.|

187 Henry Ireton succeeded Sir Michael Livesey as colonel before 21/4/45, but did not take over his troop: W.S. Library, SMS 463, unfol. This fell to William Cecil. According to Sprigg, Cecil succeeded Hoskins who was killed at Naseby. This is incorrect. In a pay warrant dated 26/6/45, Cecil is described as having the troop formerly commanded by Sir Michael Livesey: *Anglia Rediviva*, p. 331; TNA, SP 28/30, fo. 569. Elsewhere John Bury is clearly identified as Hoskins's successor: ibid, SP 28/31, fos. 296, 303. The fact that James Wilson served as an officer under Ireton in both the Eastern Association and the New Model Armies suggests that Ireton took his troop with him: Spring i; Worc. College, Clarke Ms 67, fo. 17.

188 Bury had been lieutenant colonel in Colonel King's regiment of foot in the Eastern Association but was dismissed for his religious radicalism in 1644. He was either a reformado or out of the army until late 5/45 when he became captain lieutenant in Oliver Cromwell's Eastern Association horse: TNA, SP 28/31, fo. 367 (14 days' pay only). Bury became captain in the 11th regiment of horse under the circumstances mentioned above, and his troop is mentioned in a warrant dated 4/46, but he left soon afterwards for a position in the Exeter garrison: ibid, SP 28/33, fo. 122; ibid, SP 28/38, fo. 34; ibid, SP 28/41, fos. 7, 178; ibid, E 121/4/8/40B, entries 879-85; W.S.Library, SMS 463, unfol. 18/4/46. There is little doubt that Bury was serving as adjutant general from before 1/49 until his death in the early 1650s. In 6/53 his widow Priscilla was allowed to retain his quarters in Whitehall until further notice: ibid, SP 28/58, fo. 48; CSPD 1653-4, p. 26. Thus Major. Later Colonel James Berry cannot have been adjutant general, even though this is claimed in The Clarke Papers, C.H. Firth ed., *Camden Society* 3rd series (4 vols., 1891-1901) ii, p. 282.

189 The first mention of Gwilliam as a captain of horse in the 11th regiment is in a warrant dated 5/5/45: W.S. Library, SMS 463, unfol.

190 Cecil was in post by the end of 5/45: TNA, SP 28/30, fo. 569. He may have been Sir Michael Livesey's captain lieutenant. For this see the career of James Jeffries in note 187 above and ibid, SP 28/30, fo. 334..

191 Degennis was lieutenant of Henry Ireton's troop at the start of the Civil War: Peacock, *Army Lists*, p. 55. Spring claims he became Ireton's captain lieutenant in 4/45: Spring i. Admittedly Degennis was to die in Ireland as Ireton's captain lieutenant, but he did not join the 11th regiment of horse until 1649: CJ vii, p. 39. Ireton's captain lieutenant on 26/6/45 was Robert Kirkby: TNA, SP 28/29, fo. 531. He was still captain lieutenant in 5/47: Worc. College, Clarke Ms 41, fo. 102. Kirkby had been cornet in Sir Michael Livesey's regiment in Waller's army: TNA, E 121/4/6/16A, entry 8. Before that he may have served in Ireton's troop in the army of the Eastern Association, but the reference I have seen is incorrect.

Lifeguard H[192]	Name	Military career
Captain	Charles Doyley[193]	Capt. 10th regt. H. N.M. army| Left c.8/45. Succeeded by Henry Hall|
Capt. Lt.	Henry Hall[194]	Cor. Sir Phillip Stapleton's troop Essex's lifeguard.

192 Fairfax's Lifeguard is included for the first time here as it was not established until late 4/45: CJ iv, p. 123. Doyley and Hall were in active command by 8/5/45: W.S. Library, SMS 463, unfol.

193 Doyley was at Naseby but gave up his troop on becoming governor of Newport Pagnell and colonel of the garrison regiment there in 8/45: Whitelock, *Memorials*, p. 151; CSPD 1645-7, pp. 45-7, 75; ibid 1625-49, p. 689. He is wrongly described as John Doyley in the 1645-7 volume of the Calendar of State Papers and as Edward Doyley by Temple: 'Original Army List', p. 68.

194 Turton, *Chief Strength*, p. 63. See also TNA, E 121/3/3/111, entry 4; ibid, E 315/5, fos. 5-6.

Company and Troop Commanders in early December 1646

Infantry

1st Regiment	Name	Military career
Colonel	Sir Thomas Fairfax	
Lt. Col.	Thomas Jackson	
Major	Samuel Gooday	
Captains	Vincent Boyce	
	Fulk Muskett	
	Francis White	
	Thomas Highfield	
	Michael Bland[195]	XXX Succeeded Capt. Beamont c. 6/45|
	William Leigh[196]	XXX. Succeeded Major Cooke c. 9/45|
	Thomas Wolfe[197]	Succeeded Capt. Maneste in 10/45|
Capt. Lt.	Lewis Audley[198]	XXX. Prob. succeeded William Fortescue|

195 Bland's arrears as captain in the regiment were from 14/7/45. As his commission ended on 22/2/47, Sprigg was mistaken to claim that Captain Leigh succeeded him: *Anglia Rediviva*, p. 329. By the time Bland left the regiment Leigh had been in post for quite a number of months: TNA, SP 28/44, fos. 215, 218; SP28/41, fo. 185. Bland's first name was Michael, not William as Gentles believes: *New Model Army*, p. 487. He was probably the man who had been a captain in Sir William Fairfax's regiment in Essex's army in 1642: Peacock, *Army Lists*, p. 44.

196 Leigh must have taken command of Major Cooke's company as Wolfe succeeded Maneste. He was certainly a company commander by 5/46: TNA, SP 28/38, fo. 272. He may have served in Lord Fairfax's regiment in the Northern army as lieutenant colonel, but it is not absolutely clear that the man claiming arrears was this William Leigh. It would, however, explain his rapid promotion in the army in Ireland. Within a year of arriving there he was a full colonel: ibid, E 121/4/1/16, unnumbered.

197 Wolfe's pay arrears as a captain began in early 10/45: ibid, E 315/5, fo. 79.

198 Audley could have been in post as early as 23/12/45 when Fortescue's connection with the regiment ended: ibid, SP 28/38, fo. 438. Before that he had served for a time as a private soldier in Thomas Harrison's troop in Manchester's army, but nothing is yet known about the rest of his military service prior to being commissioned as captain lieutenant: ibid, E 121/3/4/83C, entry 1.

2nd Regiment	Name	Military career
Colonel	Phillip Skippon	
Lt. Col.	Richard Ashfield	
Major	Samuel Clarke	
Captains	Edward Streater	
	James Harrison	
	John Clarke	
	Maurice Bowen	
	Devereux Gibbon	
	John Cobbett	
	William Symonds[199]	Capt. Lt. in the regt.|
Capt. Lt.	John Rogers?[200]	
Possible		
Captain	XXX Wingfield[201]	Capt. William Davies's regt. L.G. army|

199 It is clear that Symonds took command of Lieutenant Colonel Francis's company at some stage as he was the only new captain to appear in Sprigg's listing of the regiment: *Anglia Rediviva*, p. 329. Francis's subordinate officers, Lieutenant Norman and Ensign Green, had both been killed at Naseby alongside their company commander: ibid, SP 28/173/1, fos. 1-4. However, Symonds may have followed Captain Wingfield.

200 Rogers was a non-commissioned officer in Captain Turner's and Harrison's companies in Essex's army and ensign and lieutenant to Captain Clarke in Skippon's New Model Army regiment. He then became a captain lieutenant (but possibly in Skippon's Bristol garrison regiment) before becoming a full captain in the New Model regiment: ibid, E 121/2/3/unnumbered, entries 49-51.

201 A Captain Wingfield appears as an officer in the 2nd regiment of foot some of whose men were wounded at Naseby: ibid, SP 28/173/1, fo. 3. This was almost certainly Captain Wigfall of the 11th regiment commanding men who had not been impressed in time to take part in the march to the relief of Taunton which began at the end of 4/45. Like others in the same circumstances, they were temporarily attached to another regiment for the Naseby campaign: ibid, SP 28/31, fos. 13, 25. The evidence for Wingfield and Wigfall being the same man comes from the claim for pay arrears presented by Ensign Francis Farmer, who served in the company from 1643 until 1647,which was attested by most of the 11th regiment's surviving company commanders: ibid, E 315/5, fo. 26. Other evidence, however, suggests that Captain Wingfield was alive in 12/45, ten weeks after Captain Wigfall had been slain at Berkeley Castle in Gloucestershire, and that his company was still in Skippon's regiment: ibid, SP 28/41, fos. 185, 367; ibid, SP 28/37, fo. 187. It is, however, interesting that the 2nd and the 11th were two of the three regiments in the brigade involved in the capture of Berkeley Castle: F. and D.

3rd Regiment	Name	Military career
Colonel	Sir Hardress Waller	
Lt. Col.	Edward Salmon[202]	Major in the N. army. Succeeded Cottesworth|
Major	Thomas Smith	
Captains	John Gorges[203]	
	William Howard	
	John Clarke	
	Daniel Thomas	
	Richard Hodden[204]	Previously the surgeon of the 12th regt. F.|
	Richard Aske[205]	Cor. in Capt. Thomas Howard's troop. 4th regt. H.|
	XXX[206]	
Capt. Lt.	XXX	

202 There were no officers from the Army of the North in Fairfax's listings of 2/45. Salmon was one of several who entered the New Model officer corps from late 1645 onwards. Salmon had been a company commander in Lord Fairfax's regiment of foot and a troop commander and major in John Lambert's regiment of horse: TNA, E 121/3/3/117, entry 2; ibid, E 121/5/5/37, entry 1. His career in the New Model probably began in 2/46 as captain in the 11th regiment of horse, but he left that command on Cottesworth's death, see note 271 below.

203 Captain Gorges received a payment from John Rushworth in 7/45 for his service in the army and for cure of his wounds: TNA, SP 28/140/2, fo. 34. However, this did not mark the end of his direct association with the New Model. He was still apparently commanding a company in the 3rd regiment of foot in 12/46. However, he was no longer doing so in 4/47. Instead he was governor of Exmouth fort. Later he was in the garrison of Exeter Castle, and there he remained until 5/50 at the earliest: Sprigg, *Anglia Rediviva*, p. 329; TNA, E 315/6, fos. 6-16; LJ ix, p. 237; Worc. College, Clarke Ms 69, unfol. (20/5/50).

204 Richard Hodden had taken over from Benjamin Holden by the time of the siege of Oxford where Owen Robbins, one of his soldiers, was wounded: TNA, SP 28/56, fo. 407. For Richard Hodden's earlier career in the army, see ibid, E 121/1/6/63, entry 302.

205 According to Sprigg Aske succeeded Hill who was killed at Bristol, but his wording does not rule out another officer succeeding Hill and his being succeeded by Aske. This seems very likely as Aske was only a cornet in the summer of 1645: ibid, E 121/1/6/66, entry 67.

206 Sprigg has Waad (Wade) as both captain in this regiment and major in the 11th regiment of foot: *Anglia Rediviva*, p. 329. The mistake lies here rather than in Herbert's regiment. The resignation of James Gray, Herbert's lieutenant colonel, in 7/46 had occasioned the move: ibid, SP 28/265, fo. 454. The major of that regiment, Thomas Read, moved up a rank and Wade took his place. The missing captain's name was Amor Stoddard or possibly Phillip Ebzery or a Captain Furnice mentioned as serving in the 3rd regiment of foot at the storming of Basing House in 10/45. Furnice was still in the regiment in 12/45: ibid, SP 28/33, fo. 189.

4th Regiment	Name	Military career
Colonel	Robert Hammond	
Lt. Col.	Isaac Ewer	
Major	Robert Saunders	
Captains	Israel Smith	
	Charles O'Hara	
	William Disney	
	John Boyce	

4th Regiment	Name	Military career
	John Puckle	
	William Stratton	
	Edmund Rolfe[207]	Lt. in Cromwell's regt. H. E.A. army. Succeeded Capt. Eaton in 8/45|
Capt. Lt.	XXX	

207 Firth and Davies assumed that Rolfe and Stratton were captains from 4/45, but they were working from Sprigg's list, not the one in the House of Lords Journal. Stratton first appears as a company commander in the list of officers whose soldiers were wounded at Naseby, whilst Rolfe's commission can be no earlier than 11/8/45: LJ vii, p. 279; TNA, SP 28/173/1, fo. 8; ibid, SP 28/38, fo. 181.

5th Regiment	Name	Military career
Colonel	Richard Fortescue	
Lt. Col.	Ralph Cobbett	
Major	Thomas Jennins[208]	
Captains	Arthur Young	
	Richard Pooley[209]	Lt. to Capt Dursey in Fortescue's regt. F. L.G. army	
	John Denison[210]	XXX Took over Major Dursey's co.|
	XXX Whitton[211]	XXX
	John Cox[212]	Reformado under Capt. Knight 8th regt. H. to 8/45|
	John Bushell[213]	Capt. Lord Grey's Leicestershire regt. F.|
	XXX Farley[214]	XXX Succeeded Capt. Edward Gittins|
Capt. Lt.	XXX	

208 Thomas Jennins was major by 8/46: Rushworth, *Historical Collections* vi, p. 295.

209 Pooley was promoted to captain on 14/7/45 six weeks before Dursey's death. He must therefore have taken over the company of one of the captains killed at Taunton: ibid, SP 28/58, fo. 284. For his earlier career, see ibid, E 121/2/11/17B, entries 130, 151.

210 Evidence that Denison and not Pooley succeeded Dursey is to be found in ibid, SP 28/53, fo. 113.

211 Denison, Whitton, Cox, Bushell and Farley entered the regiment thanks to the regiment's heavy loss of officers during 1645. A Captain Whitton was serving in Colonel Ayloffe's regiment in 1/45: ibid, SP 28/27, fos. 109-10.

212 Cox is not mentioned in Sprigg's list and he is incorrectly described as captain Cope in the Vindication of the Army of 4/47 printed in Rushworth: *Anglia Rediviva*, p. 330; *Historical Collections* vi, p. 466. He was commissioned on or before 22/12/45: TNA, SP 28/56, fo. 262; ibid, SP 28/44, fos. 165-6.

213 Ibid, E 121/2/11/17B, entry 51.

214 F. and D. have Farley as captain in 4/45, but they must be wrong. His predecessor's army service did not end until 8/46: TNA, SP 28/265, fo. 427. They also wrongly identify Farley with the William Farley who was captain in the 1st regiment of foot in the summer of 1647, as that officer had previously been a lieutenant in that regiment: Clarke Papers i, pp. 48-57. One possible candidate is Richard Farley who had served as an ensign in Captain John Stente's company in Colonel John Weare's regiment in Dorset: TNA, E 121/3/4/143, entry 7. Another is a Captain Farley listed in Colonel Sydenham's regiment in the Weymouth garrison: ibid, E 121/2/1/53, entry 185. Farley may have left the army by 4/47. For this see note 291 below.

6th Regiment	Name	Military career
Colonel	Richard Ingoldsby	
Lt. Col.	Thomas Kelsey	Succeeded Farrington c. 12/45 and took over his co.[215] Formerly major in 10th regt. F. N.M. army|
Major	Charles Duckett	
Captains	Henry Ingoldsby	
	Francis Allen	
	John Mill	
	John Grime[216]	XXX. Prob. succeeded to Major Richard Cromwell's co.|
	Edward? Stephens[217]	XXX Succeeded Capt. Job Gibson|

6th Regiment	Name	Military career
	Thomas Ingoldsby[218]	XXX Succeeded Capt. Williams[219] who had succeeded Capt. Arthur Ward|
	Richard Wagstaffe	XXX Succeeded Capt. Warwick Bamfield|
Capt. Lt.	William Duckett	Left c. 4/47|

215 Ibid, SP 28/58, fo. 214.

216 A lieutenant John Grime had served in Major Alexander Urry's company in Lord Robartes' regiment in Essex's army but had been laid aside in 4/45: ibid, SP 28/29, fo. 334. Grime was certainly a captain in Ingoldsby's regiment in the New Model by 7/46: ibid, SP 28/56, fo. 231. A tenuous link between the officer in Robartes' regiment and the captain in Ingoldsby's is supplied by the claim for pay arrears by a soldier in Essex's army who described Grime as captain, which he was not prior to 4/45: ibid, E 121/3/1/45, entry 57.

217 I have not discovered any evidence for the suggestion made by Kishlansky that this officer's first name was Edward: *Rise of the New Model Army*, p. 336.

218 This man may have been the Captain Ingoldsby who was captured by the royalists with Captain Cambridge at Gunnersby near Grantham on 5/12/44: Luke, *Letter Books*, p. 408. F. and D. describe him as a company commander at the storming of Bristol, but there does not appear to have been a vacancy and Sprigg shows Williams, not Ingoldsby, succeeding Captain Ward: *Anglia Rediviva*, p. 330.

219 Williams may have signed the petition of Essex's infantry officers presented to Parliament in 12/44. If so, his first name was John: HLRO, Main Papers 177, fo. 102. He may also have been the Captain Williams who intercepted a letter from the king's ministers to the governor of Pendennis Catle in 1646, as Ingoldsby's was one of the regiments in the besieging force: BL, Thomason Tracts E 506 (12, 25). The claim for pay arrears made by Richard Bentley, who had served as a sergeant in the company Williams commanded, gives the succession Ward, Williams, Ingoldsby: TNA, E 121/1/7/unnumbered, entries 10-11.

7th Regiment	Name	Military career
Colonel	Thomas Rainborough	
Lt. Col.	Henry Bowen	
Major	John Edwards[220]	Formerly capt. in the regt.|
Captains	George Drury	
	Thomas Dancer	
	Thomas Creamer	
	John Browne[221]	
	Henry Whittle?[222]	Lt. to Capt. Crosse|
	Henry Flower?[223]	Lt. in the regt.	
	XXX Philpot?[224]	XXX. Succeeded by Lt. Thomas Walker c. 6/47|
Capt. Lt.	XXX	

220 Edwards's appointment as major was no earlier than mid-December: ibid, SP 28/33, fos. 375, 577-8.

221 Browne had had a chequered career in Parliament's armies, having served as captain of horse under Lord Brooke, engineer at the siege of Lathom House and captain of horse in Lancashire, major of horse to Sir William Brereton in Cheshire, and captain of foot under Colonel Sydenham in Weymouth garrison: TNA, E 121/2/11/11A, entries 1-6; BL, Additional Ms 11332, fo. 38; Dore, *Brereton Letter Books* ii, pp. 186-7; TNA, SP 28/152/7, fo. 12. Browne's career in the 7th regiment of foot is also complex. He was in post as captain on 11/8/45 but is not mentioned by Sprigg: TNA, SP 28/34, fo. 400. Despite Firth and Davies's comment that he left the regiment in 6/47, he was still serving as captain during the suppression of the uprising in South Wales in the summer of 1648, but he did not take part in the Preston campaign. Instead he served as governor of Tenby in South Wales, and he was still there in 10/48: TNA, SP 28/56, fo. 186. However, Browne was twice referred to as major in pay warrants even at a time when Edwards was clearly major of the regiment e.g. ibid, SP 28/41, fo. 305; SP 28/37, fo. 390 (3/46). All that I can suggest is that as he had briefly held the rank of major he was sometimes referred to by his previous rank. See note 437 below for another example of this practice. However, this does not explain why Browne was sometimes described as lieutenant colonel in claims for pay arrears when Henry Bowen held that position from 1645 to 1652: e.g. ibid, E121/2/3, unnumbered.

222 Whittle was a full captain in 3/47. Even though his name does not appear in Sprigge's list, command of Crosse's company almost certainly passed directly to him in 8/45: ibid, SP 28/35, fo. 105; ibid, SP 28/61, fo. 19.

223 Flower was a company commander in the regiment by 16/3/47: ibid, SP 28/42, fo. 105. He had previously been a lieutenant in the regiment, and before that lieutenant in Captain Ralph Cobbett's company in Colonel Holmstead's regiment in the earl of Essex's army: ibid, E 121/2/5/27A, entry 64 and /27B, entries 6-8; ibid, E 121/2/5/27A, entry 64.

224 Philpot was a company commander in the regiment by 3/47: ibid, SP 28/35, fo. 1055. The only Philpots I have encountered are Guy, who was captain lieutenant to Colonel William Davies in Essex's army, and a Captain Bartholomew Philpot who had a company in the earl of Manchester's regiment in the Eastern Association army: ibid, SP 28/27, fo. 444; ibid, SP 28/28, fo. 192.

8th Regiment	Name	Military career
Colonel	Robert Lilburne[225]	Col. H. N. Army 6/45 to 6/46. Succeeded Weldon|
Lt. Col.	Nicholas Kempson	
Major	William Masters	
Captains	Christopher Peckham	
	Nicholas Fenton	
	Francis Dormer	
	Jeremiah Tolhurst	
	Stephen Caine[226]	Left regt. in early 47|
	Abraham Holmes	Lt. N. army. Succeeded Capt. Francklin[227]|
	George Weldon	XXX Succeeded Capt. Munday|
Capt. Lt.	XXX	

225 The new colonel took charge at the beginning of July: ibid, SP 28/39, fos. 30-1. His appointment caused resentment amongst the officers who would have liked Lieutenant Colonel Kempson to have succeeded Weldon: CSPD 1625-49, p. 706. Lilburne also took over Weldon's company: TNA, SP 28/50, fo. 80. For his earlier colonelcy, see F. and D.

226 Caine resigned on or about 25/1/47: TNA, SP 28/44, fo. 198; ibid, SP 28/49, fo. 268. He was then commissioned as a captain in the regiment that James Gray, formerly of the 11th regiment of foot, was raising for service in Ireland. This was disbanded in 9/47 before leaving England, but Caine was commissioned as captain in Colonel Huncks's regiment in 1649, also raised for service in Ireland: CSPD 1645-47, pp. 547, 570; Worc. College, Clarke Ms 67, fo. 42. Caine was succeeded as captain by Robert Lilburne's brother Henry.

227 Holmes had been lieutenant to Captain Henry Lilburne in Robert Lilburne's regiment of horse in 7/45: TNA, SP 28/122, fo. 371.

9th Regiment	Name	Military career
Colonel	Edward Harley	
Lt. Col.	Thomas Pride	
Major	William Cowell	
Captain	William Goffe	
	George Gregson	
	Sampson/Hinder[228]	Gone by 3/47[229]|
	John Ferguson	
	John Mason	
	Waldine Lagoe	
	Thomas Parsons[230]|	
Capt. Lt.	XXX	

228 Sprigg has both Hinder and Sampson as captains in the regiment in 12/46, but one must have left by 7/46 to make room for Captain Parsons. Hinder subsequently served as a militia officer in Cornwall, and then as lieutenant colonel in Colonel Robert Bennett's regiment raised in 1650: *Anglia Rediviva*, p. 329; CSPD 1649-50, p. 521; TNA, E 121/4/5/86B, entry 1. Sampson was heavily involved in local administration in Somerset from c. 1647 and commissioned as major of the militia in that county in 2/50: CSPD 1649-50, p. 521; CCC passim; D. Underdown, *Somerset in the Civil War and Interregnum* (Newton Abbot 1973).

229 Roger Alsop was captain in the regiment by the end of March 1647: BL, Thomason Tracts, E 396 (26).

230 Parsons probably succeeded Captain Hinder rather than Captain Sampson. He had been lieutenant to George Gregson's company in Essex's army and presumably continued to serve at that rank in the New Model Army: TNA, E 121/4/8/40B, entry 592. He was a company commander by 7/46 at the latest: ibid, SP 28/39, fo. 38. Walter Crocker, commissioned as lieutenant to Captain Hinder in 11/45, was lieutenant to Captain Parsons in 5/47: Worc. College, Clarke Ms 67, fo. 12; Rushworth, *Historical Collections* vi, p. 467.

10th Regiment	Name	Military career
Colonel	John Lambert[231]	Col. H. N. army|
Lt. Col.	Mark Grime	
Major	Wroth Rogers[232]	
Captains	John Biscoe	
	Francis Blethin	
	Lawrence Nunney	
	Giles Saunders	
	Thomas Disney	
	Matthew Cadwell[233]	XXX Succeeded Capt. William Wilkes|
	William Style[234]	XXX
Capt. Lt.	Samuel Ross[235]	Previously ens. in the col's. co.|

231 Lambert succeeded to the colonelcy before the siege of Dartmouth in 1/46. Montagu had resigned on 27/10/45: TNA, SP 28/37, fo. 373.

232 Rogers was promoted soon after Lieutenant Colonel Kelsey moved to the 6th regiment of foot and Mark Grime took his place. Sprigg has him as both captain and major but this is a similar mistake to the one which he made in his listing of the 3rd regiment of foot: *Anglia Rediviva*, p. 329.

233 Cadwell had been a trooper in Colonel Rich's troop and quartermaster to Captain Ireton's troop, but it is not known what position he held in the New Model Army immediately prior to his being commissioned as captain in the 10th regiment of foot : TNA, E 121/5/7/21, entry 335. He may not have been lieutenant in the company he took over. William Shelley was ensign to both Wilkes and Cadwell, which suggests that the lieutenant was not promoted on Wilkes's death: ibid, SP 28/27, fos. 300-26.

234 Style may have been the immediate beneficiary of Rogers' promotion but I have not come across him earlier than 8/46: ibid, SP 28/39, fo. 378. He was probably the Quartermaster William Style who had served in Montagu's regiment in the Eastern Association army: Spring i.

235 TNA, E 121/5/7/21, entry 257; BL, Thomason Tracts E 390 (26).

11th Regiment.	Name	Military career
Colonel	William Herbert	Succeeded Lloyd by 21/6/45[236]|
Lt. Col.	Thomas Read[237]	Replaced James Gray[238]|
Major	John Wade	Transfer from the 3rd regt. F. by 9/46. Succeeded Major Read|
Captains	John Melvin	
	John Spooner	
	Richard Lundy[239]	
	Nathaniel Short	
	Robert Read[240]	Lt. in Col. Lloyd's co. 11th regt. F. and then capt. lt.|
	William Meredith[241]	Lt. to Capt. Disney's co. 10th regt. F. Prob. succeeded Capt. Wigfall|
	XXX	
Capt. Lt.	XXX	
Possibles Captains	Edward Orpin[242] Robert Anderson [243]	Former commissary general victuals for the E.A. and N.M. armies. Prob. Succeeded Capt. Meredith| XXX

236 W.S. Library, SMS 463, unfol. Between 9/44 and the early summer of 1645 Herbert was supervising the refortification of Tonbridge Castle in Kent. His pay ceased on 16/6/45: ibid, SP 28/130, fos. 31, 84. He was probably the Colonel William Herbert authorised by the earl of Essex to raise a regiment to fight in Pembrokeshire: HMC, Portland Mss I, pp. 222-3.

237 For Gray's resignation from this regiment in 7/46, see ibid, SP 28/39, fos. 429-30.

238 Gray was arrested in England in June 1650 at the time of the outbreak of war with Scotland whilst acting as a courier for the Scottish government: CSPD 1650, p. 221

239 Lundy appears to have been acting major before Wade's appointment: TNA, SP 28/51, fo. 38. He was subsequently commissioned as major in Colonel Herbert's regiment for service in Ireland, see below p. 153.

240 Robert Read, lieutenant to Lieutenant Colonel William Lloyd in Essex's army and Herbert's captain lieutenant in the 11th regiment of foot, almost certainly became company commander before the end of 1645 given the death of his colonel and four captains

during the campaign, and also his own length of service. He had served as lieutenant to three company commanders before 4/45: TNA, E 121/4/5/94B, entry 73; ibid, E 121/5/7/unnumbered, entry 32.

241 Captain William Meredith served in Herbert's regiment at some time between 6/45 and 6/47: ibid, E 121/1/6/48, fo. 3.

242 See note 308 below. William Cowling was commissary general by 12/46: Sprigg, *Anglia Rediviva*, p. 328.

243 Robert Anderson was a company commander in the regiment by 4/47: BL, Thomason Tracts E 385 (19). A Robert Anderson had been lieutenant to captain Hezekiah Haynes in Colonel John Holbourne's regiment in Essex's army, later Colonel Davies's. Two of that regiment's company commanders entered the 11th regiment of foot: TNA, E 121/1/7/57, entry 102.

12th Regiment	Name	Military career
Colonel	John Hewson[244]	
Lt. Col.	John Jubbs	
Major	Daniel Axtell	
Captains	John Silverwood[245]	Left the regt. between 12/46 and 3/47. Prob succeeded by Capt. Lt. Brayfield|
	John Carter	
	Thomas Price	
	John Toppendene[246]	Lt. to Lt. Col. Hewson's co. F. E.A. army|
	Samuel Grime/Graeme	Lt. to Capt. Silverwood's co. F. Montagu's regt. E.A. army. Succeeded Capt. Husbands c. 5/46|
	Henry Davies?[247]	XXX
	Thomas Atkinson?[248]	XXX
Capt. Lt.	William Arnop[249]	XXX

244 Sprigg only gives the names of Captains Grime, Toppendene, Silverwood, Carter and Price: *Anglia Rediviva*, pp. 329-30.

245 Silverwood left between 12/46 and 4/47. Only Lieutenant Alexander Brayfield can have succeeded him.

246 TNA, SP 28/27, fo. 262. Toppendene, whose name is spelled in a number of different ways, probably succeeded Tomkins who succeeded Jenkins. He was in post by 4/46 at the latest, but probably straight after Naseby: TNA, SP 28/37, fo. 615; ibid, SP 28/56, fo. 459.

247 Davies was lieutenant to Capt. Jenkins in the Eastern Association army: Spring i. The officer who succeeded Captain Gayle slain at Bristol in 9/45 was probably Henry Davies rather than Thomas Atkinson. Whoever did not probably took over Pickering's company a few weeks later. Both signed the Vindication with three of the other captains in the regiment in the order Toppendene, Davies, Graeme, Brayfield followed by the captain lieutenant William Arnop: BL, Thomason Tracts E 385 (19). For Davies's earlier career see note 163 above.

248 Atkinson, having served as lieutenant in the regiment, was a captain by 2/46: TNA, E 121/3/5/45,entry 91; ibid, SP 28/59, fo. 428. He had probably served in Colonel Ayloffe's regiment: ibid, E 121/2/1/53, entries 171, 181-4.

249 William Arnop became captain lieutenant in or just before 12/46: TNA, SP28/56, fo. 236.

Dragoons

Regiment	Name	Military career
Colonel	John Okey	
Major	Nicholas Moore	
Captains	John Farmer	
	Christopher Mercer	
	Daniel Abbott	
	Ralph Farr	
	Tobias Bridge	
	Harold Scrimgeour	
	Edward Wogan	
	William Neale[250]	XXX. Succeeded Capt. Turpin|
Capt. Lt.	XXX	

250 Neale had been lieutenant to Lieutenant Colonel John Lilburne in Manchester's regiment of dragoons in the Eastern Association army. It is likely that he moved into the New Model Army with that rank, but the troop in which he served is not yet known. William Turpin left the regiment in or before 12/45: ibid, E 121/1/4/56, entry 74; ibid, SP 28/33, fo. 420.

Cavalry

1st Regiment	Name	Military career
Colonel	Thomas Fairfax	
Major	John Disbrowe	
Captains	John Browne	
	Adam Lawrence	
	James Berry	
	William Packer	Capt. Oliver Cromwell's regt. H. E.A. army|
Capt. Lt.	John Gladman	

2nd Regiment	Name	Military career
Colonel	John Butler	
Major	Thomas Horton	
Captains	Edward Foley	Discharged from the army in early 47[251]|
	Samuel Gardiner	
	Thomas Pennyfather	
	Walter Bethell[252]	Capt. in Hugh Bethell's regt. H. N. army|
Capt. Lt.	Josias Mullineaux	

251 Worc. College, Clarke Ms 69, unfol. 16/4/50.
252 Bethell came out of Yorkshire to join General Fairfax in the west in 7/45: TNA, SP 28/140/2, fo. 8. He was troop commander by 2/46 at the latest: ibid, SP 28/37, fo. 251.

3rd Regiment	Name	Military career
Colonel	Thomas Sheffield	
Major	Richard Fincher	
Captains	Arthur Evelyn	
	William Rainborough	
	Gabriel Martin	
	Robert Robotham	
Capt. Lt.	Richard Young[253]	

253 Young was in Major John Hales's troop in Colonel James Sheffield's regiment and had seemingly been cashiered in 4/45: ibid, E 121/4/8/57B, entry 10; ibid, SP 28/29, fo. 422. However, he was captain lieutenant of the regiment by late 7/45: ibid, SP 28/38, fo. 130.

4th Regiment	Name	Military career
Colonel	Charles Fleetwood	
Major	Thomas Harrison	
Captains	William Coleman	
	Hon. Thomas Howard	
	Richard Zanchy/Sankey	Lt. to Capt. Le Hunt|
	James Laughton[254]	Lt. in the regt. Succeeded Capt. Selby|
Capt. Lt.	Joseph Blissett	

254 Laughton's name is given as troop commander in a warrant issued at the very end of June 1645: ibid, SP 28/30, fo. 600. He had served as lieutenant to either Captain Coleman or Captain Howard. A former trooper claiming pay arrears in 1651 remembered

him as James Lawson and another possibly as James Lloyd. If Lloyd and Lawson are the same man, Laughton's troop commander was Coleman: ibid, E 121/1/1/26B, entry 245; ibid, E 121/4/7/5, entry 7; ibid, E 121/1/1/26B, entry 245.

5th Regiment	Name	Military career
Colonel	Edward Rossiter	
Major	Phillip Twistleton	
Captains	Anthony Markham	
	John Nelthorpe	
	Original Peart	
	Henry Markham[255]	Capt. in Rossiter's regt. H. E.A. army. Succeeded Capt. Bushy|
Capt. Lt.	Richard Curzon??[256]	

255 For Henry Markham's service at the rank of captain in Manchester's army, see ibid, E 121/3/3/113B, entries 318, 339, 349, 429. As there were more than six troops in Rossiter's Eastern Association regiment, Markham did not immediately get command of a troop in the New Model. It is probable that he became captain in the regiment in the summer of 1645. He can only have replaced Captain Bushy: *Anglia Rediviva*, p. 331.

256 See note 176 above.

6th Regiment	Name	Military career
Colonel	Oliver Cromwell[257]	Lieutenant General H. E.A. army|
Major	Robert Huntington	
Captains	John Jenkins	
	John Reynolds	
	Henry Middleton	
	John Blackwell	Capt. in Edmund Harvey's regt. H. London brigade. Succeeded Capt. Bush X at Naseby[258]|
Capt. Lt.	Joseph Wallington[259]	Lt. to Capt. Bush. Replaced Richard Curzon c.7/45[260]|

257 Cromwell succeeded Bartholomew Vermuyden who returned to the continent in early 6/45: F. and D.

258 Symonds, Diaries of the Marches of the Royal Army, p.73. Blackwell entered the New Model Army as captain during 7/45: TNA, SP 28/31, fos. 119, 185.

259 Wallington was lieutenant in 7/45 and captain lieutenant by 3/46: ibid, SP 28/31, fo. 119; ibid, SP 28/37, fo. 268.

260 Ibid, SP28/31, fo. 367; ibid, SP28/32, fo. 243.

7th Regiment	Name	Military career
Colonel	Nathaniel Rich[261]	Succeeded Algernon Sidney as col. in 5/45|
Major	John Alford	
Captains	Thomas Neville	
	Thomas Ireton	
	Azariah Husbands	
	Francis Hawes[262]	Lt. to Major Rich in the N.M. army in 4/45. Capt. Lt. 5/45. Succeeded Bough 5/46|
Capt. Lt.	John Danvers[263]	XXX

261 Rich had been lieutenant colonel of Manchester regiment of horse in the Eastern Association army. For his shaky start in the New Model, see note 95 above. It seems probable that Rich's troop moved with its commander from the 8th regiment to the 7th just before Naseby with Sidney's troop replacing it in the 8th. Cromwell asked Fairfax for Thomas Rawlins to take command of Colonel Sidney's troop and one of the veterans claiming for arrears of pay had fought in Sidney's and Rawlins's troop: Thomas Carlyle, *Letters and Speeches* (3rd ed., 3 vols., 1849) i, p. 170; TNA, E 121/1/1/unnumbered, entry 154. For Rawlins being in the 8th not the 7th regiment of horse, see note 264 below.

262 A pay warrant issued on 26/4/45 shows Hawes as lieutenant in Rich's troop in the 8th regiment of horse: TNA, SP 28/29, fo. 72. He then followed Rich into the 7th regiment in 5/45 when Rich succeeded Algernon Sidney as colonel: ibid, SP28/31, fo. 67.

263 Danvers served as captain lieutenant from 6/46 to 12/46. He died before 1650: ibid, SP 28/50, fo. 65.

8th Regiment	Name	Military career
Colonel	Sir Robert Pye	
Major	Matthew Tomlinson	
Captains	Ralph Knight	
	Ralph Margery	
	Samuel Barry	
	Thomas Rawlins[264]	Capt. E.A. Army|
Capt. Lt.	Edward Hamden	

264 Thomas Rawlins was a captain in the regiment at Naseby but very new to the command. He had served as one of the earl of Manchester's staff officers at the Second Battle of Newbury in the Eastern Association army and gave testimony against the earl on Cromwell's behalf in 12/44. He took charge of what had been Colonel Sidney's troop after 4/6/45 when Cromwell wrote to Fairfax in his support as 'a most honest man' for the next captaincy: CSPD 1644-5, p. 153; TNA, SP 28/173/1, fo. 10; ibid, E 121/1/1/ unnumbered, entries 154, 205; Abbott, *Writings and Speeches* i, p. 352.

9th Regiment	Name	Military career
Colonel	Edward Whalley	
Major	Robert Swallow	Capt. 1st regt. H. N.M. Army. Succeeded Capt. Horseman in 6/45. Major on the death of Christopher Bethell[265]|
Captains	John Grove	
	Henry Cannon[266]	
	William Evanson	
	John Pitchford[267]	
Capt. Lt.	Daniel Dale[268]	XXX Succeeded William Evanson c. 7/45|

265 F. and D.

266 See note 185 above.

267 Pitchford is not mentioned by Sprigg, but he was captain of the troop by 11/45: *Anglia Rediviva*, p. 332; TNA, SP 28/33, fo. 69.

268 Spring suggests that Dale became captain lieutenant in Whalley's regiment in the New Model army in 4/45. This cannot be so as William Evanson is known to have held that position at that date. However, Dale certainly succeeded Evanson before c. 2/46 and probably as early as 7/45: ibid, SP 28/140/7, fo. 282.

10th Regiment	Name	Military career
Colonel	Richard Graves	
Major	Adrian Scroop	
Captains	Christopher Fleming	
	William, Lord Caulfield	
	Nicholas Bragg	
	Nathaniel Barton	
Capt. Lt.	Charles Holcroft	

11th Regiment	Name	Military career
Colonel	Henry Ireton	
Major	George Sedascue	
Captains	Robert Gibbon	
	William Cecil	
	Henry Pretty[269]	Lt. to Capt. Foley 2nd regt. H.[270] Took over Capt. Gwilliam's troop|
	Anthony Morgan[271]	Capt. in S.E. Wales 45. Succeeded John Bury after 4/46 and before 7/46|
Capt. Lt.	Robert Kirkby	

Lifeguard	Name	Military career
Captain	Henry Hall	Lt. to Capt. Doyley|
Capt. Lt.	Andrew Goodhand[272]	XXX|

269 Pretty was in post by 12/45: TNA, SP 28/140/7, fo. 280. There is a possibility that a Captain Forster came between Gwilliam and Pretty: ibid, E 121/2/3/40, entry 5. Corporal Thomas Purslow claimed to have served under him in Ireton's regiment and this is the only gap.

270 Ibid, SP28/253/A/1, fo. 46.

271 Morgan was a former royalist who had been pardoned for the invaluable assistance he had given in securing South Wales for Parliament: F. and D.; BL, Thomason Tracts, E 506 (34). Edward Salmon succeeded Bury in 4/46, but Morgan was signing for the troop's pay in 6/46 on Salmon's behalf. He was its commander by the following month. Benjamin Gifford, Bury's lieutenant, remained at that rank under Morgan's command: F. and D.; TNA, SP 28/140/7, fo. 285; ibid, SP 28/38, fo. 348; ibid, SP 28/39, fo. 253; W. Salt Library, SMS 463, unfol. 30/5/46; Worc. College, Clarke Ms 41, fo. 102; CSPD 1645-7, pp. 312-13. For a possible identification of Salmon and the reason for his departure, see note 202 above.

272 Goodhand held this rank in 1/46 and so he probably succeeded Hall: TNA, SP 28/36, fo. 148.

Company and Troop Commanders on 31 May 1647

Infantry

1st Regiment	Name	Military career
Colonel	Sir Thomas Fairfax	
Lt. Col.	Thomas Jackson *	Left regt. 6/47. Successor Major William Cowell 9th regt F.|
Major	Samuel Gooday *	Ditto. Co. went to Ens. Charles Bolton|
Captains	Vincent Boyce *	Ditto. Succeeded by Lt. James Priest|
	Fulk Muskett *	Ditto. Succeeded by Capt. James Pitson|
	Thomas Highfield *	Ditto. Succeeded by Lt. Clement Keene|
	Francis White	Major of the regt. in c. 7/47|
	William Leigh +	
	Thomas Wolfe *[273]	Left the N.M. army in 6/47. Succeeded by Lt. Farley|
	William Wayne *[274]	XXX Succeeded Capt. Bland| Left the N.M. army in 6/47. Succeeded by George Baldwin[275]|
Capt. Lt.	Lewis Audley	

273 A Captain Thomas Wolfe was captain in the garrison at Harwich in 1648-9 and possibly militia captain in Essex in the following year: CSPD 1650, pp. 366-7, 509.

274 Wayne took over Bland's company c. 2/47: TNA, SP 28/41, fo. 185; Worc. College, Clarke Ms 41, fo. 136; ibid, Clarke Ms 67, fo. 3; BL, Thomason Tracts, 669 f11 (15). Having 'deserted' the army in early 6/47 Wayne was appointed captain in the Blue Auxiliary regiment by the London Militia Committee later in the month: Clarke Papers i, p. 154. Whoever transcribed evidence from the company commanders concerning misbehaviour in Fairfax's regiment in 5/47 mistakenly wrote Bland instead of Wayne: ibid i, p. 48.

275 See note 344 below.

2nd Regiment	Name	Military career
Colonel	Phillip Skippon[276]	
Lt. Col.	Richard Ashfield	
Major	Samuel Clarke[277]	Gone before 8/47. Succeeded by John Cobbett as major but prob. by John Rogers as co. commander|
Captains	Edward Streater *[278]	Gone before 8/47|
	James Harrison	
	John Clarke	
	Maurice Bowen	
	Devereux Gibbon	
	John Cobbett	
	William Symonds	
Capt. Lt.	John Rogers?	

276 Skippon's regiment was in garrison at Newcastle from 1/47 until the late autumn of 1648. Its officers therefore played little part in the struggle between the army and Parliament in London and its environs which produced much of the evidence concerning the changing composition of the officer corps in 1647. Its isolation also probably explains why few newly commissioned officers are recorded earlier than 3/49 when Colonel Cox took over the regiment. I have therefore reproduced Sprigg listing for 12/46: *Anglia Rediviva*, p. 331. The bolded names are officers who may have left the regiment for whatever reason between 1/47 and 8/48 when the accounts for the Newcastle garrison provide the next complete listing of company commanders.

277 Major Clarke was cashiered before the end of July 1647: Perfect Occurences, issue 31, 30/7-6/8/47. He was at Bristol in 8/47 and may have joined Skippon's other regiment. For this see Appendix III below. A Major Samuel Clarke also contracted to take prisoners captured at the battle of Dunbar to work in England's North American colonies: CSPD 1650, pp. 346, 418, 421.

278 Lieutenant Arthur Helsham was Streater's successor: TNA, E 121/5/5/44A, entry 1. He will have taken over the company in 8/47: Perfect Occurences, issue 31, 31/7/-6/8/47.

3rd Regiment	Name	Military career
Colonel	Sir Hardress Waller	
Lt. Col.	Edward Salmon +	
Major	Thomas Smith+	
Captains	William Howard *	Left the regt. c. 6/47[279]|
	John Clarke	
	Daniel Thomas *	Left the regt. c. 6/47[280]	
	Richard Hodden	
	Richard Aske	
	Philip Ebzery[281]	XXX
	Amor Stoddard[282]	Capt. Lt. to Robert Lilburne's regt. H. N. army|
Capt. Lt.	James Knight *[283]	XXX

279 The fact that Lieutenant John Byfield was the assignee for Howard's claim for pay arrears suggests that Howard was probably overseas at the time. He was clearly not dead: TNA, E 121/5/1/25, entry 1.

280 Thomas was captain of a company raised in 4/50 to fight in Ireland and major in a regiment there by 7/53: CSPD 1650, p. 575; ibid, 1653-4, p. 429.

281 Ebzery had been lieutenant to Benjamin Holden in Sir Hardress Waller's regiment of foot in Waller's army, which provided several company commanders for his regiment in the New Model: Spring ii. Ebzery was a company commander by 4/47 and probably replaced John Gorges: BL, Thomason Tracts E 385 (19).

282 TNA, E 121/5/7/146, entry 32.

283 There is no further mention of Knight's serving in this regiment but the same man was almost certainly the captain lieutenant of Colonel Phayre's regiment raised for service in Ireland in 1649: Worc. College, Clarke Ms 67, unfol. section.

4th Regiment	Name	Military career
Colonel	Robert Hammond +	
Lt. Col.	Isaac Ewer +	
Major	Robert Saunders	
Captains	Israel Smith	
	Charles O'Hara *	Left the regt. c. 6/47[284]|
	William Disney[285]	
	John Boyce	Left the regt. c. 6/47|
	John Puckle +	
	William Stratton	
	Edmund Rolfe +	
Capt. Lt.	Edward Humphreys	Possibly lt. in James Hobart's regt. E.A. army who enlisted as a private soldier in the N.M. army.[286]	

284 See below Appendix II. In 1649 O'Hara was commissioned as lieutenant colonel in a regiment raised for service in Ireland: TNA, E 121/3/4/unnumbered, entry 5; TNA, SP 28/64, fo. 40.

285 Worc. College, Clarke Ms 41, fo. 102.

286 Spring i, p. 43. The evidence that Edward Humphreys was captain lieutenant in 5/47 is compelling. A man of that name was a captain lieutenant in the New Model in 4/47 and a company commander in this regiment in the late 1640s: Worc. College, Clarke Ms 41, fo.103; Clarke Papers i, p. 436; BL, Thomason Tracts E 390 (26).

5th Regiment	Name	Military career
Colonel	John Barkstead[287]	Former col. and gov. of Reading. Replaced Richard Fortescue who became gov. of Pendennis Castle|
Lt. Col.	Ralph Cobbett	
Major	Thomas Jennins[288]	Left the regt. c. 6/47. Succeeded by Robert Cobbett and then Capt. Biscoe of the 10th regt. F.|

5th Regiment	Name	Military career
Captains	Arthur Young	
	Richard Pooley *	
	John Denison *[289]	
	XXX Whitton	Left the regt. c.6/47
	John Cox *	
	John Bushell *[290]	Ditto|
	XXX Farley[291]	Possibly succeeded as capt. by William Read
Capt. Lt.	William Read?[292]	

287 Colonel in 3/47, Fortescue was described as late colonel of the regiment in a warrant dated 17/4/47: TNA, SP 28/45, fos. 248, 268. Barkstead had begun his military career as captain under Colonel Venn in the Windsor Castle garrison: ibid, E 121/2/11/17B, entries 1-2. Later he was governor of the Reading garrison but had been discharged from the military or was seeking a different employment in 3/46 when Oliver Cromwell wrote to Fairfax on his behalf: BL, Sloane MS 1519, fo. 129.

288 Jennins, Whitton and Farley are mentioned by Sprigg as being in service in 12/46 and their companies received pay on 1/6/47: *Anglia Rediviva*, p. 330; TNA, SP 28/46, fo. 221. For Cobbett, see note 365 below.

289 For the durations of Denison's and Cox's commissions see notes 367 and 368 below.

290 Bushell was in custody by 11/47 having fallen foul of Colonel Henry Ireton: Worc. College, Clarke Ms 66, fo. 29. In 1649 a Captain John Bushell was serving in Oliver Cromwell's lifeguard: CSPD 1653-4, p. 265.

291 Farley had certainly left the regiment by 7/47 but his name does not appear on any of the declarations or petitions of the period leading up to the first Army coup.

292 Read was described as a captain in a petition submitted to Parliament in late 3/47: ibid, Thomason Tracts E 390 (3). He can only have been captain lieutenant or Farley's successor. The latter seems the more likely as eight other officers who signed the petition gave their rank as captain lieutenant.

6th Regiment	Name	Military career
Colonel	Richard Ingoldsby	
Lt. Col.	Thomas Kelsey +	
Major	Charles Duckett[293]	Gone by 9/47|
Captains	Henry Ingoldsby	Left the regt. c. 6/47. Lt. Col. in Ireland 49; Col. Dr. in Ireland 50-c.55|
	Francis Allen +	
	John Mill +	
	John Grime +	
	Edward? Stephens[294]	Prob. left the regt. in 6/47|
	Thomas Ingoldsby	
	Richard Wagstaffe +	
Capt. Lt.	John Shrimpton[295]	XXX. He succeeded William Duckett[296]|

293 F. and D have identified a Charles Duckett who was captain lieutenant and then captain in the 7th regiment of horse of which Ingoldsby was colonel in the late 1650s. They suggest that he was Major Duckett, but a son or nephew seems the more likely..

294 According to both Kishlansky and Gentles, Stephens left the army during the army coup but I can find no confirmation of this in the sources they cite: Kishlansky, *Rise of the New Model Army*, p. 336; Gentles, *New Model Army*, p. 487.

295 BL, Thomason Tracts, E 390 (3).

296 Duckett ceased to be captain lieutenant in c. 4/47. He was subsequently commissioned as lieutenant to Lieutenant Colonel Kelsey: Worc. College, Clarke Ms 67, fo. 13.

7th Regiment	Name	Military career
Colonel	Thomas Rainborough	
Lt. Col.	Henry Bowen	
Major	John Edwards	
Captains	George Drury	

	Thomas Dancer	
	Thomas Creamer	
	John Browne	
	Henry Whittle	
	Henry Flower	
	Thomas Walker?	Possibly lt. to Capt.Philpot[297]|
Capt. Lt.	XXX	

297 Thomas Walker had served as lieutenant to Captain Drury in Colonel Ayloffe's regiment in the army of the Eastern Association. He had certainly replaced Philpot by 7/47. At the Council of War held at Reading on 5/7/47 he signed immediately after Drury and Flower. Walker was a friend of Richard Elton, the author of *The Compleat Body of the Art Military* (1650): Spring ii; Worc. College, Clarke Ms 41, fo. 158; TNA, E 121/4/1/156, entry 30; F. and D.

8th Regiment	Name	Military career
Colonel	Robert Lilburne +	
Lt. Col.	Nicholas Kempson *[298]	Col. of a regt. intended for Ireland 5/47|
Major	William Masters *	Left regt. c. 6/47|
Captains	Christopher Peckham *	Lt. Col. in Kempson's regt. 5/47|
	Nicholas Fenton	
	Francis Dormer *[299]	Major in Kempson's regt. 5/47|
	Jeremiah Tolhurst	
	Abraham Holmes +	
	George Weldon *	Capt. in Kempson's regt. 5/47. Succeeded by Capt. Earwood|
	Henry Lilburne[300]	Major in N. Army. Replaced Stephen Caine c.1/47|
Capt. Lt.	Robert Fish *	XXX Capt. in Kempson's regt. 5/47|
Possible Captain	John Wells[301]	

298 In April Kempson had been commissioned to raise a new regiment for service in Ireland and many of its officers were to come from this regiment: see Appendix II below. However, he and they appear to have retained their positions in the old regiment until the end of May despite Fairfax addressing Kempson as the colonel of a regiment in April: CSPD 1645-47, p. 706; BL, Thomason Tracts 669 f11 (15). In 1659 Nicholas Kempson, who was Major General Edmund Ludlow's brother-in-law, was major of his regiment of foot in Ireland: R. Dunlop, *Ireland under the Commonwealth* (2 vols., 1913) ii, p. 715.

299 Dormer was described as major in late 4/47 but may only have been acting major as Master was still apparently in post in the following month: LJ ix, pp. 154-5; BL, Thomason Tracts 669 f11 (15).

300 Henry Lilburne served as major in his brother Robert's regiment of horse in the Army of the North until 6/45 but then left the military. On 26/8/46 Cromwell wrote to Fairfax on his behalf as he was out of employment: BL, Sloane Ms 1519, fo. 146. By 4/47 he was a captain in the 8th regiment of foot: TNA, SP 28/39, fo. 497; LJ ix, p. 153. This and his subsequent promotion to lieutenant colonel c. 6/47 are recounted by his widow Anne in her plea for his arrears to be paid: TNA, E 121/4/1/unnumbered, entries 108, 111; CSPD 1648-9, p. 286. This seems a bit cheeky as he had died defending Tynemouth Castle on the king's behalf. For his fate, see note 384 below.

301 TNA, E 121/3/3/31, entry 19. Wells may have replaced Captain Fenton who does not appear in any document dating from 1647. There was a Francis Wells in the regiment in that year: ibid, SP 18/539, fo. 439.

9th Regiment	Name	Military career
Colonel	Edward Harley[302]	Left the army in 6/47|
Lt. Col.	Thomas Pride +	
Major	William Cowell +	Lt. Col. to the 1st regt. F. 6/47|
Captains	William Goffe +	
	George Gregson +	Major of the 9th regt. F. by 8/47|
	John Ferguson +	
	John Mason +	

9th Regiment	Name	Military career
	Waldine Lagoe +	
	Thomas Parsons +	
	Roger Alsop +[303]	XXX
Capt. Lt.	Joseph Salkeld[304]	XXX

302 The full listing of captains is in Worcester College, Clarke Ms 41, fos. 120, 123.

303 BL, Thomason Tracts, E 385 (19). Alsop had been lieutenant to Captain Anthony St. John in the earl of Essex's regiment of foot: TNA, E 121/4/8/40B, entry 582. Nothing is known of his career in the New Model Army before 3/47 when his name appears as captain on a petition: BL, Thomason Tracts, E 390 (3).

304 Salkeld appears in the list of company commanders of this regiment in 4/47 but is wrongly described as a full captain: BL, Thomason Tracts, E 370 (3). He took over Colonel Harley's company in 6/47: Worc. College, Clarke Ms 41, fo. 120.

10th Regiment	Name	Military career
Colonel	John Lambert +	
Lt. Col.	Mark Grime +	
Major	Wroth Rogers +	
Captains	John Biscoe +	
	Francis Blethin	
	Lawrence Nunney +	
	Giles Saunders +	
	Thomas Disney +	
	William Style +	
	Matthew Cadwell +	
Capt. Lt.	Samuel Ross +	

11th Regiment	Name	Military career
Colonel	William Herbert[305]	Left the regt. in 6/47 to command a regt.intended for Ireland. Succeeded by Col. Robert Overton|
Lt. Col.	Thomas Read +	
Major	John Wade	
Captains	John Melvin	Left the regt. c. 5/47 for lt. col. position in Herbert's regt. intended for Ireland|
	John Spooner	
	Richard Lundy *	Left the regt. c. 6/47|
	Nathaniel Short *[306]	Ditto
	Robert Read[307]	
	Edward Orpin +[308]	
	Robert Anderson[309]	
Capt. Lt.	Thomas Hughes[310]	XXX

305 A Colonel William Herbert was commanding troops in Colonel Horton's brigade in southwest Wales in 5/48, but he was the former high sheriff of Monmouthshire and so probably a different man: TNA, SP 28/51, fos. 196-7; ibid, SP 28/56, fo. 217.

306 Short left the army before Overton took charge and was alive on 26/4/1649: Worc. College, Clarke Ms 69, unfol.

307 Robert Read was a captain in the regiment on 15/5/47: ibid, Clarke Ms 41, fo. 102.

308 Orpin was captain in the regiment in 4/47 and possibly in 12/46. He probably took charge of the company originally commanded by Captain Benjamin Wigfall and then, it seems, by Captain William Meredith : TNA, SP 28/140/2, fo. 3; ibid, E 315/5, fo. 26.

309 Anderson was captain by 4/47: Worc. College, Clarke Ms 41, fo. 102.

310 Hughes was captain lieutenant in 4/47. He became a full captain in the regiment in the summer: ibid, Clarke Ms 41, fo. 102; ibid, Clarke Ms 67, fo. 11; F. and D.

12th Regiment	Name	Military career
Colonel	John Hewson +	
Lt. Col.	John Jubbs +	
Major	Daniel Axtell +	
Captains	John Carter +	
	Thomas Price +	
	John Toppendene +	
	Samuel Grime +[311]	
	Henry Davies +[312]	
	Thomas Atkinson +	
	Alexander Brayfield +[313]	Prob. succeeded Capt. Silverwood|
Capt. Lt.	William Arnop +	

311 Graeme succeeded Captain Azariah Husbands c. 5/46. For this see note 162.

312 Silverwood left early in 1647. Davies signed the Vindication as a captain alongside all the other company commanders in the regiment: BL, Thomason Tracts E 385 (19). For speculation about his earlier career in the army, see note 247 above.

313 Brayfield had been promoted from lieutenant to captain by 5/47 at the latest: Rushworth, *Historical Collections* vi, p. 456.

Dragoons

Regiment	Name	Military career
Colonel	John Okey +	
Major	Nicholas Moore *	Left the regt. in 6/47. Later major in Henry Ingoldsby's regt. Dr. Ireland 50|
Captains	Daniel Abbott	
	Ralph Farr *	Left the regt. in 6/47. Nothing further known|
	Tobias Bridge	
	John Farmer *[314]	Left the regt. in 6/47 but returned to the army in 51|
	Christopher Mercer +[315]	
	Harold Scrimgeour *	Left the regt. in 6/47. Capt. in Daniel Abbott's regt. Dr. in Ireland[316]|
	Edward Wogan *	Left the regt. in 6/47. Royalist activist from 48 to his death in 1654[317]|
	William Neale	
Capt. Lt.	XXX	

314 Farmer became captain in the regiment of dragoons raised by Colonel Thomas Morgan in 1651 for service in Scotland. By 1656 he was major, but his career probably came to an end in 11/59 when he failed to secure Carlisle for General Monck: F. and D.

315 Mercer may have been replaced in 6/47, but an officer of that name carried the message informing Parliament of Colonel Horton's victory over the Welsh royalists at St. Fagans in 5/48. He served as acting major of 3 companies of dragoons in the war with Scotland in 1650/51 by which time he had seemingly left the regiment: CJ v, p. 556; F. and D.

316 TNA, SP 28/83, fo. 25.

317 Despite leaving the regiment, Wogan was allowed to keep some of his troop under arms. He persuaded them to change sides at the start of the Second Civil War in 2/48, whereupon they rode to Scotland. For Fairfax's grovelling apology, see *Old Parliamentary History*, xvii, pp. 79-80. Wogan died of his wounds in 1/54: F. and D.

Cavalry

1st Regiment	Name	Military career
Colonel	Thomas Fairfax	
Major	John Disbrowe +	
Captains	John Browne	
	Adam Lawrence +	
	James Berry +	Major 5th regt. H. c. 6/47. His lt. William Disher succeeded him|
	William Packer +	
Capt. Lt.	John Gladman +	

2nd Regiment	Name	Military career
Colonel	John Butler *	Left the regt. in 6/47|
Major	Thomas Horton +	Col. of the regt. 6/47|
Captains	Samuel Gardiner +	
	Thomas Pennyfather +	
	Walter Bethell +	Major of the regt. 6/47|
	Benjamin Burgess +[318]	Lt. to Capt. Edward Foley and his successor|
Capt. Lt.	Josias Mullineaux	

318 Burgess was captain by 1/3/47: TNA, SP 28/45, fo. 301.

3rd Regiment[319]	Name	Military career
Colonel	Thomas Sheffield *	Left the regt. in 6/47. Succeeded by Major Harrison of the 4th regt. H.|
Major	Richard Fincher *	Ditto. Succeeded by Capt. Henry Cromwell as troop commander|
Captains	Arthur Evelyn[320]	Succeeded as capt. by Stephen Whitehead after 6/47|
	William Rainborough	Replaced Fincher as major|
	Gabriel Martin *	Left the regt. in 6/47.[321] Succeeded by John Peck, lt. to Capt. Evelyn|
	Robert Robotham *	Ditto. Succeeded by Stephen Winthrop|
Capt. Lt.	Richard Young*	Left the regt. c. 6/47. Succeeded by John Spencer, Major Thomas Harrison's lt. in the 4th regt. H.|

319 For the extensive changes in this regiment, see Worc. College, Clarke Ms 67, fo. 25.

320 Evelyn was governor of Wallingford Castle from 7/46, but he retained his troop of horse probably until c. 7/47. After leaving the New Model Army he was promoted to major and took command of a non-New Model Army troop of horse: TNA, SP 28/58, fo. 330; ibid, E 121/3/4/71, entries 1-2.

321 Martin was a militia commissioner in Wiltshire in 1650: CSPD 1650, p. 505.

4th Regiment	Name	Military career
Colonel	Charles Fleetwood	
Major	Thomas Harrison	Col. 3rd regt. H. 6/47. Succeeded by Capt. Coleman|
Captains	William Coleman	Major 6/47|
	Hon. Thomas Howard	Left the regt. c. 6/47|
	Richard Zanchy +	
	James Laughton[322]	D 8/47|
Capt. Lt.	Joseph Blissett[323]	

322 Laughton's widow presented a petition for pay arrears from 6/45 to 9/8/47: ibid, SP 28/50, fos. 8-9.

323 Blissett was described as a full captain in 4/47 but this must have been in error: BL, Thomason Tracts E 370 (3).

5th Regiment	Name	Military career
Colonel	Edward Rossiter	Left the regt. c. 7/47[324]
Major	Phillip Twistleton	Succeeded Rossiter as col.
Captains	Anthony Markham[325]	Left the regt. c. 7/47
	John Nelthorpe	
	Original Peart	
	Henry Markham[326]	Left the regt. c. 7/47 but still in arms
Capt. Lt.	Richard Curzon??	Left the regt. c. 7/47 if he was ever in it

324 Rossiter was still colonel on 23/6/47: LJ ix, pp. 206, 289.

325 Anthony Markham and his brother Henry were paid their arrears in 4/48. The warrant shows that they had resigned from the army. They had not been cashiered: TNA, SP 28/53, fos. 333, 337. Anthony succeeded his brother as governor of Belvoir Castle in mid-1649: CSPD 1649-50, pp. 140, 279.

326 Henry Markham held the rank of major and was garrison commander at Belvoir Castle, Leicestershire in 11/47 and 1/49. He was a commissioner for Parliament in Ireland in 1651, and colonel of a regiment of horse there in 1/60: TNA, SP28/58, fo. 64; Edmund Ludlow, *Memoirs 1625-1672*, C. Firth ed. (2 vols. Oxford, 1894) i, p. 261; F. and D; Chequers Ms 782, fo. 46.

6th Regiment	Name	Military career
Colonel	Oliver Cromwell	
Major	Robert Huntington	
Captains	John Jenkins +	
	John Reynolds +	
	Henry Middleton	
	John Blackwell +	
Capt. Lt	Joseph Wallington +	

7th Regiment	Name	Military career
Colonel	Nathaniel Rich +	
Major	John Alford *[327]	Left the regt. c. 6/47
Captains	Thomas Neville *	Ditto
	Thomas Ireton	
	Azariah Husbands +	
	Francis Hawes +	
Capt. Lt.	William Weare/Warre +	Lt. in Col. Rich's troop[328]

327 In 1648 Alford was ordered by the House of Commons to raise horse for Parliament's defence. In 1651 at the time of the war with Scotland he was a prisoner in the Tower of London, presumably on account of his Presbyterian sympathies: CSPD 1648-9, p. 152; ibid, 1651, p. 225.

328 Weare was successively corporal, quartermaster, cornet and lieutenant in Rich's troop: TNA, E 121/4/5/81, entry 2.

8th Regiment	Name	Military career
Colonel	Sir Robert Pye *	Left the army 6/47. Succeeded as col. by major Tomlinson
Major	Matthew Tomlinson	Succeeded Pye as col.
Captains	Ralph Knight	
	Ralph Margery	
	Samuel Barry *[329]	Left the regt. 6/47. Succeeded by Lt. Robert Glyn
	Thomas Rawlins +	
Capt. Lt.	Edward Hamden*	Left the regt. in 6/47[330]

329 For Barry's later career, see note 449 below.

330 He was in London with Sir Robert Pye and most of the rest of the troop by 6/6/47: CSPD 1625-49, p. 709; F. and D.

9th Regiment	Name	Military career
Colonel	Edward Whalley +	
Major	Robert Swallow	
Captains	John Grove +	
	Henry Cannon	
	William Evanson +	
	John Pitchford	
Capt. Lt.	Daniel Dale	

10th Regiment	Name	Military career
Colonel	Richard Graves *	Left the army 6/47|
Major	Adrian Scroop	Succeeded Graves as col.|
Captains	Christopher Fleming *	Left the army. 6/47. Prob. succeeded by Capt. Woolf[331]|
	William, Lord Caulfield *	Left the army in 6/47.[332] Succeeded by Thomas Goddard|
	Nicholas Bragg *[333]	Left the regt. in 6/47|
	Nathaniel Barton	Succeeded Scroop as major|
Capt. Lt.	Charles Holcroft *[334]	Left the regt. 6/47|

331 Francis Pick was cornet to Fleming and lieutenant to Wolfe: TNA, SP 28/44, fo. 419; ibid, SP 28/53, fo. 418. Fleming was appointed governor of Pembroke Castle early in 1648: Worc. College, Clarke Ms 66, fo. 20; BL, Thomason Tracts, The Impartial Intelligencer no. 7 (11-18/4/48).

332 Lord Caulfield was serving as a cavalry captain in Ireland by 10/50: TNA, SP 28/71, fo. 184.

333 Bragg's withdrawal from the army is implicit in the petition of Richard Atkins, one of his troopers: ibid, SP 28/56, fo. 309.

334 A Captain Charles Holcroft was in the army of occupation in Ireland in 1/54: Dunlop, *Ireland under the Commonwealth* ii, p. 397.

11th Regiment	Name	Military career
Colonel	Henry Ireton	
Major	George Sedascue[335]	Left the regt. in 6/47|
Captains	Robert Gibbon	
	William Cecil	
	Henry Pretty +	
	Anthony Morgan	
Capt. Lt.	Robert Kirkby[336]	

335 Gibbon was major by 30/6/47: TNA, SP 28/46, fo. 167. Sedascue returned to the New Model Army as adjutant general of horse in 10/48: F and D.

336 James Wilson, Kirkby's cornet, was seemingly captain lieutenant by 3/47: TNA, SP 28/38, fo. 41. However, this must be a mistake on the clerk's part. Kirkby signed a petition in 4/47 as captain lieutenant: Worc. College, Clarke Ms 41, fo. 102.

Lifeguard	Name	Military career
Captain	Henry Hall *	Left the regt. in 6/47. Succeeded by Richard Cromwell|
Capt. Lt.	Andrew Goodhand[337]	Ditto. Succeeded by John Ingram|

337 Goodhand had been replaced by 30/6/47: TNA, SP 28/46, fo. 145.

Company and Troop Commanders on 31 August 1647

Infantry

1st Regiment	Name	Military career
Colonel	Sir Thomas Fairfax	
Lt. Col.	William Cowell[338]	Major 9th regt. F. N.M. army| X or D c. 9/48|
Major	Francis White[339]	Capt. F. in the regt.|
Captains	William Leigh	
	James Priest[340]	Lt. in the regt. Succeeded Vincent Boyce|
	James Pitson[341]	Scout-master W. army 1644. Took over Muskett's co.|
	Clement Keene[342]	Lt. in the regt., he took over Highfield's co.|
	William Farley[343]	Lt. in the regt., he took over Wolfe's co.|
	Charles Bolton	Ex ens. in the col's co. He took over Gooday's co.[344]|
	George Baldwin	XXX he took over Wayne's co.[345]| Left the regt. soon after being appointed.[346] Succeeded by Lt. Hadfield|
Capt. Lt.	Lewis Audley[347]	Left the regt. before 6/48|

338 News of Cowell's death reached London after 20/9/48 but before 3/10/48: TNA, SP 28/56, fos. 372-4.

339 The officer's name is given as William White in Worc. College, Clarke Ms 67, fo. 3, but this is an error.

340 Information relating to Matthew Garrett, ensign to Boyce and lieutenant to Priest, plus Priest's claim that he was lieutenant and then captain, makes it certain that Priest was Boyce's lieutenant: TNA, E 121/2/9/unnumbered, entries 317-18.

341 Like Thomas Rawlins in the 8th regiment of horse, Pitson had given evidence in Cromwell's support against the earl of Manchester in December 1644: CSPD 1644-5, pp. 150-1.

342 For Keene and Farley's previous ranks, see TNA, E 121/2/9/46, entries 232-3, 270-1.

343 This was not the Captain Farley of the 5th regiment who transferred to 1st regiment in 6/47. In 5/47 William Farley had signed a letter from the officers of Fairfax's regiment as a lieutenant: F. and D.

344 Both Baldwin and Bolton appear as new captains in c. 6/47 in Worc. College, Clarke Ms 67, fo. 3.

345 A George Baldwin had been cornet to Captain Martin's troop in the 3rd regiment of horse: TNA, E 121/4/1/61, entry 14. He was succeeded by Robert Dawes before the end of 1645. Thus there is a possibility that he was a serving as a junior officer in the 1st regiment of foot in 5/47 before becoming a captain.

346 Baldwin left the regiment well before 5/49 as very few soldiers claimed to have served under him: TNA, E 121/2/9/46, entries 500-2. Baldwin or a man of the same name was a captain in the Buckinghamshire militia in 1649: CSPD 1649-50, p. 521. A Lieutenant Colonel George Baldwin is mentioned as sharing quarters in Whitehall with Colonel George Fleetwood in 1653: ibid 1653-4, p. 3.

347 Audley represented the regiment in 10/47 as an officer/agitator, but by 6/48 he was a major in the 7th regiment of foot: see F. and D. and note 513 below.

2nd Regiment	Name	Military career
Colonel	Phillip Skippon[348]	Retired as col. by 2/1/49[349]|
Lt. Col.	Richard Ashfield	
Major	John Cobbett[350]	Capt. in the regt. Replaced Samuel Clarke|
Captains	James Harrison	
	John Clarke	
	Maurice Bowen	
	Devereux Gibbon[351]	
	William Symonds	
	Arthur Helsham	Lt. to Capt. Harrison and then to Cap. Streater. Succeeded Streater in or soon after 8/47[352]|
	Thomas Butler?	XXX Capt. by 8/48. Prob. succeeded Capt. Gibbon|
Capt. Lt.	John Rogers?[353]	Full capt. in the regt. by 8/48 at the latest|

2nd Regiment	Name	Military career
Possibles[354]		
Capt. Lt.	Samuel Clarke[355]	XXX

348 I give the same list as that for May 1647 (but with little confidence). None of Skippon's company commanders is cited by Kishlansky or Gentles as having resigned or been forced out in June and July 1647: Kishlansky, *Rise of the New Model Army*, p. 336; Gentles, *New Model Army*, p. 487. However, there are gaps in their coverage of expulsions and resignations. For this see notes 366, 368.

349 In a warrant of that date the regiment is described as late Major General Skippon's: TNA, SP 28/58, fo. 191.

350 Cobbett was major of the regiment by 11/47: F. and D.

351 Gibbon had left the regiment by 7/8/48 as shown by a list of the regiment on that date given in the Newcastle garrison accounts: TNA, SP 28/133/1, fos. 55-9.

352 Ibid, E 121/3/3/130, entry 7; ibid, SP 28/133/1, fos. 55-9. For his lieutenancy in the regiment, see ibid, E 121/1/7/49, entries 4-6; ibid, E 121/1/2/49, entries 4-6; ibid, SP 28/29, fo. 237.

353 For Captains Butler and Rogers and Captain Lieutenant Clarke, see ibid and Worc. College, Clarke Ms 67, fo. 4. Nicholas Copland was ensign to Clarke and lieutenant to Rogers: TNA, E 121/4/7/48B, entry 9. Rogers was captain by 7/8/48: ibid, SP 28/133/3, fo. 11.

354 F. and D.; TNA, SP 28/133/1, fos. 55-9; Spring ii.

355 Worc. College, Clarke Ms 67, fo. 4. It is surely a coincidence that Rogers's successor as captain lieutenant had a name identical to that of the major who had recently left the regiment.

3rd Regiment	Name	Military career
Colonel	Sir Hardress Waller	
Lt. Col.	Edward Salmon	
Major	Thomas Smith	
Captains	John Clarke	
	Richard Hodden	
	Richard Aske	
	Phillip Ebzery	
	Amor Stoddard[356]	
	Nathaniel Chase[357]	Lt. to Capt. Daniel Thomas in 4/47. Succeeded Capt. Howard|
	XXX[358]	
Capt. Lt.	Ralph Wilson	Lt. to Capt. Clarke in 4/47. Succeeded James Knight|
Possible		
Capt.	Brian Smith[359]	

356 Stoddart must have left the army during the coup of June 1647 or quite soon after. He transferred to Lambert's regiment of horse and fought in his brigade which had been formed from Northern Army regiments in the Second Civil War: ibid, E 121/4/1/30, entry 262; ibid, E 121/3/1/57, entry 146; Akerman, Letters of Roundhead Officers, pp. 171, 173.

357 Worc. College, Clarke Ms 67, fo. 5. Chase had served as ensign in Capt. Thomas's troop in the dragoon regiment of Sir William Waller and Sir Hardress Waller in 1644-5: Spring ii. He was discharged in 4/45: TNA, SP 28/35, fo. 635. For his rank in 5/47, see Worc. College, Clarke Ms 41, fo. 28.

358 The names John Lane and Phillip Desborough both appear as captains in the regiment in 5/48 when it took over responsibility for garrisoning Exeter: F. and D. However, their source, *The Old Parliamentary History of England* (24 vols., 1763) xvii, pp. 164-7 contains errors of transcription. The House of Lords Journals shows that Desborough was Ebzery: LJ vii, pp. 271-2. Lane (who also appears as S. Larks) was John Clarke.

359 Smith was a lieutenant in the regiment in 3/47: BL, Thomason Tracts, E 390 (26); TNA, E 121/1/6/unnumbered, entry 17.

4th Regiment	Name	Military career
Colonel	Robert Hammond[360]	Resigned from regt. by 9/47. Succeeded by Lt. Col. Ewer|
Lt. Col.	Isaac Ewer	
Major	Robert Saunders[361]	Succeeded Ewer as lt. col.|
Captains	William Disney[362]	Acting major in the winter of 47/48. Full major 49|
	Israel Smith	
	John Puckle	

4th Regiment	Name	Military career
	William Stratton	
	Edmund Rolfe	Major in 48. No longer in post in 3/49[363]|
	Francis Wheeler[364]	XXX Succeeded Capt. O'Hara|
	Edward Humphreys	Ex. capt. lt. in the regt., he succeeded Capt. Boyce|
Capt. Lt.	XXX	

360 Hammond's resignation followed his being named as governor of the Isle of Wight in 8/47: F. and D. The decision that Robert Hammond (4th regiment), Thomas Rainborough (7th regiment) and John Lambert (10th regiment) should be replaced by Isaac Ewer, Richard Deane and Sir William Constable was taken on 29/9/47: Worc. College, Clarke Ms 66, fo. 18.

361 It is not totally clear who the field officers were for the rest of 1647 and the first half of 1648. Saunders had been promoted to lieutenant colonel by 5/48, but the position of major may have remained vacant longer with Hammond recommending Rolfe for the position in a letter dated 22/5/48: F. and D. Rolfe was certainly major by late 6/48: LJ x, p. 351. The acting major was apparently William Disney, who received pay on the regiment's behalf in 11/47 and was described as major in the warrant: TNA, SP 28/48, fo. 458.

362 A Captain Disney attended Councils of War in late 1648. He was probably Thomas of the 10th regiment as the company in this regiment commanded by William Disney had been ordered to garrison the Isle of Wight in 11/47: Worc. College, Clarke Ms 66, fo. 18. If Disney refused and Rolfe agreed to take his place, this might explain why Disney was not confirmed as major. However, he did become major of the regiment in 1649. See note 491 below.

363 Rolfe's promotion is not recorded in the commissions' book. This is not surprising as there is a gap in the record of the commissions issued to officers in Ewer's regiment between 9/47 and 6/49, but he was certainly major in 6/48 when he was accused of plotting to poison the king. Rolfe left the regiment before it left for Ireland in 8/49, but was still governor of Carisbrook Castle in 1/51: *Old Parliamentary History* xvii, p. 257; CJ vii, pp. 18-19; CSPD 1651, p. 23.

364 Wheeler was a lieutenant in the regiment in 4/47 but not in O'Hara's company: Clarke Papers i, p. 28. The appointment of Wheeler and Humphreys is recorded in the commissions' book: Worc. College, Clarke Ms 67, fo. 6.

5th Regiment	Name	Military career
Colonel	John Barkstead	
Lt. Col.	Ralph Cobbett	
Major	Robert Cobbett John Biscoe?[365]	Succeeded by John Biscoe capt. in 10th regt. F. in 12/47 Formerly capt. 10th regt. F. N.M. army|
Captains	Arthur Young	
	Richard Pooley[366]	
	John Denison[367]	Left regt. c. 3/49|
	John Cox[368]	
	John Miller[369]	Lt. in the regt.|
	Henry Dorney[370]	Lt. to Major Wroth Rogers 10th regt. F.|
	John Groome?	Lt. in Haselrig's regt. F. W. army[371]|
Capt. Lt.	Thomas Buckner[372]	XXX. He may have replaced William Read[373]|

365 Robert Cobbett was major on 23/6/47, but he was cashiered in 12/47: TNA, SP 28/46, fos. 142, 317; ibid, E 121/4/5/64B, entry 6; ibid, E 121/4/9/95, entry 2; Perfect Occurences, issue 51 17-24/12/47.

366 Kishlansky states that Denison and Pooley did not serve in the regiment after June 1647: *Rise of the New Model Army,* p. 336. The commissions' book shows that they did: Worc. College, Clarke Ms 67, fo. 8. Pooley was involved in a skirmish in London in 5/48 in which the regiment was involved: BL, Thomason Tracts E 443 (29).

367 Denison commanded his company until 12/48 at the earliest: Clarke Papers ii, p. 272. He transferred to Colonel Peter Stubber's regiment raised for service in Ireland before 5/49: Worc. College, Clarke Ms 67, unfol. section; CSPD 1649, p. 131.

368 Cox continued to serve in the regiment after 6/47 despite recent claims that he did not: Kishlansky, *Rise of the New Model Army,* p. 336; Gentles, *New Model Army,* p. 487. He signed a letter from the army in 11/47, and he also appears in a list of the company commanders of Barkstead's regiment which must be later than 6/47, as it has Biscoe as major and Buckner as a captain: Clarke Papers i, p. 416; TNA, E 121/4/5/67B, entry 28; ibid, E 121/2/1/43, entry 1. Cox was mortally wounded early in the siege of Colchester: ibid, SP 28/56, fo. 262; ibid, SP 28/315/5, fo. 70; HMC, Duke of Portland Mss i, p. 459; BL, Thomason Tracts 669 f13 (6).

369 Miller had served as ensign under Captain Robert Cobbett in Colonel James Carre's regiment in Waller's army: TNA, E 121/11/17B, entries 157-9. He was a lieutenant in the 5th regiment of foot in 4/47, probably in Lieutenant Colonel Ralph Cobbett's company: BL, Thomason Tracts E 390 (3); Worc. College, Clarke Ms 41, fo. 102. He, Dorney and Groome became captains in 6/47 or not long afterwards: ibid, Clarke Ms 67, fo. 8: Spring i; TNA, SP 28/56, fo. 376.

370 Ibid, E 121/2/11/17A, entry 138.

371 Spring ii. For Groome's commission, see Worc. College, Clarke Ms 67, fo. 8, but the entry does not make it clear whether it was issued as early as 8/47. He was certainly a full captain in the regiment in 3/48: BL, Thomason Tracts E 443 (5). Nothing is yet known about his earlier career in the military.

372 Commissioned as captain lieutenant in c. 6/47 Buckner became a full captain well before 1650, his replacements as captain lieutenant being first William Bayly and then Roger Jones: Worc. College, Clarke Ms 67, fo. 8. Bayly had been lieutenant to Capt. Denison in 4/47 and Jones lieutenant to Capt. Whitton: Rushworth, *Historical Collections* vi, p. 466.

373 Read's position in the regiment in 1647 and 1648 is unclear. Although seemingly a captain in 4/47, by 5/48 he was a mere lieutenant. Possibly he had been promoted when Cox volunteered for Ireland and then demoted when he was reinstated. See Appendix II for the officers reinstated.

6th Regiment	Name	Military career
Colonel	Richard Ingoldsby	
Lt. Col.	Thomas Kelsey	
Major	John Mill	
Captains	Francis Allen	
	John Grime	
	Edward? Stephens[374]	Succeeded by Francis Messervy|
	Thomas Ingoldsby[375]	Probably succeeded by Captain Cooke and then by Captain Duckett[376]|
	Richard Wagstaffe	
	John Shrimpton	Capt. Lt. in 5/47, he succeeded Capt. Henry Ingoldsby|
	John Hunt[377]	Capt. H. in Monmouthshire. Succeeded Major Charles Duckett|
Capt. Lt.	Abraham Davies[378]	Lt. in the regt. he succeeded John Shrimpton|

374 For Stevens's successor see Worc. College, Clarke Ms 67, fo. 13; Clarke Papers ii, p. 276. If Kishlansky and Gentles are right, the change of captain took place in 6/47, but I have not found any evidence to substantiate the claim.

375 Thomas Ingoldsby was still seemingly a captain in the regiment in 11/47, but the number of known company commanders in the regiment in 4/49 means that he must have left the regiment before then: Chequers Ms 782, fo. 53; Worc. College, Clarke Ms 67, fo.13. He or his namesake was a captain in the 3rd regiment of horse in c. 1656: F. and D.

376 For Duckett's career in the New Model Army pre 1648, see note 508 below. For Cooke and Duckett, see TNA E 121/5/1/unnumbered B, entry 29.

377 Ibid, E 121/2/10/49, entry 622. In the First Civil War Hunt had been a captain in Colonel John Fiennes' regiment of horse: Spring ii.

378 Ensign to Captain Wroth Rogers in Edward Montagu's regiment of foot in the army of the Eastern Association and later in the 10th regiment of foot, Davies was a lieutenant by 3/47: TNA, E 121/3/3/115, entry 58; Worc. College, Clarke Ms 41, fo. 103. The fact that his signature was next to that of Thomas Day, another lieutenant in the 6th regiment of foot, in two documents in which officers from the same regiment were grouped together, suggests strongly that Davies was already in the 6th regiment by the spring of 1647: BL, Thomason Tracts, E 390 (3); Rushworth, *Historical Collections* vi, p. 456.

7th Regiment	Name	Military career
Colonel	Thomas Rainborough	Naval commander from 9/47. Succeeded by Richard Deane[379]|
Lt. Col.	Henry Bowen	
Major	John Edwards[380]	
Captains	George Drury	
	Thomas Dancer	
	Thomas Creamer[381]	
	John Browne[382]	Left regt. early in 49.[383]|
	Henry Whittle	
	Henry Flower	
	Thomas Walker	
Capt. Lt.	XXX	

379 Deane was controller of the ordnance in Essex's army and in the New Model Army at Naseby. He was also captain of the company of firelocks which guarded the train, and later adjutant general and as such deputy to Major-General Skippon: TNA, E 121/2/5/14, entries 1-3; ibid, SP 28/27, fo. 458.

380 F. and D. suggest that Edwards may have left the regiment in the autumn of 1647 after being half-killed by his soldiers when they mutinied and expelled their officers. He may have lasted a little longer, but his eventual successor was Lewis Audley, who was major of the regiment from the summer of 1648 to the summer of 1649: F. and D.; Clarke Papers ii, p. 270; TNA, SP 28/58, fo. 686.

381 It is almost certain that Creamer left the regiment well before 5/49. He did not attend any of the councils of war held during the winter months of 1648/9. Moreover, his claims for back pay, submitted in 6/49, only went up to 24/12/47: TNA, SP 28/61, fo. 22. Subsequently Creamer was one of the guardians of the heir of Sir Thomas Tyldesley, a Catholic royalist killed at the skirmish at Wigan Lane in 8/51: Calendar of the Committee of Compounding iv, pp. 2568-9.

382 Browne's company was in garrison at Tenby Castle possibly until 10/48, but it was in the London area in 11 and 12/49: TNA, SP28/56, fos. 37, 186; ibid, SP 28/57, fos. 484, 507. The last mention I have of Browne in the 7th regiment is in a document dated 1/49, whilst the commission issued to his successor Thomas Segrave shows that Browne had resigned by 4/49 and that he still held the rank of captain when he left the army: ibid, SP 28/58, fo. 187; Worc. College, Clarke Ms 67, unfol. section. The reason why Browne was often described as Major Browne has been set out in note 221 above, but after he left his former soldiers frequently referred to him as lieutenant colonel, despite the fact that Henry Bowen held that position in the regiment from 1645 to 1652. This is particularly puzzling as Browne did not refer to himself as lieutenant colonel in his own claim for pay arrears. It is, however, unlikely to be a clerical error as Bowen's and Browne's names sometimes appear very close together in the lists of soldiers claiming arrears as, for example, in TNA, E 121/1/4/6C, entries 79, 88.

383 Browne was governor of Upnor Castle in Kent, which guarded the mouth of the river Medway and the naval base at Chatham, from 7/49 to c. 11/50: ibid, SP 28/61, fo. 538; CSPD 1650, pp. 389, 600.

8th Regiment	Name	Military career
Colonel	Robert Lilburne	Commissioned as col. H. N.M. army c.1/48. Succeeded by Sir Arthur Haselrig|
Lt. Col.	Henry Lilburne	Capt. in the regt.|X at Tynemouth Castle 8/48[384]|
Major	Paul Hobson[385]	Capt. F. in non N.M. Army regt.|
Captains	**Nicholas Fenton**[386]	
	Jeremiah Tolhurst	
	Abraham Holmes	
	William Mitchell[387]	Capt. Overton's regt. Pontefract garr.| Transferred in 48 to Maleverer's regt. F. or to 11th regt. F.	
	Robert Hutton[388]	Capt. Robert Lilburne's regt. H. N. army|
	Richard Deane[389]	XXX
	Gabriel Earwood[390]	Lt. in the regt. Succeeded Capt. George Weldon|
Capt. Lt.	William Bray[391]	Successor appointed c. 3/48.
Possibles Captains	Ethelbert Morgan[392] John Topping[393]	Lt. in the regt. in 3/47| Ditto|

384 For Lilburne's military career in 1647-8, see note 300 above.

385 TNA, E 121/1/7/unnumbered, entry 62. Hobson was captain in Fleetwood's regiment of horse in the army of the Eastern Association in late 1644. He was not chosen as a troop commander at the formation of the New Model Army, but he probably enlisted as a reformado in Fleetwood's new regiment for a few weeks. He then served in the Leicester garrison: Luke, Letter Books, pp. 322-9. 582; CSPD 1645-47, p. 82; TNA, SP 28/140/7, fo. 283. Hobson was major in the 8th regiment of foot by 11/47 at the latest: ibid, SP 28/48, fo. 100.

386 F. and D. believed, and Gentles implies, that Fenton continued as captain post 6/47, but there is no evidence that he did. Fenton's successor was probably Captain Ethelbert Morgan, a lieutenant in the regiment.

387 TNA, E 121/4/1/30, entry 36; ibid, E121/4/6/23, entries 1-4. For Mitchell's previous command, see ibid, E 121/4/6/23, entries 1-4; ibid, E 121/5/7/55B, entries 18-22; ibid, E 121/4/6/79, entries 1-2. James Hart, who had served as lieutenant to Fenton, was also Mitchell's lieutenant: Worc. College, Clarke Ms 67, fo. 10. However, this does not necessarily mean that Mitchell succeeded Fenton, as junior officers moved from company to company. Mitchell left the regiment by 8/48 as he does not appear in a list of company commanders of that date: ibid, SP28/133/1, fos. 55-9. His successor was Lieutenant Hart. Mitchell subsequently served as field officer in the 15th regiment of foot: F. and D.: Worc. College, Clarke Ms 67, fo. 10. For Mitchell's possible service in the 11th regiment of foot, see note 548.

388 TNA, SP 28/122, fos. 391-2.

389 Deane was serving as a trooper in Fairfax's Lifeguard immediately before becoming captain: ibid, E 121/5/1/13A, entry 1. This was not an impossible jump if, like many others, he had been a commissioned officer in another unit before volunteering to serve in the ranks in the Lifeguard. He was almost certainly the Richard Deane junior discharged as clerk of the train of artillery in Essex's army in 4/45, who was also a cousin of Colonel Richard Deane senior and executor of his will: ibid, SP 28/29, fo. 325; ibid, SP 28/33, fo. 347; Deane, *Admiral Deane*, p. 693.

390 Earwood became captain whilst Lilburne was colonel: Worc. College, Clarke Ms 41, fo. 118; TNA, E 121/4/8/40B, entries 223-4. There is a possibility that he was Lilburne's captain lieutenant: ibid, E 121/1/7/ 13, entry 11. See ibid, SP 28/53, fo. 201 for Earwood as Weldon's successor.

391 CJ vi, p. 297. Bray was in serious trouble for involvement in the Leveller mutiny in November 1647. He was pardoned but denied his old command by Lieutenant Colonel Henry Lilburne c. 2/48. In trouble again in 3/49 for defending Leveller principles, he was by then a full captain in a cavalry regiment raised for service in Ireland by John Reynolds, formerly captain in the 6th regiment of horse: BL, Thomason Tracts E 546 (30); ibid, E 552 (10). For his second offence Bray was imprisoned for two years in Windsor Castle, see CJ vi, p. 168.

392 In a document dated 3/47 in which names of officers in the same regiment are grouped together Morgan's name comes between those of Lieutenants Earwood and Topping: BL, Thomason Tracts E 390 (26).

393 LJ ix, pp. 153-6. In an account of the storming of Tynemouth Castle, Topping appears as a captain together with Major Cobbett and Captains Holmes and Hutton: National Library of Scotland, Adv. Ms 35.5.11, unfol. (reproduced in Harvester Microfilms, Clarke Manuscripts, roll 16).

9th Regiment	Name	Military career
Colonel	Thomas Pride	Lt. Col. in the 9th regt. F.|
Lt. Col.	William Goffe	Capt. in the 9th regt. F.| Lt. Col. 1st regt. F. 9/48|
Major	George Gregson	Retired due to wounds in 9/48 as major [394]|
Captains	John Ferguson[395]	
	John Mason	Major 9/48, Lt. Col. by 12/48[396]|
	Waldine Lagoe	Major 11/48|
	Thomas Parsons	
	Roger Alsop	
	Joseph Salkeld[397]	Capt. Lt to Col. Harley, he took over his company|
	John Hawes[398]	Lt. in the regt.|
Capt. Lt.	William Galhampton[399]	Ens. in 4/47. He succeeded Joseph Salkeld|

394 Gregson died soon afterwards as his arrears were claimed by his administrator: TNA, SP 28/56, fo. 387.

395 Gentles is mistaken in claiming that Ferguson left the regiment in 6/47. The petition of John Kelvin who served in his company shows that he was in post until 12/47 at the earliest: TNA, SP 28/56, fo. 284-7.

396 Clarke Papers ii, p. 276.

397 For Salkeld's predecessors, see Worc. College, Clarke Ms 67, fo. 12.

398 For Hawes's rank in 4/47, see ibid, Clarke Ms 41, fo. 102.

399 Galhampton had served as a sergeant in Pride's company in the earl of Essex's army: TNA, E 121/4/8/40B, entry 591. Subsequently an ensign in the New Model Army, he was commissioned as captain lieutenant in 8/47 and may have served in the regiment until 1660 when he was a full captain, but he could have left during the 1650s and then returned: BL, Thomason Tracts E 390 (3); Worc. College, Clarke Ms 67, fo. 12

10th Regiment	Name	Military career
Colonel	John Lambert	Succeeded by Sir William Constable in 9/47|
Lt. Col.	Mark Grime	
Major	Wroth Rogers	
Captains	Francis Blethin[400]	Prob. left by late 47. Succeeded by his lt. Roger Lewis|
	Lawrence Nunney	
	Giles Saunders	
	John Biscoe	Major in the 5th regt. F. c. 12/47. Succeeded by Lt. John Nicholas|
	Thomas Disney	
	William Style	
	Matthew Cadwell	
Capt. Lt.	Samuel Ross	

400 The last record of Blethin's career in the New Model Army is as an officer who had gone into Wales in 10/47. This probably signalled his retirement from the regiment: Harvester Microfilms, Clarke Manuscripts, reel 17, Chequers Ms 782, fo. 44. He subsequently

served under Colonel John Jones in South Wales: TNA, E 121/5/7/unnumbered, entry 150. In 1655 a Francis Blethin was a captain of militia horse in Monmouthshire: C. Durston, *Cromwell's Major-Generals* (Manchester, 2001), p. 142.

11th Regiment	Name	Military career
Colonel	Robert Overton[401]	Col. H. N. Army. Succeeded Herbert 6/47|
Lt. Col.	Thomas Read	
Major	John Wade	
Captains	John Spooner[402]	X at the siege of Pembroke 6/48|
	Robert Read	
	Edward Orpin	
	Robert Anderson	
	William Knowles[403]	Lt. to Capt. Kelsey in Col. Fleetwood's non-N.M. army regt. F. Succeeded Capt. Lundy|
	William Gough[404]	Lt. to Capt. Melvin in 4/45. Succeeded him c. 6/47|
	Thomas Hughes[405]	Formerly the capt. lt., he succeeded Capt. Short|
Capt. Lt.	XXX Kingston??[406]	

401 Overton's previous command had been as colonel in the garrison of Pontefract Castle: TNA, E 121/4/1/30, entry 96. In 1647 he was either out of employment or seeking a new post. Both Lord Fairfax and Oliver Cromwell wrote to Fairfax on his behalf: F. and D.; Carlyle, *Letters* i, p. 217.

402 Spooner's widow petitioned for his arrears: TNA, SP28/55, fos. 506-7. I am grateful to Professor Peter Gaunt for this reference.

403 Worc. College, Clarke Ms 67, fo. 11. For Knowles's earlier career, see ibid, E 121/1/7/13, entries 96-7. Fleetwood's regiment appears to have been in garrison at Boston.

404 Gough was a lieutenant in 4/47 but a company commander by 6/47 or soon afterwards: Worc. College, Clarke Ms 41, fo. 103; ibid, Clarke Ms 67, fo. 11.

405 Ibid, Clarke Ms 67, fo. 11. See note 310 above for his previous post.

406 A Captain Lieutenant Kingston was associated with Lieutenant Colonel Read in an entry in Fairfax's order book dated 1/5/1649: Worc. College, Clarke Ms 69, unfol.

12th Regiment	Name	Military career
Colonel	John Hewson	
Lt. Col.	John Jubbs	Left c. 3/48[407]|
Major	Daniel Axtell	Capt. 45-48. Succeeded Jubbs as lt. col. by 5/48|
Captains	John Carter	Capt. 45-48. Succeeded Axtell as major by 5/48|
	Thomas Price[408]	X at the battle of Maidstone 6/48[409]|
	John Toppendene	D before 11/47. Succeeded by Lt. Gayle[410]|
	Samuel Grime	
	Henry Davies	Not listed for Ireland. Left the regt. before 5/49[411]|
	Thomas Atkinson	
	Alexander Brayfield	
Capt. Lt.	William Arnop[412]	

407 BL, Thomason Tracts, E 552 (28).

408 Price was not the captain lieutenant in 1648 as Temple has claimed: 'Original Officer List', p. 62. He probably confused him with William Arnop, who was badly wounded but not killed at Maidstone.

409 R. Bell, *Memorials of the Civil War* (2 vols., 1849) ii, p. 33.

410 A letter signed by Hewsons' company commanders in 11/47 has those in post in August 1647 apart from Toppendene. Ralph Gayle was his replacement: BL, Thomason Tracts, E 413 (6). Interestingly Gayle's claim for pay arrears shows that he had been lieutenant to Henry Davies, not to Toppendene, in the New Model Army: TNA, E 121/4/7/50, entry 24. However, he had been ensign to the company in Pickering's regiment in the army of the Eastern Association in which Toppendene had been lieutenant: Spring i. For evidence that Toppendene had died, not resigned or been cashiered, see TNA, SP 28/59, fo. 201.

411 Worc. College, Clarke Ms 67, fo. 44. This man was almost certainly the Captain Henry Davies who was commissioned in c. 4/50 to raise a company for the 3rd regiment of foot to help make it up to a full regiment. His ensign at that juncture was William Powell who had been ensign to Captain Price: ibid, Clarke Ms 67, fos. 5, 44; TNA, E 121/4/7/48B, entry 90.

412 Although paralysed by wounds received at the battle of Maidstone in 6/48, Arnop appears to have made a complete recovery. A Major William Arnop was serving in Hewson's regiment in 1650, but not when it left for Ireland in 8/49: ibid, SP 28/56, fo. 236; F. and D.; Worc. College, Clarke Ms 67, fo. 44.

Dragoons

Regiment[413]	Name	Military career
Colonel	John Okey	
Major	Daniel Abbott	
Captains	Tobias Bridge	
	Christopher Mercer	
	William Neale	
	John Garland	Previously capt. lt. in Robert Lilburne's regt. H. N. army.[414] Took over Capt. Farmer's troop|
	Francis Bolton[415]	Lt. to Capt. Abbott. Took over to Capt. Farr's troop|
	Francis Barrington	Cor. to Capt. Abbott in 6/45.[416] Took over the remnant of Capt. Wogan's troop|
	Francis Freeman[417]	XXX. Took over Major Moore's troop|
	Henry Fulcher[418]	Lt. to Capt. Scrimgeour and succeeded him|
Capt. Lt.	XXX Baldwin[419]	XXX| Succeeded by Richard Nicholetts by 5/48|

413 For the changes in the troop commanders in 6/47 see ibid Clarke Ms 67, fo. 26.
414 For Garland's career in the Army of the North see TNA, E 121/1/6/66, entry 32; ibid, SP 28/122, fo. 390.
415 As lieutenant Bolton had signed a warrant on his troop commander's behalf in 3/47: ibid, SP28/47, fo. 422. He was a full captain by 15/6/47: ibid, SP 28/51, fo. 1.
416 Barrington was cornet in Abbott's troop in 6/45: ibid, SP 28/30, fo. 319.
417 Captain Francis Freeman was part of the force besieging Dunster Castle in 1646: BL, Thomason Tracts E 343 (6).
418 Garland and Fulcher were troop commanders by the end of 6/47: TNA, SP 28/43, fos. 129, 176.
419 Baldwin had left the regiment by the time of the battle of St. Fagans in 5/48. He may have commanded a troop of dragoons in Scotland, initially in Sir Arthur Haselrig's regiment, from late 1650 until 1652. If so, his first name was Ralph: Chequers Ms 782, unfol. section; CSPD 1650, p. 359; TNA, SP 28/73, fo. 55. However, a Ralph Baldwin was lieutenant to Captain Tolhurst in the 8th regiment of foot after 5/47, and this was a regiment that was stationed in the far north of England from early 1648 onwards: Worc. College, Clarke Ms 67, fo. 10: F. and D.

Cavalry

1st Regiment	Name	Military career
Colonel	Thomas Fairfax	
Major	John Disbrowe[420]	Col. of the 6th regt H. 4/49. Succeeded by his lt. William Covell|
Captains	John Browne	Succeeded Disbrowe as major|
	Adam Lawrence	X at siege of Colchester 6/48. Richard Merest his lt. succeeded him|
	William Packer	
	William Disher	Lt. to Capt. Berry. He succeeded him as troop commander|
Capt. Lt.	John Gladman	

420 F. and D. claim that Disbrowe ceased to be major in 9/48 when he became governor of Yarmouth. However, he was still major in the regiment c. 2/49: Clarke Papers ii, p. 195. Disbrowe, described as colonel on 1/3/49, gave up direct command of his troop a few weeks later: BL, Thomason Tracts, E 545 (30).

2nd Regiment	Name	Military career
Colonel	Thomas Horton	
Major	Walter Bethell[421]	
Captains	Samuel Gardiner	
	Thomas Pennyfather	
	Benjamin Burgess	
	Josias Mullineaux[422]	Capt. Lt. in the regt.|X in Wales c. 5/48|
Capt. Lt.	William Forster?[423]	

421 Walter Bethell, whose commission as major was granted before 28/ 6/47, seems to have leapt over the heads of Captains Gardiner and Pennyfather who were senior captains in the regiment, but he had a commission as captain in the Army of the North, which probably predated theirs: TNA, SP 28/46, fo. 148; ibid, SP 28/140/2, fo. 8.

422 Mullineaux took over Butler's troop on 14/6/47: ibid, E 315/5, fo. 35. He probably received his death wound a few days before the battle of St. Fagans when in an encounter with Welsh royalists he was shot through the thigh: J.R. Phillips, *Memoirs of the Civil War in Wales and the Marches* (2 vols. 1874) ii, p. 356.

423 Forster had been a cornet in Sir Arthur Haselrig's regiment in Waller's army when Horton was captain lieutenant, and lieutenant in Thomas Horton's troop in the 2nd regiment of horse in the New Model Army: ibid, E 315/5, fo. 60; ibid, SP 28/31, fo. 259; ibid, SP 28/40, fo. 253. One of his former soldiers claimed to have served under him in Colonel Horton's troop. He therefore probably became captain lieutenant when Horton received his commission as colonel: ibid, E 121/1/1/26, entry 94.

3rd Regiment	Name	Military career
Colonel	Thomas Harrison	Replaced Col. Thomas Sheffield in 6/47|
Major	William Rainborough	Capt. in this regiment, he replaced Fincher as major| Left the regt. early in 1649.[424] Col. Northants. militia 8/59[425]|
Captains	Henry Cromwell[426]	Prob. capt. under Col. Thomas Morgan H. in Gloucestershire. Took over Fincher's troop|
	Stephen Winthrop[427]	XXX Succeeded Capt. Robotham by late 6/47|
	John Peck[428]	Lt. to Capt. Evelyn. Succeeded Capt. Martin|
	Charles Whitehead	Succeeded Evelyn as capt. after 6/47[429]|
Capt. Lt.	John Spencer[430]	Lt. to Major Harrison|

424 The date of Rainborough's dismissal or resignation is given by F. and D. as 1648 and by Gentles as 1649. The last mention I have found of Major Rainborough is in 1/49: F. and D; Gentles, *New Model Army*, p. 500; TNA, SP 28/58, fo. 195.

425 CSPD 1659-60, p. 198.

426 Worc. College, Clarke Ms 67, fo. 25. Morgan's regiment had formerly been Major General Edward Massey's: ibid, E 121/1/1/26, entries 55, 60, 89, 120.

427 Ibid, SP 28/46, fo. 237. Stephen Winthrop was the son of John Winthrop, governor of Massachusetts. He was in England by 3/46. According to F. and D., he may have served as a junior officer in Sheffield's regiment under Captain Rainborough whose sister he had married. However, I have not found any evidence of this.

428 Ibid, E 121/4/8/ 57A, entry 1. Peck had been cornet to Lieutenant General Thomas Hammond's troop in the army of the Eastern Association: Spring i.

429 Charles Whitehead had been quartermaster in General Thomas Hammond's troop in Manchester's regiment in the Eastern Association army when John Peck was the cornet. In 4/47 Whitehead was still only a cornet: Spring i; BL, Thomason Tracts E 385 (19), E 390 (3); TNA, E 121/3/4/71, entries 1-2.

430 Spencer was in post by late 6/47: ibid, SP 28/46, fo. 240.

4th Regiment	Name	Military career
Colonel	Charles Fleetwood	
Major	William Coleman	Succeeded Thomas Harrison as major|
Captains	Richard Zanchy	
	Gilman Taylor	Lt. to Capt. Howard whom he succeeded[431]|
	Griffith Lloyd[432]	Lt. in 5/47 in Harrison's troop. He took it over when Harrison became col. of the 3rd regt. H.|
	Stephen White[433]	Lt. to Capt. Laughton whom he succeeded|

4th Regiment	Name	Military career
Capt. Lt.	Joseph Blisset	

431 Ibid, SP 28/56, fo. 290. The troop is described was ex Captain Howard's on 13/6/47, but with Taylor still as lieutenant: ibid, SP 28/46, fo. 195. He was captain by 11/47: ibid, SP 28/48, fo. 60.

432 For Lloyd's regiment, see Gentles, *New Model Army*, p. 151.

433 When Laughton died, Cornet Joyce was recommended for the vacant captaincy but Fairfax refused to appoint him. Instead White, who had been Laughton's lieutenant in 6/46, was promoted. He was in post by 11/47: TNA, SP 28/140/7, fo. 288 ibid, SP 28/48, fo. 439; BL, Thomason Tracts E 385 (19); F. and D.

5th Regiment[434]	Name	Military career
Colonel	Phillip Twistleton	Major in the regt. Replaced Col. Rossiter|
Major	James Berry[435]	Capt. 1st regt. H. Succeeded Twistleton in c. 6/47|
Captains	John Nelthorpe	
	Original Peart	
	Owen Cambridge	Major in Col. John Needham's Leicester garr. regt. F. Seemingly replaced Anthony Markham in 7/47[436]|
	Hezekiah Haynes[437]	XXX Replaced Henry Markham in 7/47[438]|
Capt. Lt.	Richard Franklin?[439]	XXX
Possible		
Captain	Ezard[440]	

434 This regiment seems to have been the last to be reformed in the summer of 1647. Twistleton was major and both Markhams still captains in late June: ibid, SP 28/46, fos. 228, 232, 233. Pay warrants for all six of the troops in the regiment, however, show that all the changes had taken place by 8/47: ibid, SP 28/47, fo. 470

435 Worc. College, Clarke Ms 67, fo. 23. Berry continued as major of the regiment until given the colonelcy of Sir Arthur Haselrig's regiment of horse in 1651.

436 Ibid.

437 TNA, E 121/3/3/113B, entries 93-4. Haynes was an officer in the Eastern Association in 1645 and held the rank of a major by 1647, but although no more than a captain in the 5th regiment of horse, he continued to be described as major: Worc. College, Clarke Ms 67, fo. 23. Similar examples of titles being retained when the holder was give a more lowly role in another regiment are to be found in the case of Majors Henry Lilburne, Owen Cambridge and George Smithson.

438 Ibid, Clarke Ms 67, fo. 23.

439 Ibid. There is no indication of the date when Franklin took up his commission, but it could have been as early as the second half of 1647 or as late as 6/49.

440 The crossings out in folio 23 of Clarke Ms 67 suggest that an officer named Ezard was initially lieutenant to Henry Markham and Hezekiah Haynes. This man was almost certainly Thomas Izod who had served as lieutenant to Captain Henry Markham: TNA, E 121/4/7/104, entry 2. He did not become a full captain until 12/55 and then in a different regiment: F. and D. Captain Ezard appears again in 6/59 when he was displaced as a captain in the 1st regiment of horse: CSPD 1658/9, pp. 376, 378.

6th Regiment	Name	Military career
Colonel	Oliver Cromwell	Left 4/49. Succeeded by Major Disbrowe of the 1st regt. H.
Major	Robert Huntington	Resigned 6/48 after breaking with Cromwell. Major Oxfordshire militia regt. H. 8/59|
Captains	John Jenkins	
	John Reynolds	Major by 11/48. Col. of regt. H. raised for service in Ireland before 3/49[441]|
	Henry Middleton[442]	Cashiered in late 1647 for misconduct. Succeeded by his lieutenant George Ensor|
	John Blackwell	
Capt. Lt.	Joseph Wallington	

441 Reynolds was almost certainly Huntington's immediate successor as major: BL, Thomason Tracts, E 526 (28). He received two weeks' pay for his new regiment on 3/3/49: TNA, SP 28/59, fo. 95.

442 Middleton was apparently court-martialled: F. and D. He is last named as captain of his troop in 11/47: TNA, SP 28/48, fo. 437. A Captain Henry Middleton was keeper of the Privy Garden at Whitehall Palace in 1649: CSPD 1649, p. 332.

7th Regiment	Name	Military career
Colonel	Nathaniel Rich	
Major	Azariah Husbands[443]	Capt. in the regt. Succeeded Major Alford|
Captains	Thomas Ireton	
	Francis Hawes	
	Henry Barton[444]	Lt. in the regt. 5/47. Took command of Alford's troop|
	John Merriman[445]	Lt. in the regt. Succeeded Capt. Neville|
Capt. Lt.	William Weare[446]	Left c.10/48. Went to Ireland in 49 as capt. in Oliver Cromwell's regt. H.|

443 The order of entries in the commissions' book suggests that Husbands became major after the rest of the troop commanders had been appointed: Worc. College, Clarke Ms 67, fo. 21. He was still described as captain in a pay warrant dated 26/6/47: TNA, SP 28/46, fo. 143.

444 Ibid, SP 28/49, fo. 341. Barton had been quartermaster to Major Rich's troop in Manchester's regiment of horse in the Eastern Association army: Spring i. In 7/46 he was lieutenant to Major Alford: ibid, SP 28/140/7, fo. 289.

445 Merriman had been cornet in the regiment, and then lieutenant (probably to Captain Husbands). He was a captain by 7/47 or soon afterwards: ibid, SP 28/31, fo. 313; BL, Thomason Tracts E 390 (3); Clarke Papers i, pp. 161, 176, 276, 363. Neville had left in 6/47 and his lieutenant was regarded as unacceptable by the soldiers of the regiment: F. and D.

446 Weare became commander of a troop in Colonel Henry Marten's regiment in 1648: Worc. College, Clarke Ms 67, fo. 21; Chequers Ms 782, fo. 63. In the following year he enlisted for service in Ireland: TNA, SP 28/61, fo. 343; ibid, E 121/3/4/122, unnumbered. It is most likely that his immediate successor as captain lieutenant was Thomas Babbington, see note 591 below.

8th Regiment	Name	Military career
Colonel	Matthew Tomlinson[447]	
Major	Ralph Knight	
Captains	Ralph Margery	
	Thomas Rawlins	
	Thomas Johnson[448]	Lt. to Capt. Knight in the regt., he took over Sir Robert Pye's troop|
	Robert Glyn	Lt. to Major Tomlinson in the regt., he took over Capt. Barry's troop[449]|
Capt. Lt.	William Raunce?	Cor. to Tomlinson when Tomlinson was major[450]|

447 The earliest reference I have of Tomllinson as colonel is in August 1647, but Pye and his troop had truly deserted the army having fled to London in early June: F. and D. There is no record of changes in the officers of the 8th regiment of horse in the commissions' book earlier than 9/48: Worc. College, Clarke Ms 67, fo. 24.

448 TNA, E 121/2/11/24A, unnumbered; ibid, E 121/4/1/16, unnumbered; Clarke Papers i, p. 439.

449 Barry is said by Kishlansky to have left the regiment in 6/47, but not according to F. and D. who place the date between 12/47 and 1653. He must, however, have resigned or been dismissed in or before 22/6/47 as Glyn was troop commander at that date: TNA, SP 28/46, fo. 164; ibid, E 121/1/1/unnumbered, entry 63. Barry may have commanded a regiment in the Jamaica garrison from 1656 to 1662, but a lieutenant colonel Samuel Barry was serving in George Twistleton's regiment of foot in 1660. They cannot be the same man and so there must have been two Samuel Barrys: F. and D.; Worc. College, Clarke Ms 53.

450 See note 592 below for evidence to support the hypothesis.

9th Regiment	Name	Military career
Colonel	Edward Whalley	
Major	Robert Swallow	
Captains	John Grove	
	Henry Cannon	
	William Evanson	
	John Pitchford	Succeeded by John Savage his lt. in 5/48[451]|
Capt. Lt.	Daniel Dale	

451 BL, Harleian Ms 427, fos. 31-2, 35, 91-2. Savage's commission was dated 5/5/49, but it should be 5/5/48: ibid, Clarke Ms 67, fo. 20. Pitchford was still a troop commander in 4/48: TNA, SP 28/53, fo. 321.

10th Regiment	Name	Military career
Colonel	Adrian Scroop	Major in the regt. Succeeded Col. Graves in 6/47|
Major	Nathaniel Barton	Capt. in the regt. Succeeded Major Scroop in 6/47[452]|
Captains	Richard Watson	Lt. to Capt. Scroop in James Sheffield's regt. H. L.G. army. He then served under Sir John Gell[453]|
.	Thomas Goddard	Lt. to Capt. Lord Caulfield[454]|
	Edward Wolfe[455]	
	XXX[456]	
Capt. Lt.	William Peverell	Officer in Scroop's troop[457]|

452 Ibid, SP 28/46, fo. 162.

453 Ibid, E 121/3/3/78, entries 15, 22; ibid, E 121/1/2/49, entry 56; Worc. College, Clarke Ms 67, fo.18.

454 Thomas Goddard was lieutenant to Captain Nathaniel Chute in the earl of Essex's regiment of horse: Turton, *Chief Strength*, p. 25. Chute, chosen to serve in the New Model in this regiment, died in March 1645. He was succeeded as troop commander by Lord Caulfield who left the army in the spring of 1647: CSPD 1644-5, pp. 98-9. Goddard, still a lieutenant, succeeded Caulfield: TNA, SP 28/41, fo. 50; ibid, SP 28/58, fo. 588.

455 Wolfe was a troop commander in the regiment on 29/6/47: ibid, SP 28/46, fo. 395. He had served as captain in Sir William Constable's regiment of foot in Essex's army and as lieutenant colonel to Colonel Needham in the Leicester garrison: ibid, SP 28/30, fo. 119; ibid, SP 28/35, fo. 59. He became a field officer under Colonel Robert Hammond in the Exeter garrison but left in 9/46. He was paid £552 for his services (unspecified) between 9/46 and 6/47: ibid, SP 28/41, fo. 129; ibid, E 121/4/7/50, entries 9-11.

456 Following Bragg's departure Lieutenant John Lewis may have taken temporary command, but when Skippon resigned early in 1649 William Peverell became captain: Worc. College, Clarke Ms 67, fo. 17; F. and D; TNA, E 121/1/7/46B, entry 1; ibid, E 121/4/1/ unnumbered, entry 24; ibid, E 121/3/3/81, unnumbered.

457 In his claim for arrears of pay Peverell described himself first as cornet and then as lieutenant in the colonel's troop, but he does not give any dates: ibid, E 121/3/5/47, unnumbered. He was cornet in James Sheffield's regiment in the earl of Essex's army: ibid, E 121/3/3/78, entry 2.

11th Regiment	Name	Military career
Colonel	Henry Ireton	
Major	Robert Gibbon	Capt. in the regt. Succeeded Sedascue as major|
Captains	William Cecil	Left in c. 12/48.[458] Succeeded by George Hutchinson|
	Henry Pretty	
	Anthony Morgan	
	Robert Kirkby[459]	Capt. Lt. in the regt. Capt. of Sedascue's troop 6/47|
Capt. Lt.	James Wilson[460]	

458 The troop was described as Captain Cecil's on 15/12/48: ibid, SP 28/57, fo. 454.

459 The first mention of Kirkby as full captain is in a pay warrant dated 23/6/47: ibid, SP 28/46, fo. 168.

460 Wilson had served as quartermaster in Ireton's troop in the army of the Eastern Association. In 4/47 he was Ireton's cornet in the New Model Army. He was killed at the battle of Maidstone in 6/48; Spring ii; BL, Thomason Tracts E 390 (3); TNA, SP 28/44, fo. 370; ibid, SP 28/ 56, fo. 355; ibid, E 121/4/2, unnumbered, entry 112.

Lifeguard[461]	Name	Military career
Captain	Richard Cromwell[462]	Succeeded Capt. Hall|
Capt. Lt.	John Ingram[463]	Cor. or corporal in the troop 4/47. Cashiered 12/47|

461 The lifeguard was disbanded as a troop in 2/48: F. and D.

462 A Captain Richard Cromwell was in command between 7/47 and 2/48: BL, Thomason Tracts, E 430 (15). F. and D. named him as Richard, Oliver Cromwell's elder son and the future second Lord Protector. They were right as the other Richard Cromwell in Fairfax's army was killed at Bristol in 9/45. For this see note 132 above.

463 For Ingram's former rank, see TNA, SP 28/39, fo. 74. He was dismissed in 12/47 for publicly declaring his Leveller sympathies: F. and D. His successor, albeit briefly, was Captain Lieutenant Thomas Ellis: ibid, SP 28/51, fo. 134; BL, Thomason Tracts E 430 (15). Ingram was dead by 1650: ibid, E 315/5, fo. 3.

Company and Troop Commanders on 10 May 1649

Infantry

1st Regiment	Name	Military career
Colonel	Sir Thomas Fairfax	
Lt. Col.	William Goffe[464]	Lt. Col. 9th regt. F. Succeeded William Cowell 9/48|
Major	Francis White[465]	
Captains	William Leigh[466]	Left the regt. in 6/49|
	James Priest	
	James Pitson	
	Clement Keene	
	William Farley	
	George Hadfield[467]	In the regt. by 7/48 and so must have succeeded Capt. Baldwin[468]|
	Charles Bolton[469]	Left the regt. in the middle of 49. Succeeded by Capt. Hammond|
Capt. Lt.	Robert Luson?[470]	Ens. in Fairfax's own co.|
Possibles Captains	Richard Combes[471]	XXX Capt. in 12/49|
	XXX Straghan[472]	XXX Capt. in 50|

464 Goffe transferred in 9/48 from the 9th regiment of foot where he had been lieutenant colonel. This was to all intents and purposes a promotion as he was *de facto* colonel of his new regiment, and he was listed as such in a petition dated 3/49: BL, Thomason Tracts E 545 (30).

465 White was allegedly passed over for promotion to lieutenant colonel on Cowell's death because of his forthright radical opinions, but he was granted that rank for the bravery he displayed at the battle of Dunbar in September 1650 when Goffe was promoted to full colonel: F. and D.

466 Leigh was commissioned as major in Henry Ireton's regiment of foot raised for service in Ireland, but was seemingly promoted to lieutenant colonel after the death of Edward Wolfe later in the year: TNA, SP 28/61, fo. 363; ibid, SP 28/65, fo. 25. He was a colonel in Ireland for much of the 1650s: F. and D.

467 Hadfield had been ensign and lieutenant in the regiment: TNA, E 121/2/9/46, entry 126. He died in or just before 1/50: ibid, SP 28/65, fo. 250.

468 Hadfield fought at Appelby against the Scottish army in 7/48: Perfect Occurences, issue 82, 21-28/7/48.

469 Charles Bolton became major in Ireton's regiment of foot in Ireland before 5/50 as he was mortally wounded at the storming of Clonmel in that month: ibid, SP 28/67, fo. 339; CSPD 1653-4, p. 391. For Captain Hammond see TNA, E 121/2/9/46, entry 502.

470 Ibid, E 121/2/9/unnumbered, entry 65. Luson was certainly captain lieutenant by the time Fairfax left the regiment and captain at a later date, but somebody else may have directly succeeded Lewis Audley in c. 6/48.

471 Worc. College, Clarke Ms 69, unfol. 6/12/49.

472 This man cannot be identified as there were several officers with that surname in Parliament's armies. The most likely is the Captain Straghan who had served in the earl of Manchester's regiment of foot in the Eastern Association army and been discharged at the formation of the New Model Army. Subsequently he had some connection with the garrison at Abingdon in Oxfordshire in 4/46: Davies, 'Army of the Eastern Association', p. 92; Spring i; TNA, SP 28/42, fo. 1066. If this was he, his first name was James: ibid, SP 28/301, fo. 803.

2nd Regiment	Name	Military career
Colonel	William Sydenham[473]	Gov. of Weymouth and col. F. to 9/48. Succeeded Skippon in early 49| Succeeded by Col. Cox in 6/49|
Lt. Col.	Richard Ashfield	
Major	John Cobbett[474]	Gone by 7/49. Succeeded by Major Barber by 12/49. Lt. James Mayer took command of Cobbett's co.|
Captains	James Harrison	
	John Clarke	
	Maurice Bowen[475]	Gone by 15/11/49. Transferred to the 3rd regt. F. by 4/50. Succeeded by Capt. Lt. Samuel Clarke|

2nd Regiment	Name	Military career
	William Symonds	
	John Rogers	Left the regt. c. 6/49 but he probably resumed his military career later[476]
	Arthur Helsham	
	Thomas Butler	Left in or before 11/49. Militia commissioner for Oxfordshire 4/50. Succeeded by James Symcock, his lt[477]
Capt. Lt.	Samuel Clarke[478]	He took over Captain Bowen's co. in 11/49. Succeeded as capt. lt. by an officer named Heyrick|

473 Skippon had resigned by 9/1/49 when Lieutenant Colonel Ashfield was described as belonging to Skippon's former regiment : TNA, SP 28/58, fo. 192. Sydenham replaced him on 13/2/49, but left after two or so months. In 6/59 Sydenham became colonel of the 6th regiment of foot but was displaced in 12/59: F. and D.

474 Cobbett was in trouble for Leveller sympathies in 11/47 but pardoned. He was cashiered after the Leveller revolt in the army in May 1649. His replacement was a Major John Barber who does not appear to have had any previous connection with the regiment: Gentles, *New Model Army*, p. 347; F. and D. By September 1649 Cobbett, described as a moderate Leveller, was trusted to serve as an intermediary with units of the 6th regiment of foot garrisoning Oxford which had imprisoned their officers. He seems to have been restored to favour soon afterwards. He was major of John Lambert's regiment of foot before the battle of Dunbar in 9/50: Perfect Occurences, issue 141; F. and D.

475 Bowen and Butler's successors were commissioned in 11/49: Worc. College, Clarke Ms 67, fo. 4. However, Bowen is mentioned on 12/12/49 as if he was still in the regiment: ibid, Clarke Ms 69, unfol.

476 Rogers became embroiled in Leveller intrigues in the garrison of Bristol in 5/49 and was committed prisoner to the marshal general of the army in the following month: F. and D. Unlike Major Cobbett there is no unimpeachable evidence that he was restored to favour, but a Captain John Rogers served in Charles Fairfax's regiment of foot in the New Model Army from 1652 or earlier. By 1660 he was lieutenant colonel: Chequers Ms. 782, unfol. section.

477 Worc. College, Clarke Ms 67, fo. 4. For Butler's first name and his serving under Colonel Cox, see TNA, E 121/1/1/7/ unnumbered, entry 189; CSPD 1650, pp. 81, 511.

478 Clarke was in the regiment as captain lieutenant on 7/8/48: ibid, SP 28/133/1, fo. 55. His commission as captain of Bowen's company and Heyrick's as captain lieutenant are recorded in Worc. College, Clarke Ms 67, fo. 4.

3rd Regiment[479]	Name	Military career
Colonel	Sir Hardress Waller	
Lt. Col.	Edward Salmon[480]	Left c. 6/49 to become deputy gov. of Hull; Col. F. 53|
Major	Thomas Smith	Lt. Col. 7/49. X in gunpowder explosion in 1/50[481]
Captains	John Clarke	Major 7/49 when Smith became lt. col. Became lt. col. on Smith's death, Served in England[482]
	Richard Hodden[483]	Served in Ireland|
	Richard Aske	Served in England under Lt. Col. Clarke and then in Ireland in Clarke's regiment[484]
	Phillip Ebzery	Major by 5/50 in England[485]
	Nathaniel Chase	Served in England|
	Brian Smith[486]	Served in Ireland|
	William Wade/Ward?	Lt to Capt Stoddard. Served in Ireland in the battalion[487]
Capt. Lt.	Ralph Wilson	Served in Ireland[488]

479 The regiment was one of those chosen in 4/49 for Cromwell's expedition to Ireland, but only a single battalion went. The other remained in southwest England where it took part in the capture of the Scilly Isles.

480 Lieutenant Colonel at Hull to Colonel Overton, Salmon became colonel of the 15th regiment of foot in 1653 and held that command until 1660. He also married Deane's widow: F. and D. His successor as company commander in the 3rd regiment of foot was almost certainly Lewis Northcott his lieutenant: TNA, E 121/1/6/66, entry 186.

481 Worc. College, Clarke Ms 67, fo. 5; F. and D.

482 F. and D; TNA, SP 28/65, fo. 287.

483 Hodden joined the battalion of the 3rd regiment of foot which went to Ireland with Cromwell in 1649. He was major in the regiment by 1651: ibid, SP 28/81, fo. 177.

484 Ibid, SP 28/66, fo. 446.

485 Worc. College, Clarke Ms 69 unfol. 10/5/50.

486 Smith was successively lieutenant and captain in the regiment. His company left England for Ireland in late 1649: TNA, E 121/1/6/ unnumbered, entry 17; F. and D. He was subsequently major in Henry Ireton's regiment of foot, but it had a major and too many captains in post for Smith to have transferred any earlier than the summer of 1650: F. and D.; TNA, SP 28/61-8, passim.

487 Ibid, E 121/1/6/63, entry 187. For Wade's service in Ireland see Sir John Gilbert, *A Contemporary History of Affairs in Ireland 1641-1652* (3 vols. 1879-81) iii, p. 364; TNA, SP 28/81, fo. 177.

488 Wilson was a captain in the regiment by 10/51: ibid, SP 28/81, fo. 177.

4th Regiment[489]	Name	Military career
Colonel	Isaac Ewer	Succeeded Hammond in 9/47|
Lt. Col.	Robert Saunders	Wounded at the storming of Drogheda in 9/49. He returned to Ireland in 6/50 as col. of a newly raised F. regt. Gov. of Kinsale 1659[490]|
Major	William Disney	Major by 3/49 Wounded at Drogheda. Possibly lt. col. very briefly c. 4/50[491]|
Captains	Israel Smith[492]	
	John Puckle	Lt. Col. in the regt. in 5/50[493]|
	William Stratton	Major in the regt. in 6/50[494]|
	Francis Wheeler	
	Edward Humphreys	Prob killed at the storming of Clonmel, Ireland in 5/50[495]|
	Richard Tonson/Tomson[496]	Lt. in 3/47|
	Thomas Sharpe[497]	XXX. Prob. took over Major Rolfe's co.|
Capt. Lt.	William Ewer[498]	Ens. to Lt. Col. Ewer 4/47|

489 On 20/4/49 the regiment was chosen to serve in the expedition to Ireland led by Oliver Cromwell: F. and D.

490 Abbott, *Writings and Speeches* ii, pp. 127-8; CSPD 1650, p. 83; F. and D; BL, Thomason Tracts, E 598 (6); TNA, SP 28/68, fo. 337.

491 For evidence of Disney's rank in 3/49, see BL, Thomason Tracts E 455 (30). In his report of the capture of Drogheda Cromwell stated that both the field officers in Ewer's regiment had been shot: Abbott, *Writings and Speeches* ii, pp. 127-8. The fact that Disney had been seriously wounded is apparent from CSPD 1650, pp 592, 604. He nevertheless returned to England in c. 7/50 as lieutenant colonel to raise two companies of infantry for Colonel Foulkes's regiment. It is possible that Disney never reached the rank of lieutenant colonel in the 4th regiment of foot. Possibly John Puckle had been preferred to him when Saunders left, Disney's compensation being a commission as lieutenant colonel in another regiment.

492 Smith was killed at the storming of Drogheda: CJ vii, p. 38.

493 TNA, SP 28/67, fo. 325.

494 Ibid, SP 28/68, fo. 347.

495 Gilbert, *Contemporary History* iii, p. 409.

496 Tonson was a captain by 12/47 when he and his company were ordered to the Isle of Wight: TNA, SP 29/49, fo. 326. His previous military career is uncertain, but in 1645 there was an Ensign Tonson in Captain O'Hara's company in Crawford's regiment in the Eastern Association army, and Crawford's regiment became Robert Hammond's and then Isaac Ewer's: F. and D.; TNA, SP 28/27, fo. 318.

497 Sharpe was a captain in the regiment in mid-1649: Worc. College, Clarke Ms 69, unfol. 29/4/49; TNA, SP 28/61, fos. 319, 454.

498 Worc. College, Clarke Ms 41, fo. 102. Information given to the House of Lords in 4/47 shows that at that time Ewer was ensign in the lieutenant-colonel's company: LJ ix, pp. 153-6.

5th Regiment	Name	Military career
Colonel	John Barkstead	
Lt. Col.	Ralph Cobbett	
Major	John Biscoe	
Captains	Arthur Young	
	Richard Pooley[499]	
	John Miller	
	Henry Dorney	
	John Groome[500]	
	Thomas Buckner[501]	Ex capt. lt. in the regt. Almost certainly succeeded Capt. Denison|

5th Regiment	Name	Military career
	William Read[502]	Succeeded Capt. Cox|
Capt. Lt.	William Bayly[503]	Lt. in the regt. to Capt. Denison. Succeeded Thomas Buckner|

499 Pooley was still in the regiment in 2/50 when an ensign was commissioned to serve in his company: Worc. College, Clarke Ms 69, unfol. ; ibid, Clarke Ms 67, fo. 8.

500 There was a Captain John Groome in the regiment in 1647. He was at Colchester siege and attended a council of war in 12/48: Chequers Ms 782, fo. 76; Clarke Papers ii, p. 274.

501 Buckner's commission was dated 5/5/49: Worc. College, Clarke Ms 16, fo. 99.

502 Read was captain in the regiment in 1650: TNA, E 121/2/11/17A, fo. 84. He had been sergeant and ensign in Sir Anthony St. John's company in the Earl of Essex's regiment of foot, and then lieutenant to Captain Richard Pooley in the 6th regiment of foot: ibid, E 121/2/11/17B, entry 190-1. He was still a lieutenant in 5/48: BL, Thomason Tracts E 443 (5). However, it is clear that he took over Captain Cox's company. Cox was killed at the start of the siege of Colchester in 6/48: BL, Thomason Tracts 669 f13 (6).

503 Bayly's commission as captain lieutenant was dated 5/5/49: Worc. College, Clarke Ms 16, fo. 99. He was replaced by Roger Jones very soon afterwards: ibid, Clarke Ms 67, fo. 8; ibid, Clarke Ms 69, unfol.

6th Regiment[504]	Name	Military career
Colonel	Richard Ingoldsby	
Lt. Col.	Thomas Kelsey[505]	
Major	John Mill	
Captains	Francis Allen	
	John Grime	
	Richard Wagstaffe	
	John Shrimpton[506]	Left army in 9/49. Succeeded by a Capt. Davies|
	John Hunt	
	Francis Messervy[507]	Officer in the Barnstable garrison. Succeeded Capt. Stephens|
	William Duckett[508]	Lt. to Lt. Col. Kelsey|
Capt. Lt.	**Abraham Davies[509]**	Succeeded by Lt. Consolation Fox[510]|

504 Six of the regiment's companies were in garrison at Oxford in the summer of 1648; the rest were at the siege of Colchester. There were five companies at Oxford a year later: F. and D.; TNA, SP 28/55, fo. 220.

505 Kelsey commanded the Oxford garrison from 1648 to 1651. After that he was governor of Dover Castle: F. and D.

506 Shrimpton was cashiered in 9/49 for alleged complicity with the Levellers. Captain Lieutenant Abraham Davies probably took over his company as a full captain. However, the Captain Davies who served in the regiment in the late 1640s could have been John Davies, Shrimpton's lieutenant: Worc. College, Clarke Ms 67, fo. 13.

507 Messervy attended the Council of War in 11 and 12/48 and in 3/49: ibid, Clarke Ms 67, fo. 13; BL, Thomason Tracts E 545 (30). For the Barnstable connection, see TNA, E 121/3/4/61, unnumbered.

508 Duckett had been commissioned as Kelsey's lieutenant in 6/47. During the siege of Colchester he was promoted from lieutenant to captain. The only person he could have replaced was Thomas Ingoldsby, but it is possible that a Captain Cooke or a Lieutenant Thomas Matthews succeeded Ingoldsby as captain between 3/48 and the start of the siege, and that Duckett replaced him before it ended. Worc. College, Clarke Ms 67, fo. 13; Chequers Ms 782, fos. 66, 74-6; TNA, E 121/5/1/unnumbered, entry 29.

509 Davies was a major of foot in Flanders in 1659: F. and D.

510 The commissions' book does not make it clear when Consolation Fox succeeded Abraham Davies, but Fox's position in the list of commissions for this regiment in the commissions' book means it is unlikely to have been in 1647 or in 1650: Worc. College, Clarke Ms 67, fo. 13. In 1644 Fox had been sergeant in Captain Nathaniel Tilly's company in the Tower Hamlet regiment of the London trained bands and then lieutenant to Captain Grime in the 6th regiment of foot: TNA, SP 28/121A, fo. 586; ibid E 121/3/3/31, entry 30.

7th Regiment	Name	Military career
Colonel	Richard Deane[511]	Oliver Cromwell succeeded Deane after 4/49[512]|
Lt. Col.	Henry Bowen	
Major	Lewis Audley[513]	Gone in late 49/early 50. Succeeded by Capt. Flower|
Captains	George Drury	
	Thomas Dancer	
	Thomas Creamer[514]	

7th Regiment	Name	Military career
	Henry Whittle	
	Henry Flower	
	Thomas Walker[515]	
	Thomas Segrave[516]	XXX Succeeded Capt. Browne|
Capt. Lt.	George Townshend[517]	XXX
Possible Captain	John Jewell[518]	XXX

511 When Deane was appointed one of the three 'generals at sea' in 2/49, the colonelcy of a regiment of foot seemed as inappropriate as it had done in the case of Rainborough two years earlier. Within three months he had been replaced by Oliver Cromwell, the designated Lord Lieutenant of Ireland, who took the regiment with him in 8/49: F. and D. ii, p. 625; Clarke Papers ii, p. 209. The last mention I have discovered of Deane as colonel is in Worc. College, Clarke Ms 69, unfol. 19/4/49.

512 All the officers apart from Audley, Creamer and Townshend are known to have served in Cromwell's regiment in Ireland: TNA, SP 28/67, fo. 284, 310; ibid, SP 28/68 fo. 329; ibid, SP 28/73 fo. 165; ibid, SP 28/125, fo. 70; J.P. Prendergast, *The Cromwellian Settlement of Ireland* (Dublin, 1875), p. 134.

513 It was the intention that Audley should continue serving as major when the regiment was chosen for service in Ireland: TNA, SP 28/61, fo. 351. If he went there, he did not stay for long. By 5/50 he was major in Colonel Robert Gibbon's newly raised regiment of foot: Worc. College, Clarke Ms 67, unfol. The connection between Audley and Gibbon is unclear, but he and Gibbon had served together in Surrey in 1648: F. and D., p. 325. By 5/56 Audley was an officer of the ordnance. For this see CSPD 1656, p. 330.

514 For Creamer's departure from the army, see note 381 above.

515 Walker was still in the regiment in 6/49 when an officer named Barber was commissioned as ensign in his company: Worc. College, Clarke Ms 69, unfol.

516 Ibid, Clarke Ms 67, fo. 42. Thomas Segrave had been lieutenant in the earl of Manchester's regiment of foot in the Eastern Association army: Spring i. I have been unable to trace his military career between 1645 and 4/49 when he succeeded Captain Browne: ibid, Worc. College, Clarke Ms 67, fo. 29.

517 Townshend was commissioned as captain lieutenant on 1/7/48: ibid, Clarke Ms 67, fo. 9. It is possible that his first name was John. I have no further record of his army career.

518 Jewell was captain in the regiment by 6/50: TNA, SP 28/68, fo. 329.

8th Regiment	Name	Military career
Colonel	Sir Arthur Haselrig	Succeeded Robert Lilburne c. 1/48[519]|
Lt. Col.	Paul Hobson[520]	Promoted from major to lt. col. c. 8/48|
Major	Jeremiah Tolhurst	Promoted from capt. c. 8/48|
Captains	Abraham Holmes	
	Robert Hutton	
	Richard Deane	Succeeded as capt. by Henry Mason in 2/50[521]|
	Gabriel Earwood	Succeeded by Lt. James Rosse before 31/8/49[522]|
	Ethelbert Morgan	Capt. by 1/48[523]|
	James Hart[524]	Lt. to Capt. Mitchell. Succeeded him by 8/48|
,	John Topping	Capt. by 8/48[525]|
Capt. Lt.	Henry Goodyear	Did not directly succeed William Bray as he was commissioned after 8/48[526]|

519 Haselrig was commissioned as governor of Newcastle on 29/12/47: CJ v, p. 410.

520 Hobson was a major in early July 1648 and must have succeeded Henry Lilburne, Robert's brother, who had gone over to the royalists: CSPD 1648-9, p. 244. The nine company commanders from Hobson downwards derive from a list of payments made to their companies whilst in garrison at Newcastle between 7/48 and early 1650: TNA, SP 28/133/3 and 4, passim.

521 Worc. College, Clarke Ms 67, fo. 10. Richard Deane became secretary and registrar of the army committee in 1/2/50, which is not surprising as he had been secretary to the earl of Essex's train of artillery earlier in the war: TNA, SP 29/28, fo. 325; ibid, SP 28/68, fo. 306; ibid, SP 28/71, fo. 235.

522 Earwood's name last appears as captain in the regiment in 7/49: TNA, SP 28/133/4, fo. 39. The reason for his leaving is not known, but he was certainly dead by 8/50: ibid, E 121/2/5/5, entry 11.

523 Morgan was commissioned as captain whilst Lilburne was still colonel: ibid, E 121/4/8/1, entry 8.

524 Hart was lieutenant to Capt. Nicholas Fenton in Weldon's regiment in Waller's army from 7/44. After 6/47 he was lieutenant to Captain Mitchell: Spring ii; Worc. College, Clarke Ms 67, fo. 10. He was a company commander by 7/8/48: TNA, SP 28/133/1, fos. 59-60.

525 See notes 393, 520 above.

526 TNA, SP 28/133/4, fo. 32. His petition for £300 recompense for loss of goods at Tynemouth Castle shows that he had served in Henry Lilburne's company: CJ vi, p. 297.

9th Regiment	Name	Military career
Colonel	Thomas Pride	
Lt. Col.	John Mason[527]	
Major	Waldine Lagoe	
Captains	Thomas Parsons	
	Roger Alsop	
	Joseph Salkeld	
	John Hawes	
	Richard Mosse[528]	Lt. in the regt. in 4/47[529]|
	John Pearson[530]	Ens. to Capt. John Hawes in the regt. in 6/47|
	Richard Kemp?	Lt. in the regt. in late 47[531]	
Capt. Lt.	William Galhampton	

527 For Mason's and Lagoe's promotion from captain to field officer, see note 396 above and Worc. College, Clarke Ms 67, fo.12.

528 Mosse was a company commander by 12/48 at the latest: Clarke Papers ii, pp. 276-7. He may have succeeded Lieutenant Colonel Goffe, who had been transferred to the 1st regiment of foot, as he had been his ensign in the earl of Essex's army: TNA, E 121/4/8/ unnumbered, entry 580.

529 BL, Thomason Tracts, E 390 (3).

530 Pearson became ensign when Hawes was commissioned as captain in 6/47. He received his captain's commission in 9/48 with Nicholas Andrews as his lieutenant: Worc. College, Clarke Ms 67, fo. 12. It is highly likely that Pearson took over the company hitherto commanded by Lieutenant Colonel Goffe or Major Gregson both of whom left the regiment in 9/48.

531 Kemp was captain by 11/49: ibid, Clarke Ms 41, fo. 103; ibid, Clarke Ms 67, fo. 12.

10th Regiment[532]	Name	Military career
Colonel	Sir William Constable	Col. F. L.G. and N. Armies 1642-47. Succeeded Lambert 9/47|
Lt. Col.	Mark Grime[533]	Cashiered in c. 6/49. Lt. Gov. of Carlisle 8/59|
Major	Wroth Rogers[534]	Lt. Col. of the regt. 8/49. Gov. of Hereford well into the 1650s|
Captains	Lawrence Nunney	
	Giles Saunders[535]	
	Thomas Disney	
	William Style	
	Matthew Cadwell	
	John Nicholas	Lt. of Rogers's and then Biscoe's co. he succeeded Biscoe as capt.. Gov. of Chepstow Castle 8/48.[536]|
	Roger Lewis	Lt. to Capt. Blethin[537]|
Capt. Lt.	Samuel Ross[538]	
Attached Co.		
Captain	Thomas Pury junior[539]	Capt. Col. Morgan's regt. F. Gloucester garr.|

532 The 10th regiment had been placed in garrisons in the southern Welsh borderland in early 1648 with six companies at Gloucester, one at Chepstow and several at Hereford: F. and D. See also entries above and below for Wroth Rogers and John Nicholas.

533 Grime was accused of grievous crimes by some of his officers in 4/49, but he contested the case they brought against him. He was therefore probably still in post in May. An order for his arrears to be paid on 7/6/49, however, suggests that by that date he had resigned or been cashiered: F. and D: Worc. College, Clarke Ms 69, unfol.

534 TNA, SP 28/62, fo. 13; ibid, E 121/5/7/unnumbered, entry 1.

535 Saunders was still captain in the regiment in 8/49: TNA, SP 28/62, fo. 344.

536 F. and D. suggest that Biscoe left the regiment in about 7/47. His successor appears from the commissions' book to have been Ethelbert Morgan: Worc. College, Clarke Ms 67, fo. 7. This was a clerical error. The entry gives as Morgan's junior officers Lieutenant Thomas Cartwright and Ensign Indigo who held those positions in his company in the 8th regiment of foot in 1648: TNA, SP28/122, fo. 247. Biscoe's true successor was his lieutenant: E 121/5/7/52, entry 79. For Chepstow see ibid, SP 28/55, fo. 218.

537 Spring i; TNA, E 121/5/7/21, entry 260.

538 Ross was involved in the arrest of Lieutenant Colonel Grime and was described as captain: HMC, Leybourne-Popham Mss, p. 16. However, the lieutenant component of his rank had almost certainly been omitted. All the full captains in the regiment are known for that date.

539 A Gloucester man, Pury had previously served under Colonels Massey and Morgan in the city's garrison regiment: TNA, SP 28/55, fo. 119. A warrant dated 7/48 shows that Pury's company had been added to the 10th regiment of foot in the same way that Captain Jones's was later to be added to the 3rd regiment of horse: ibid, SP 28/55, fo. 119. This may be an indication of the influence of Thomas Pury senior, Captain Pury's father, who sat as MP for Gloucester. His signature appears many hundreds of times on warrants issued by the House of Commons' committee in charge of army administration in the period covered by this volume.

11th Regiment[540]	Name	Military career
Colonel	George Fenwick	Col. of H. newly raised in Northumberland in 6/48. Succeeded Overton on 9/5/49[541]
Lt. Col.	Thomas Read	
Major	John Wade[542]	Major 10th regt. F. late 49
Captains	Robert Read	Replaced Wade as major
	Edward Orpin[543]	
	Robert Anderson[544]	Possibly succeeded by Capt. Lt. Fann
	William Knowles	
	William Gough	
	Thomas Hughes	
	XXX Andrews	XXX. He replaced Capt. Spooner[545]
Capt. Lt.	**Matthew Fenn/Fann**[546]	Succeeded by William Collinson before 6/49[547]
Possible		
Captain	William Mitchell[548]	

540 541 BL, Thomason Tracts E 451 (34). F. and D. give the date of his commission.

542 Wade fought at the battle of St. Fagans in 5/48. His transfer to the 10th regiment of foot based at Gloucester took place after the disgrace of Lieutenant Colonel Grime and the promotion of Major Rogers. It was possibly because of his knowledge of ironworks. He was to manage the former royal blast furnaces and forges in the Forest of Dean on the state's behalf for the next ten years: Phillips, *Wales and the Marches* ii, p. 366; CJ vii, p. 85; CSPD 1650-59, passim.

543 This officer's ensign was commissioned on 17/4/49, but he appears to have retired soon afterwards: Worc. College, Clarke Ms 69, unfol. The most likely date is soon after 1/50 when General Fairfax granted him permission to remain in London for six months: Worc. College, Clarke Ms 69, unfol.

544 The latest piece of evidence of Anderson's serving in the regiment is his signature on a petition dated 11/48: Worc. College, Clarke Ms 16, fo. 9. If he left before 5/49, the new company commander was probably William Collinson who was a full captain in the regiment in 1650: F. and D; Worc. College, Clarke Ms 69, unfol. 25/2/50.

545 For Andrews, see TNA, E121/5/7/18, entries 72-5. It is not known when he left the New Model Army.

546 Fenn was captain lieutenant in 5/48 and 11/48: Phillips, *Wales and the Marches* ii, p. 365; Worc. College, Clarke Ms 16, fo. 9. A man of that name served as cornet of Captain Rainborough's troop in Colonel Sheffield's regiment in the earl of Essex's army. Fenn was not been given a commission in the New Model Army in 4/45: TNA, SP 28/28, fo. 432.

547 Ibid, E 121/5/5/30A, entry 65;

548 Several claims for arrears of pay have Captain William Mitchell of the 8th regiment of foot serving in Colonel Overton's regiment. See, for example, ibid, E 121/4/5/82D, entry 12. This was almost certainly not in the 11th regiment of foot but in one of Overton's earlier regiments. Overton fought in the north of England as a colonel under Lord Fairfax and Major General Poyntz.

12th Regiment[549]	Name	Military career
Colonel	John Hewson	
Lt. Col.	Daniel Axtell	
Major	John Carter	
Captains	Samuel Grime	

12th Regiment[549]	Name	Military career
	Alexander Brayfield	
	Thomas Atkinson	
	Ralph Gayle[550]	Lt. to Capt. Henry Davies. Succeeded Capt. Toppendene|
	George Smith[551]	Lt. to Capt. Alexander Brayfield, he apparently took over Lt. Col. Jubbs's co.|
	George Jenkins[552]	Lt. and successor to Capt. Thomas Price who was X at Maidstone| X at the storming of Drogheda in 9/49[553]|
	Samuel Axtell[554]	Lt. to Capt. Thomas Atkinson. Succeeded Capt. Davies|
Capt. Lt.	XXX Ramsey[555]	XXX. Succeeded Capt. Lt. Arnop|

549 The regiment was chosen in 4/49 for service in Ireland under Oliver Cromwell. Its officers' names are given in Worc. College, Clarke Ms 67, fo. 44.

550 For Gayle's earlier career, see note 410 above. It is likely that he was the Lieutenant Ralph Gill who signed the Vindication of 4/47 given the extent to which the names of the junior officers are garbled in the printed list: BL, Thomason Tracts E 385 (19).

551 TNA, E 121/2/1/18, entries 10-12.

552 Spring i; Temple, 'Original Army List', p. 62. Jenkins and Smith may have been present at the councils of war held in the winter of 1648/9 but at the time there were men with the same surnames serving in other regiments: Clarke Papers ii, pp. 272, 276.

553 BL, Thomason Tracts, E 575 (7).

554 TNA, E 121/2/1/18, entries 17-19. Axtell had been ensign in Daniel Axtell's company in the mid-1640s: ibid, E 121/2/1/18, fo. 17-19. He, Jenkins and Smith were lieutenants by 4/47: BL, Thomason Tracts, E 385 (19).

555 Worc. College, Clarke Ms. 67, fo. 44. Ramsey, like Jenkins, was killed at the storming of Drogheda in 9/49: CJ vii, p. 38.

Dragoons

Regiment	Name	Military career
Colonel	John Okey	Troop to remain in England|
Major	Daniel Abbott	Troop chosen to serve in Ireland in 4/49. Col. Dr. in Ireland by 8/49[556]|
Captains	Tobias Bridge	Troop to remain in England. Succeeded Abbott as major of the regt. c. 8/49|
	Christopher Mercer	Troop chosen to serve in Ireland but remained in England[557]|
	William Neale	Troop to remain in England.
	John Garland	Troop chosen to serve in Ireland but it did not do so. Garland left regt. c. 6/49. Military service thereafter not known. Succeeded by John Daborne his lt.[558]|
	Francis Bolton	Troop chosen to serve in Ireland. Bolton major in Abbott's regt. Dr. and then in Henry Pretty's regt. H. Drowned 8/59 whilst in transit to England[559]|
	Francis Barrington	Troop chosen to remain in England. Barrington left the regt. c. 12/49[560]|
	Francis Freeman	Troop chosen to remain in England.
	Henry Fulcher	Troop chosen to serve in Ireland in 4/49 and probably did. Fulcher was listed in Abbot's new regt. but left c. 8/49. Possibly he served as reformado in Capt. Palmer's troop in the 14th regt. H. in 3/50.[561] Nothing further is known about his military service|
Capt. Lt.	Richard Nicholetts[562]	Succeeded Capt. Lt. Baldwin by 5/48[563]| Capt. in Henry Cromwell's regt. H. in Ireland c. 12/49. X during operations around Limerick 9/51|

556 Major Abbott and Captains Mercer, Bolton, Fulcher and Garland and their troops were chosen for service in Ireland in 4/49: Clarke Papers ii, p. 209. Only Abbott's, Barrington's and Fulcher's seem to have gone there as dragoons. For this, see F. and D; TNA, SP 28/62, fo. 115. A full discussion of the changes to Okey's regiment in 1649 and 1650 will appear in volume 2.

557 Mercer was in the regiment in England early in 1650: Worc. College, Clarke Ms 69, unfol. 15/3/50. He was still commanding a troop of dragoons in 6/50 but appears to have left the regiment. In the campaigns in Scotland and England in 1651 he served as acting major of some unregimented troops of dragoons: TNA, SP 28/68, fo. 55; CSPD 1651, pp. 193, 236.

558 Daborne did not go to Ireland. He continued to serve in Colonel Okey's regiment: Worc. College, Clarke Ms 69, unfol. (20/05/1650).

559 F. and D; TNA, SP 28/62, fo. 46.

560 He became a captain in Colonel Henry Cromwell's regiment being raised for service in Ireland, and was later colonel of a regiment of foot in the West Indies where he died by accident in 1660:F. and D.

561 Worc. College, Clarke Ms 69, unfol. 5/3/50. For the 14th regiment of horse, see below Appendix IV.

562 A man of the same name was lieutenant to Major Clutterbuck in Colonel Turner's regiment in Waller's army, and then captain in the same regiment under Colonels Thompson, Popham and Starr: Spring i; TNA, E 121/1/1/26, entry 91. It served in Massey's brigade in the west of England after 4/45 and was disbanded with the rest of his regiments in 10/46: Spring ii. For Nicholetts' career in Ireland, see F. and D.

563 Nicholetts fought in Okey's regiment at the battle of St. Fagans: Phillips, *Wales in the Marches* ii, p. 366.

Cavalry

1st Regiment	Name	Military career
Colonel	Thomas Fairfax	
Major	John Browne[564]	Succeeded John Disbrowe|
Captains	William Packer	
	William Disher	
	Richard Merest[565]	Lt. to Capt. Lawrence|
	William Covell[566]	Lt. to Major Disbrowe|
Capt. Lt.	John Gladman	

564 Browne's commission was dated 23/4/49. College, Clarke Ms 69, unfol.

565 Merest sat in a council of war as captain on 25/8/48. Most of Merest's troopers who claimed arrears of pay in 1650 had served under Lawrence: Clarke Papers ii, p. 276; TNA, E 121/5/7/14, entries 585-623, 641-2.

566 William Covell, often incorrectly written as Cowell, was lieutenant to Major Disbrowe in Cromwell's regiment in the New Model Army: TNA, SP 28/140/7, fo. 280. After Disbrowe became governor of Portsmouth in 4/49, the troop still carried his name, but Covell commanded it as a full captain following the precedent set by Captain Nicholas Bragge, commander of Major General Skippon's troop in the 10th regiment of horse between 1645 and 1647: Worc. College, Clarke Ms 67, fo. 15; ibid, Clarke Ms 69, unfol. 17/4/49, 23/4/49 Worc.

2nd Regiment[567]	Name	Military career
Colonel	Thomas Horton	D of disease in Ireland just before 25/10/49[568]| Succeeded by Jerome Zanchy, major in Oliver Cromwell's regt. H. in Ireland[569]|
Major	Walter Bethell[570]	Allegedly refused to serve in Ireland in 8/49|
Captains	Samuel Gardiner	Ditto|
	Thomas Pennyfather	Succeeded Bethell as major c. 10/49. D in Ireland in before 11/51[571]|
	Benjamin Burgess[572]	Allegedly refused to serve in Ireland in 8/49|
	Elias Green[573]	Lt. to Capt. Josias Mullineaux whom he succeeded in c. 5/48. Major of the regt. by 1/51[574]|
Capt. Lt.	William Forster	Capt. 11th regt. H. in Ireland[575]|

567 The regiment was chosen for service in Ireland in 4/49.

568 BL, Thomason Tracts, E 579 (13).

569 TNA, SP 28/62, fo. 8. Zanchy had been major of Sir William Brereton's regiment of horse: F. and D.

570 The issue of The Moderate of 21-8 November 1649 cited a letter written three months earlier accusing Bethell, Gardiner and Burgess of refusing go to Ireland in the hope of obtaining commands in England: F. and D. If this was their plan, it did not work. Bethell was no longer in the regiment by 10/49. In 12/49 he was issued with a document which stated that he had left the army with the general's consent: TNA, SP 28/63, fo. 14; Worc. College, Clarke Ms 69, unfol. 24/12/49. A Walter Bethell was commissioned as captain in Colonel Hugh Bethell's New Model Army regiment of horse by General Monck in 2/60: F. and D. Nothing further is known about the military career of Samuel Gardiner.

571 CJ vii, p. 38.

572 Burgess was wounded at the storming of Pembroke Castle, which may explain his leaving the regiment: BL. Thomason Tracts, E 451 (21). He was commissioned as a captain of the militia in Berkshire in 1651: CSPD 1651, p. 513.

573 Green was captain whilst Horton was colonel and seemingly whilst Bethell was still major: TNA, E 121/5/7/9, entry 13; ibid, E 121/4/6/91B, entries 30-1. He therefore probably succeeded Captain Mullineaux. For Mullineaux's death, see ibid, SP 28/54, fo. 687; ibid, E 315/5, fo. 35.

574 Ibid, SP 28/74, fo. 656.

575 Ibid, E 121/4/5/64B, entry 4; ibid, E 121/2/3/40, entry 5.

3rd Regiment	Name	Military career
Colonel	Thomas Harrison	
Major	Henry Cromwell?[576]	Succeeded William Rainborough| Col. H. in Ireland in 12/49|
Captains	Stephen Winthrop	
	John Peck	
	John Spencer	Cor. 4/47 and later capt. lt. Took over Capt. Whitehead's troop by 11/48[577]|
	John Barker	In post in early 5/49 at the latest. Lt. to Major Rainborough. He took over his troop[578]|
Capt. Lt.	Joseph Deane[579]	Capt. Henry Cromwell's regt. H. in Ireland[580]|
Possible Captain	XXX Perry[581]	

576 Henry Cromwell was major in the regiment during the course of 1649 as he is addressed as such, but possibly not immediately after Rainborough's expulsion from the regiment: CSPD 1649-50, p. 558.

577 Whitehead does not appear in any document relating to the army later than the second half of 1648. His claims for arrears indicate that he was still alive in 1650: TNA, E 121/3/4/71, entries 1-2. It is possible that he was followed by a Captain George Lee rather than by Spencer. Lee signed a pay warrant for the regiment in 5/48: TNA, SP 28/54, fo. 206. However, Spencer was no longer captain lieutenant in 11/48: ibid, SP 28/57, fos. 507-11.

578 Ibid, SP 28/60, fo. 690; ibid, E 121/3/4/unnumbered, entry 1. See p. 140 below for discussion of Barker as Rainborough's lieutenant.

579 Joseph Strange was Colonel Harrison's cornet: Worc. College, Clarke Ms 67, fo. 25. It would have been logical for him to have succeeded Spencer as captain lieutenant when Spencer became a full captain. However, the Surrey quartering documents for late 1648 give Deane as captain lieutenant. This would be Joseph Deane who had been lieutenant to Major Rainborough before John Barker: TNA SP 28/57, fos. 507-11.

580 F. and D.

581 He and Captain Winthrop, both in Harrison's regiment, were involved in putting down the Leveller mutiny at Burford in 5/49: Perfect Occurences, issue 124, 11-18/5/49. Perry may be a garbled vesrion of Peck.

4th Regiment	Name	Military career
Colonel	Charles Fleetwood	
Major	William Coleman[582]	Succeeded by Capt. Hezekiah Haynes 5th regt. H. c. 10/49|
Captains	Richard Zanchy	
	Gilman Taylor	
	Griffith Lloyd	
	Stephen White	
Capt. Lt.	Joseph Blissett	

582 Coleman was still in command of the troop in 9/49: TNA, SP 28/62, fo. 547.

5th Regiment	Name	Military career
Colonel	Phillip Twistleton	
Major	James Berry	
Captains	John Nelthorpe	
	Original Peart	
	Owen Cambridge[583]	
	Hezekiah Haynes	Moved as major to the 4th regt. H. in c. 10/49|

5th Regiment	Name	Military career
Capt. Lt.	Richard Franklin[584]	Left for a command in Ireland in late 49|

583 In the record of attendances at councils of war in the winter of 1648/9 Cambridge is described as major. This was not because he had succeeded James Berry. Instead it is explained by the fact that he had held that rank in his previous regiment: Clarke Papers ii, p. 272; TNA, E 121/3/3/113B, entry 145. Elsewhere he is described as captain: eg. Worc. College, Clarke Ms 16, fo. 67.

584 Franklin was captain lieutenant of a troop going to Ireland. In 4/56 he was a captain in the army of occupation there in what had been Henry Ireton's regiment of horse and by then was Fleetwood's: CSPD 1649-50, pp. 584-6; Dunlop, *Ireland under the Commonwealth* ii, p. 597.

6th Regiment	Name	Military career
Colonel	John Disbrowe	Succeeded Oliver Cromwell in 4/49|
Major	John Blackmore	Lt. Col. of John Humphrey's regt. F. in Herefordshire. Succeeded John Reynolds as major[585]|
Captains	John Jenkins	
	John Blackwell[586]	
	Edward Scotton	Lt. to Capt. Reynolds of the 6th regt. H. in 3/47[587]|
	George Ensor	Lt. to Capt. Middleton in 5/47. He succeeded him as troop commander in c. 11/47|D at sea 2/50[588]|
Capt. Lt.	Joseph Wallington	

585 See note 14 above for Blackmore's military career during 1645-7. Blackmore succeeded John Reynolds as major in 12/48: BL, Thomason Tracts, E 526 (28); Clarke Papers ii, p. 270.

586 F. and D. claim that Blackwell left the regiment in 6/48, but the entry in the commissions' book can be read as 6/49. The latter date is in fact correct. Blackwell's successor Joseph Wallington was still captain lieutenant in 1/49: BL, Thomason Tracts E 557 (10).

587 F. and D. state that Scotton did not become a troop commander until 7/49 but he was described as captain in a document dated 11/48: TNA, SP 28/57, fo. 369. For his former troop, see ibid, SP 28/33, fo. 619.

588 Ibid, SP 28/44, fo. 408. Ensor and most of his troop drowned in transit to Ireland in 2/50, but the 6th regiment of horse never served in Ireland: Whitelock, *Memoirs*, p. 451; Worc. College, Clarke Ms 67, fo. 16. Ensor was probably conducting a draft of men from the regiment to reinforce the army there. Several cavalry regiments had been required to supply recruits for that purpose in 11/49: CSPD 1649-50, pp. 406-7.

7th Regiment	Name	Military career
Colonel	Nathaniel Rich	
Major	Azariah Husbands	
Captains	Thomas Ireton	
	Francis Hawes[589]	Succeeded by Lt. George Elsmore, prob in 1/49|
	Henry Barton[590]	Succeeded by Capt. Lt. Thomas Babbington in 6/49|
	John Merriman	
Capt. Lt.	Thomas Babbington[591]	Troop commander in provincial regts. Succeeded William Weare as capt. lt.| Succeeded by Thomas French in 6/49|

589 The exact date on which Elsmore, who was Hawes's lieutenant, succeeded him is not known. Hawes commanded the only troop of cavalry on the Isle of Wight in 11/48 as Elsmore did a year later: LJ x, p. 615; TNA, SP 28/58, fo. 44; ibid, SP 28/64, fo. 182. It is possible that Hawes resigned because of the forcible abduction of Charles I from the Isle in 12/48. He disapproved but did nothing to prevent it: Bodleian, Tanner Ms 57, fo. 481. A petition from the Isle of Wight asking for justice on the king dated January 1649 has Elsmore between Major Rolph and Captain Baskett: BL, Thomason Tracts 669 f13 (71).

590 Babbington became Barton's successor on 5/6/49: Worc. College, Clarke Ms 67, fo. 21. Barton was commissioned to raise a troop of horse in Northamptonshire in 7/59, but does not seem to have had any military command in between: CSPD 1659-60, p. 562.

591 Babbington was captain lieutenant of the regiment in 12/48 and possibly a little earlier: Clarke Papers ii, p. 270. For his earlier military service as a captain of horse in Leicestershire under Lord Grey of Groby, as major under Colonel Thomas Waite at Burghley House, and then as a captain in Herefordshire, see TNA, E 121/2/11/19, entry 118; ibid, SP 28/121A, fo. 384. Babbington brought several men from his Herefordshire troop into his New Model Army troop: ibid, E 121/2/3/21, entries 25-8.

8th Regiment	Name	Military career
Colonel	Matthew Tomlinson	
Major	Ralph Knight	
Captains	Ralph Margery	
	Thomas Rawlins	
	Thomas Johnson	
	Robert Glyn	
Capt. Lt.	William Raunce[592]	

592 He had been cornet to Major Tomlinson in the Eastern Association army and also in the New Model Army where Robert Glyn had been Tomlinson's lieutenant. It is highly probable that Raunce became captain lieutenant of the 8th regiment of horse in the summer of 1647 when Glyn received his captaincy, but he certainly held that rank in 12/49. This was when drafts from a number of cavalry regiments were being used to reinforce the army in Ireland, and Raunce was the officer in Tomlinson's regiment who undertook that task: Worc. College, Clarke Ms 17, unfol. 15/12/1649; TNA, E 121/1/1/unnumbered, entry 360.

9th Regiment	Name	Military career
Colonel	Edward Whalley	
Major	Robert Swallow	
Captains	John Grove	
	Henry Cannon[593]	
	William Evanson	
	John Savage	
Capt. Lt.	Daniel Dale	

593 Henry Chillendon, lieutenant of Evanson's troop, is named as captain in 3/49 in Clarke Papers ii, p. 196. However, the declaration of loyalty by Whalley's regiment printed in early 5/49 still gives Cannon as captain and Chillendon as lieutenant: BL, Thomason Tracts E 533 (31). Cannon had given up his troop by 4/5/50 at the latest: Worc. College, Clarke Ms 67, fo. 20.

10th Regiment[594]	Name	Military career
Colonel	Adrian Scroop[595]	Gov. of Bristol 10/49-55. Regicide. Executed 60|
Major	Nathaniel Barton	Disbanded non-mutinous soldiers 6/49 as acting col.[596]|
Captains	Richard Watson[597]	Gov. of Bristol Castle 54. Garr. disbanded 55|
	Thomas Goddard[598]	Capt. 1st regt. H. 1/60|
	Edward Wolfe[599]	
	William Peverell[600]	Succeeded Major General Skippon|
Capt. Lt.	Thomas Bayly??[601]	

594 The regiment was chosen for service in Cromwell's expedition to Ireland in 4/49 whereupon it mutinied. Surrounded and forced to surrender at Stow-on-the-Wold on 14/5/49, it was disbanded c. 7/49: F. and D.

595 Scroop was discharged as a cavalry officer on 21/12/49: Worc. College, Clarke Ms 69, unfol.

596 A London journal describes this officer as Colonel Barton in 6/49. He was to take the regiment to Ireland. Presumably the decision to disband the whole regiment had not yet been taken. Fairfax, however, continued to describe Barton as major: Perfect Occurences, issue 127 1/8/6/49; TNA, SP 28/60, fo. 244; ibid, SP28/61, fo. 321; ibid, SP 28/60, fos. 688-9.

597 For Quaker activity at Bristol which Watson supported, see Gentles, New Model Army, p. 113.

598 Goddard was listed for Ireland, but I have no record of his serving there: BL, Thomason Tracts E 563 (13).

599 This man was probably the Lieutenant Colonel Edward Wolfe who died in Ireland in 12/49: Abbott, Writings and Speeches ii, p.177.

600 Skippon relinquished command of both his regiment of foot and his troop of horse early in 1649. By 1/3/49 William Peverell had been commissioned as captain of the troop: BL, Thomason Tracts, E 545 (30). This officer had served as cornet and lieutenant in Captain Scroop's troop in the earl of Essex's army and in Colonel Scroop's regiment in the New Model Army: TNA, E 121/1/7/46B, entry 1; ibid, E 121/3/3/81, unnumbered. The disbandment did not end his military career. He was back in service in 1650 but his regiment is not yet known. In the following decade he was captain of a troop in Robert Lilburne's regiment: Worc. College, Clarke Ms 17 unfol. (17/06/1650); F. and D; TNA, SP 28/111, pt. iv, 12/56.

601 Thomas Bayly, who had been quartermaster in Scroop's troop in 1645, claimed to have been captain in the 11th regiment of horse in 1649. He can only have been the captain lieutenant. There were no other gaps amongst the troop commanders: ibid, E 121/3/4/9B, entry 41; BL, Thomason Tracts, E 574 (26).

11th Regiment[602]	Name	Military career
Colonel	Henry Ireton	Deputy to Oliver Cromwell in Ireland. D there 11/51|
Major	Robert Gibbon[603]	Left regt. c. 6/49. Succeeded as major by Capt. Morgan|
Captains	Henry Pretty	Major Oliver Cromwell's regt. H. in Ireland in 6/49[604]|
	Anthony Morgan	Served in Ireland as major of Ireton's regt.|
	Robert Kirkby[605]	Left regt. 6/49. Capt. in Edward Grosvenor's regt. H. in Scotland 51. Regt. disbanded 52|
	George Hutchinson[606]	Lt. Col. F. and Capt. H. in Nottinghamshire. Succeeded Capt. Cecil c. 12/48|Gone c. 12/49|
Capt. Lt.	Robert Browne[607]	Cor. in the col's troop. Succeeded James Wilson|

602 The regiment was chosen for service in Ireland in 4/49.

603 In 6/49 Gibbon's troop was reduced into Henry Pretty's following its involvement in the Leveller mutiny of late May: Worc. College, Clarke Ms 67, fo. 18; ibid, Clarke Ms 69, unfol. After that Gibbon was governor of Rye and then colonel of a new regiment raised to protect the south-east of England when the 2nd regiment of foot was withdrawn to take part in the invasion of Scotland: CSPD 1650, p. 165.

604 Worc. College, Clarke Ms 69, unfol. ; F. and D.

605 Kirkby does not seem to have gone to Ireland before joining Grosvenor's regiment. He was commissioned as an officer in the Nottinghamshire militia in 5/50: CSPD 1650, p. 506.

606 W. Salt Library, SMS 463, unfol. 3/7/49. It was intended that Hutchinson should serve in Ireland but he seems not to have done so: TNA, SP 28/61, fo. 366.

607 Browne was captain lieutenant at the time of the regiment's mutiny in 5/49: ibid, Clarke Ms 16, fo. 107.

Part IV

The Regimental Listings: Junior Commissioned Officers

Junior Commissioned Officers: March to May 1647

Infantry

1st Regiment Company Commanders	Lieutenants	Ensigns
Thomas Fairfax	Lewis Audley *	Charles Bolton *[1]
Thomas Jackson		
William Leigh	**David Dowley**[2]	**Stephen Baldwin**[3]
Samuel Gooday	George Watson *	Robert Wild *[4]
Fulk Muskett *	William Heydon *[5]	**William Gardner**[6]
Vincent Boyce	James Priest[7]	Matthew Garrett[8]
Thomas Woolf	Thomas Phillips *	Caleb Burgess *
Francis White		XXX Gore *
Thomas Highfield *	John Stokeham *	John Miller *[9]
William Wayne	XXX Cope *[10]	
Unplaced	Clement Keane[11] William Farley[12]	**George Hadfield**[13]

1 F. and D.

2 Dowley was lieutenant in 7/45 and 8/45: TNA, SP 28/53, fo. 95.

3 Ibid, E 121/3/4/unnumbered, entry 3. Although Baldwin's name does not appear on any of the petitions, the entry in the commissions' book giving his promotion to lieutenant appears to date from 6/47 or very soon afterwards. It is therefore very likely that he was ensign immediately before that.

4 Wild claimed pay arrears as ensign and lieutenant to Captain Bolton who succeeded Major Gooday as company commander but he had clearly served under Gooday: Ibid, E 121/3/1/unnumbered, entries 3-4.

5 Ibid, E 121/4/1/24, entry 7. He had previously served as lieutenant under Captain Warwick Bamfield: ibid, SP 28/253/B/1, fo. 39.

6 Ibid, E 121/1/1/37, entries 17-18.

7 Ibid, E 121/2/9/unnumbered, entry 318.

8 Garrett was ensign to Captain Vincent Boyce in Manchester's army and lieutenant to Captain James Priest in the 1st regiment of foot post 1647: ibid, E 121/2/9/46, entry 317. There is no evidence that Priest and Garrett were serving in different companies prior to 6/47.

9 Worc. College, Clarke Ms 41, fo. 136.

10 The list of those ready to volunteer to fight in Ireland includes a lieutenant Cope in Captain Heydon's company. There is no doubt that Heydon should be Wayne as all the other company commanders are accounted for. Cope's surname was almost certainly Cox. It was not unusual to confuse the tailed secretary's hand letter x with the letter p once that form of writing had gone out of use. The editor of Rushworth made exactly the same mistake sixty years or so later when he wrote Captain John Cox of the 5th regiment of foot as Cope: *Historical Collections* vi, pp. 465-6.

11 For Keane and Farley as lieutenants, see TNA, E 121/2/9/46, entries 232-3, 271-2.

12 F. and D., p. 321.

13 Ibid, E 121/2/9/46, entry 126. He was ensign, lieutenant and captain in the regiment.

2nd Regiment		
Phillip Skippon	William Symonds	**James Symcock**[14]
Richard Ashfield		**William Sitchell**[15]
Samuel Clarke	**John Rogers**	**Nicholas Copeland**[16]
Edward Streater	Arthur Helsham[17]	**John Streater**[18]
James Harrison	Arthur Helsham[19] Thomas Jubbs[20]	
John Clarke		**John Rogers**[21]
Maurice Bowen		
Devereux Gibbon		
John Cobbett		
William Symonds		
Possible XXX Wingfield		**Francis Farmer**[22]

14 Symcock was ensign to General Skippon and then lieutenant in another company in the regiment, possibly Captain Gibbon's, of which Thomas Butler was captain after 1647: TNA, E 121/2/49, entry 1.
15 Sitchell was wounded at Naseby: ibid, SP 28/173/1, fo. 3.
16 TNA, E 121/4/7/48B, entry 9 for Rogers also.
17 Ibid, E 121/1/2/49, entries 4-6; ibid, SP 28/29, fo. 237.
18 Ibid, E 121/1/5/59A, unnumbered.
19 Ibid, E 121/1/7/49, entries 4-6.
20 Ibid, SP 28/46, fo. 79.
21 Ibid, E 121/2/3/unnumbered, entry 50.
22 Ibid, E 121/1/7/57, entry 103. He was dead by c. 1650.

3rd Regiment		
Sir Hardress Waller	James Knight *	William Pope *
Edward Salmon	Lewis Northcott *[23]	
Thomas Smith	John Watson[24]	Samuel Chase/Case *
Phillip Ebzery	John Filkins *	William Bird[25]
Richard Hodden	Humphrey Hartwell *[26]	Edward Slow *
Amor Stoddard	William Wade/Ward[27]	Thomas Deakin*[28]
Richard Aske	William Laudgridge *	
William Howard		William Hopkins *
John Clarke	Ralph Wilson *	Robert Smith *[29]
Daniel Thomas	Nathaniel Chase *	Edward Allen *
Unplaced	Brian Smith[30]	

23 Ibid, E 121/1/6/unnumbered, entry 5.
24 Ibid, SP 28/63, fo. 532; BL, Thomason Tracts, E 390 (3).
25 TNA, E 121/2/9/46, entry 222. The clerk wrongly placed Bird and his captain in the 7th regiment of foot.
26 Ibid, E 121/1/6/63, entry 300.
27 Ibid, E 121/1/6/66, entries 186-7 for both Wade and Deakin. Northcott, Filkins, Chase, Smith and Ward are successive signatures in BL, Thomason Tracts E 390 (26).
28 TNA, E 121/4/8/14B, entry 9.
29 Ibid, E 121/1/6/30, entry 308; BL, Thomason Tracts, E 390 (3).
30 Ibid, E 121/1/6/unnumbered, entry 17. For his later career in the regiment, see p.99 above.

4th Regiment		
Robert Hammond	Edward Humphreys	
Isaac Ewer		William Ewer[31]
Robert Saunders	John Thompson *	Thomas Wood *[32]
Edmund Rolfe	Josiah Slater *	Richard Taylor *[33]
Israel Smith	John Matthews *	**Roland Harridge**[34]
Charles O'Hara	Bedingfield Creamer *	
William Disney		
John Boyce	John Toggell *[35]	Geoffrey Pert *
John Puckle	John Friend[36]	John Bishop *
William Stratton	Richard Bernard *	
Unplaced	Francis Wheeler[37] Richard Tonson?[38]	

31   LJ ix, pp. 153-6.
32   Ibid.
33   Taylor is also described as quartermaster to the company: Rushworth, *Historical Collections* vi, p. 466.
34   TNA, E 121/5/1/18, entry 404.
35   LJ ix, pp. 153-6.
36   TNA, E 121//1/1/26B, entry 3; BL, Thomson Tracts E 390 (3).
37   Clarke Papers i, p. 28.
38   See above p. 99.

5th Regiment		
Richard Fortescue		
Ralph Cobbett	**Roger Jones**[39]	
Thomas Jennins (Gimmins)		
Arthur Young	Thomas/Edward Jones *[40]	Richard Owen *[41]
XXX Farley		
John Bushell	John Ferrers/Ferrell *	Nicholas/Richard Cordes *
John Cox	Nicholas Luke *	Matthew Marwood/Martell *
Richard Pooley	William Read *	Richard Hart/Hatt *[42]
XXX Whitton	Roger Jones *	**Thomas Parry**[43]
John Denison	William Bayly *	George Forker *
Unplaced	John Miller[44]	Samuel Wise[45] William Jones[46]

39   TNA, E 121/2/11/17B, entry 8.
40   For Edward, see ibid, E 121/2/11/17A, entry 76; for Thomas, ibid, SP 28/32, fo.414; ibid, SP28/61, fo. 253.
41   Ibid, E 121/2/11/17A, entry 234.
42   Ibid, SP 28/61, fo. 70; ibid, E 121/2/11/17A, entries 83-4.
43   Ibid E 121/4/1/59, entry 82.
44   Miller was captain in the regiment after 6/47. He was a lieutenant in 3/47: BL, Thomason Tracts, E 390 (3).
45   Wise and Jones, both ensigns in 3/47, were promoted to lieutenant in 6/47: ibid, E 390 (26); Worc. College, Clarke Ms 67, fo. 8.
46   TNA, E 121/2/11/17A, entry 137: BL, Thomason Tracts E 390 (26).

6th Regiment		
Richard Ingoldsby	John Shrimpton	
Thomas Kelsey	Thomas Jones *	**Thomas Johns**[47]
Charles Duckett		**Samuel Fisher**[48]
Henry Ingoldsby		
Edward? Stevens		
Francis Allen	Thomas Day[49]	
Thomas Ingoldsby		
John Mill		
Richard Wagstaffe	Christopher Matthews *	
John Grime	Consolation Fox[50]	
Unplaced	Abraham Davies[51]	

47 Ibid, E 121/2/11/17B, entry 150.
48 Ibid, E 121/2/10/49, entry 621.
49 Ibid, SP 28/3/3/31, entry 9: BL, Thomason Tracts E 390 (26).
50 TNA, E 121/3/1/31, entry 20; Clarke Papers i, p. 437.
51 TNA, E 121/3/3/31, entry 2; BL, Thomason Tracts E 390 (26).

7th Regiment		
Thomas Rainborough		
Henry Bowen	**John Morgan**[52]	**Augustine Morris**[53]
John Edwards		
George Drury	Thomas Walker[54]	
Thomas Dancer	XXX **Walter Lorringe**[55]	**Walter Lorringe** XXX
Thomas Creamer		**John Townshend**[56]
Henry Whittle		**Stephen Shipden**[57]
John Browne	**William Barber**[58]	**John Cobbe**[59] **John Herwick** *[60]
Henry Flower		
Thomas Walker		

52 TNA, E 121/1/6/117, entry 185.
53 Ibid, E 121/4/8/58B, entry 1.
54 Spring i, p. 17.
55 TNA, E 121/4/7/36, entries 18-19.
56 Ibid, E 121/1/6/27B, entry 23.
57 Ibid, E 121/5/7/109, entry 41.
58 Ibid, E 121/4/1/50, entry 7.
59 Ibid, E 121/2/11/47, entry 7.
60 Ibid, E 121/2/11/11B, entry 6.

8th Regiment		
Robert Lilburne	Robert Fish *	Thomas Noone *
Nicholas Kempson	Alexander Fry *	Levesley Sharples *
William Masters	Abraham Clarke *	George Hope *
Christopher Peckham	Francis Wells *	
Nicholas Fenton		
Abraham Holmes		

8th Regiment		
Francis Dormer		Benjamin/ Brian Elton[61] Francis Nicholls[62]
Jeremiah Tolhurst		James Murray *
George Weldon	Shreve Parker *	James Rose *[63]
Henry Lilburne		Evan Morris *[64]
Unplaced	Richard Deedes[65] John Topping[66] Gabriel Earwood[67] Ethelbert Morgan[68]	John Mason[69]

61   Ibid, SP 28/37, fos. 568-70.

62   LJ, ix, pp. 153-6; Gentles, *New Model Army*, p. 156.

63   See LJ ix, p. 154.

64   Ibid ix, p. 156.

65   Deedes is the only signatory to a petition of early 1647 who cannot be placed amongst the commissioned officers in the regiment: TNA, SP 16/539, fo. 439.

66   LJ, ix, pp. 153-6. Topping, Earwood and Morgan signed several petitions in the spring of 1647 as lieutenants. See, for example, BL, Thomason Tracts E390 (3, 26).

67   For Earwood and Mason see also Worc. College, Clarke Ms 41, fo. 118.

68   See note p. 101 above.

69   BL, Thomason Tracts E 390 (26). See below for his later career in the regiment.

9th Regiment[70]		
Edward Harley	Joseph Salkeld	Nicholas Mitchell[71]
Thomas Pride	William Galhampton[72]	
William Cowell	John Hawes	John Ward[73]
William Goffe		
George Gregson	Thomas Parsons[74]	Ferdinando Green[75]
Roger Alsop	John/George Dirdo[76]	John Dixon
Thomas Parsons	Walter Crocker *	Moses Reynolds
John Ferguson		Henry Beale[77]
John Mason		
Waldine Lagoe		Nathaniel Portman[78]
Unplaced	Richard Mosse[79] Richard Kemp Robert Taylor Ralph Parker	William Hoorne John Gates John Pynnar[80] Nicholas Ryland[81]

70   All the officers who do not have references attached to their names signed a petition in 5/47. For this see Worc. College, Clarke Ms 41, fo. 120.

71   TNA, E 121/4/7/80A, entry 5. He was lieutenant in Salkeld's company after 16/6/47: Worc. College, Clarke Ms 67, fo. 12.

72   TNA, E 121/4/8/40,entry 591; BL, Thomason Tracts E 390 (3).

73   Ward was ensign in 3/47 and lieutenant in Hawes's company after 16/6/47: Worc. College, Clarke Ms 67, fo. 12; BL, Thomason Tracts E 390 (3).

74   He was still a lieutenant in on 25/7/45: TNA, SP 28/145 unfol..

75   BL, Thomason Tracts E 390 (26).

76   Also known as Dardoe or Dardre, he was ensign and lieutenant in Alsop's company: TNA, E 121/3/1/unnumbered, entries 1-2. His promotion to lieutenant occurred in 5/47: Worc. College, Clarke Ms 67, fo. 12.

77   TNA, E 121/4/7/105, entries 6-7.

78   If Bateman as seems most likely, he was in Lagoe's company. See note 474 below.

79   Mosse was probably in Goffe's company as he had been his ensign in the army of the Eastern Association: ibid, E 121/4/8/40B, entries 556, 580-1.

80 Pynnar's commission was dated 9/46: Worc. College, Clarke Ms 67, fo. 12.
81 TNA, SP/28/145 unfol. 7/6/45.

10th Regiment		
John Lambert	Samuel Ross	William Joyce[82]
Mark Grime	Edward Turner	Robert Baldwin[83]
Wroth Rogers	Henry Dorney[84]	**George Hopkins**[85]
John Biscoe	John Nicholas[86]	**John Madder**[87]
Francis Blethin	**Roger Lewis**[88]	**William James**[89]
Lawrence Nunney		**John Clarke**[90]
Matthew Cadwell		William Shelley[91]
Giles Saunders	Hugh Jenkins[92]	Evan Jones[93]
Thomas Disney	William Meredith[94]	Jeremiah Hand[95]
William Style		
Unplaced		Henry Hedworth[96] Thomas Lewis[97]

82 TNA, E 121/5/7/21, entry 233; BL, Thomason Tracts E 390 (26).
83 For Baldwin and Turner in Grime's company in Lambert's regiment, see ibid, E 121/3/5/25, fos. 61, 63. Turner signed the 3/47 petition, and also Baldwin but his name was transcribed as Robert Belded and Besdin: BL, Thomason Tracts E 390 (3), (26).
84 Dorney appears to have transferred to the 5th regiment of foot in c. 6/47: TNA, E 121/2/11/17A, entry 138.
85 Hopkins may appear as Lieutenant George Hegeson in a petition dated 10/48: Worc. College, Clarke Ms 17, fo. 83.
86 TNA, E 121/5/7/52, entry 79.
87 See p. 135 below. Madder was initially sergeant in the company.
88 TNA, E 121/5/7/23, entry 260.
89 Ibid, E 121/5/7/21, entry 264.
90 Ibid, E 121/5/7/21, entry 100. This man had previously been a sergeant in the 12th regiment of foot.
91 For Thomas and Shelley, see ibid, E 121/5/7/21, entry 46. Shelley was apparently ensign in the company when William Wilkes was captain: Spring i. He was the William Skelley who signed a petition in 3/47 as lieutenant: BL, Thomason Tracts E 390 (26).
92 Ibid, E 390 (26); TNA, E 121/5/7/52, entry 1.
93 For Jenkins and Evans, see ibid, E 121/5/7/52, entry 2.
94 Ibid, E 121/2/3/32, entry 4.
95 BL, Thomason Tracts E 390 (3); TNA, E 121/3/5/25, entries 79-80.
96 BL, Thomason Tracts E 390 (3); Worc. College, Clarke Ms 67, fo. 11.
97 Lewis was clearly an ensign in 3/47: ibid, Clarke Ms 41, fo. 103; BL, Thomason Tracts, E 390 (3), (26).

11th Regiment[98]		
William Herbert	Thomas Hughes	**David Tirrell**[99] Charles Awbry *
Thomas Read	Bartholomew Helby *	
John Wade	Randle Warner[100]	Richard Bourne
Nathaniel Short	William Hodgkins *	
John Melvin	William Gough	
John Spooner	William Jones[101]	John Dunckley *[102] Abraham Spooner[103]
Edward Orpin		Francis Farmer[104]
Robert Read		Edward Evans[105]
Richard Lundy		Walter Brough[106]
Robert Anderson	John Potter[107]	
Unplaced	George Clarke?[108] Thomas Cassinghurst[109] Andrew Edwards[110]	

98 The missing officers are likely to be found amongst those who opted to serve in Colonel Herbert's regiment intended for service in Ireland. For their names, see Appendix II.

99 TNA, E 121/3/3/76, unnumbered.

100 See ibid, E 121/5/7/unnumbered, entry 84 for Warner and Bourne. For both see BL, Thomason Tracts, E 390 (3).

101 Jones was lieutenant from 7/45 to 9/47: TNA. SP 28/54, fo. 109.

102 Dunckley was lieutenant in 12/45: ibid, SP 28/33, fo.574.

103 Ibid, E 121/5/7/18, entry 189; BL, Thomason Tracts E 390 (3).

104 TNA, E 121/5/7/18, entry 1; BL, Thomason Tracts E 390 (26).

105 Ibid.

106 Brough served as ensign and lieutenant to Captain Lundy: TNA, SP28/51, fo. 38.

107 Ibid, E 121/5/7/unnumbered, entry 33.

108 Hughes, Gough, Warner and Clarke signed a petition in 5/47. Only in Clarke's case is the rank not given: Worc. College, Clarke Ms 41, fo. 102.

109 Cassinghurst had been ensign to Captain Phillip Gittins in Essex's army. He was a lieutenant in 3/47: TNA, E 121/2/7/113B, entry 12; BL, Thomason Tracts, 390 (3), (26). Subsequently he was demoted to ensign under Captain Andrews. For this see note 504 below.

110 TNA, E 121/5/7/unnumbered, entry 3; BL, Thomason Tracts E 390 (26).

12th Regiment[111]		
John Hewson	William Arnop	Henry Williams
John Jubbs	Martin Jubbs[112]	Joseph Growna[113]
Daniel Axtell	John Webb[114]	Edward Hoare[115]
Samuel Grime/Graeme	Thomas Baker[116]	John Davies
Alexander Brayfield	George Smith[117]	
John Carter	Jenkin Bevan[118]	Thomas Newnham[119]
Henry Davies	Ralph Gayle[120]	
Thomas Atkinson	Samuel Axtell[121]	
Thomas Price	George Jenkins	William Powell[122]
John Toppendene	William Hill[123]	Jeremiah Campfield[124]
Unplaced		Thomas Rawlins Robert Mullins Morgan Porter[125]

111 The signatures of the commissioned officers in Hewson's regiment appear on a petition from the regiment dated 11/47. These have been compared with the names on the army petitions and the Vindication of 3/ and 4/47 to ascertain who was in post before the first Army coup: BL, Thomason Tracts E 413 (6); ibid, E 385 (19); ibid, E 390 (3); ibid, E 390 (26); Worc. College, Clarke Ms 41, fos. 102-3. The only changes that occurred between March and November were that Captain Toppendene died and was replaced by Lieutenant Gayle, and that Robert Mullins succeeded Gayle as lieutenant. Seven of the ensigns were exactly the same as in the spring of 1647 – Growna, Hoare, Newnham, Porter, Rawlins, Williams and Davies.

112 By a process of elimination Martin Jubbs must have been lieutenant to Lieutenant Colonel John Jubbs.

113 TNA, E 121/4/7/50, entries 14-17; BL, Thomason Tracts E 390 (3).

114 He was described as a sectary along with Major Axtell and Colonel Hewson: Edwards, *Gangreana,* pt. 3, p. 252-4. Webb signed the Vindication in 4/47: BL, Thomason Tracts E 385 (19).

115 TNA, E121/4/7/50, entry 45.

116 Ibid, E 121/4/7/50, entry 56.

117 Ibid, E 121/2/1/18, entry 10; ibid, E 121/4/7/50, entry 24; BL, Thomason Tracts E 390 (26). Smith was later lieutenant to Captain Atkinson and then full captain in the regiment by the spring of 1649: Worc. College, Clarke Ms 67, fo. 44.

118 TNA, E 121/4/7/50, entry 20.

119 BL, Thomason Tracts E 390 (26).

120 Possibly the Ralph Gill who as a lieutenant had signed the Vindication in 5/47: ibid, Thomason Tracts E 385 (19). He had been Hewson's ensign in the Eastern Association Army: Spring i. However, he had probably transferred to another company in 1645 as he did not become captain lieutenant when Hewson succeeded Pickering as colonel.

121 TNA, E 121/2/1/18, unnumbered.

122 Ibid, E 121/4/7/48B, entry 90. He was probably the William Powell who signed the Vindication but did not give his rank: BL, Thomason Tracts E 385 (19).

123 TNA, E 121/4/7/48B, entry 85.

124 Campfield was an ensign in April 1647. He served under Captain Toppendene and then transferred to the 5th regiment as a lieutenant on 15/7/47: ibid, E 121/2/11/17B, entry 83; Bl, Thomason Tracts E 385 (19); Worc. College, Clarke Ms 67, fo. 8. However, it is possible

that he had transferred as an ensign earlier in the year if Porter was ensign of Toppendene's company by 3/47. Nevertheless Campfield's name, like Porter's, appears amongst those of other ensigns in the regiment in an army petition of 3/47: BL, Thomason Tracts E 390 (3).
125 Porter signed the Vindication of 5/47 as ensign: BL, Thomason Tracts E 385 (19). He had a link with Toppendene's company as he had served under Captain Jenkins, Toppendene's predecessor, in the Eastern Association army: Spring i, p. 86. The position of his signature in one of the army petitions shows clearly that he was still in the 12th regiment of foot: BL, Thomason Tracts E 390 (26). However, the likelihood is that he was serving in a different company by 1647.

Quartermasters of Foot

Unlike in the cavalry where there was one quartermaster per troop, the number of quartermasters in the infantry was one per regiment. As a result they rarely appear in the documentary record. This is a list of those I have discovered in the limited number of sources in which their names appear. Dates are given where possible, but with the officers whose names derive from the E 121 series the data is not sufficiently precise. The two whose names I have obtained from Spring may not have served in the New Model Army.

Regiment	Name	Date and Source
1st	Andrew Rathwood	E 121/2/9/65.
	John Daniel	E 121/4/1/68, entry 16.
2nd	XXX Rawlins	Cashiered 7/47: Perfect Occurences, issue 31
	Benjamin Hammond	1650: Clarke Ms 67.
3rd	Jeremy Ives	After 1647: Clarke Ms 67.
	John Lane	2/5/1650: Clarke Ms 69 unfol.
4th	Thomas Tuthill??	4/1645: Spring i.
	Barnabas Bright	After 6/47: Clarke Ms 67.
5th	John Warner	6/47: Clarke Ms 67.
6th	William Illinge	E 121/3/3/31.
7th		
8th		
9th	Joseph Archer	1646 SP 28/38, fo. 280.
10th	William Style?	Spring i.
	John Thornes	c. 1648: Clarke Ms 67.
11th		
12th	John Webbe	E 121/4/7/50, entry 19.

Dragoons

Regiment	Lieutenant	Cornet	Quartermaster
1. John Okey		Thomas Okey[126]	
2. Nicholas Moore	Peter Evans[127]	William Phillips *[128]	Richard Norris[129]
3. John Farmer	John Toplady[130]	William Tinge[131]	Christopher Dobbs[132]
4. Christopher Mercer	John Ross[133]	Adam Casse/Cosse[134]	
5. Daniel Abbott	Francis Bolton[135]		
6. Ralph Farr	William Bowler[136]	Christopher Purslow[137]	
7. Tobias Bridge	John Barrow[138]		
8. Harold Scrimgeour	Henry Fulcher *	John Scrooby[139]	Henry Baker[140]
9 William Neale	John Copless[141]	Roger Carr[142]	
10. Edward Wogan	Edward Herbert[143]	Stephen Page[144]	

126 TNA, E 121/1/1/26B, entry 188. He was still a cornet at the battle of St. Fagans, see note 503 below.
127 Ibid, SP 28/45, fo. 428.
128 Ibid, SP 28/33, fo. 98. He had fled to London by 6/47: ibid, SP 28/124, fo. 335.

129 Ibid, SP 28/44, fo. 412.

130 Ibid, SP 28/30, fo. 179.

131 Ibid, SP 28/140/7 fos. 288-9. He continued as cornet under Captain Garland: see below.

132 Ibid, SP 28/41, fo. 291.

133 Ibid, SP 28/36, fo. 616; Rushworth, *Historical Collections* vii, p. 7. Barrow was the only officer in the regiment other than Colonel Okey to sign the army petitions in the spring of 1647: BL, Thomason Tracts E 390 (3).

134 TNA, SP 28/45, fo. 374.

135 Ibid, SP 28/45, fo. 422.

136 Ibid, E 121/2/3/43B, entry 2; ibid, SP 28/45, fo. 420.

137 Ibid, SP 28/41, fo. 324. He deserted the army in 6/47: CSPD 1625-49, p. 710.

138 ibid, SP 28/44, fo. 134.

139 Ibid, E 121/3/3/62, entry 1.

140 Ibid, SP 28/39, fo. 47. 7/46.

141 Copless was lieutenant to Captain Turpin in 7/45 and to his successor Neale in 7/46: ibid, SP 28/31, fo. 26; ibid, SP 28/39, fo. 78. He was probably the Lieutenant John Coplyn who deserted the army in 6/47: CSPD 1625-49, p. 710. Charles Thompson was lieutenant to the troop in 7/47: TNA, SP 28/47, fo. 340.

142 Ibid, E 121/1/1/26B, entry 96.; ibid, SP 28/140/7, fos. 288-9.

143 Stephen and Page were with Captain Wogan in London in 6/47: ibid, SP 28/124, fo. 335. For Herbert, Ross and Barrow, see ibid, SP 28/33, fos. 89, 93, 94.

144 Ibid, SP28/39, fo. 32; ibid, SP 28/44, fo. 429.

Cavalry

1st Regiment	Lieutenant	Cornet	Quartermaster
Thomas Fairfax	John Gladman	Peter Wallis[145]	George Hayes[146]
John Disbrowe	William Covell[147]	Cox Tooke[148]	
John Browne	Thomas Emerson[149]	William Barrington[150]	**Edward Rivers**[151]
Adam Lawrence	Richard Merest[152]	James Thompson[153]	**Bartholomew Chalice**[154]
James Berry	William Disher[155]	George Joyce[156]	William Newman[157]
William Packer	Robert Southwell[158]	Samuel Packer[159]	

145 Wallis was quartermaster and then cornet to Captain Packer: ibid, SP 28/33, fo. 33; ibid, E 121/5/7/unnumbered, entry 560; BL, Thomason Tracts E 390 (3).

146 Ibid, SP 28/39, fo. 229. April 1647; BL, Thomason Tracts E 385 (19).

147 TNA, E 121/5/7/14, entry 192; BL, Thomason Tracts E 385 (19).

148 TNA, E 121/5/7/14, entries 212, 313; ibid, SP 28/32, fo. 182.

149 ibid, SP 28/33, fo. 36; ibid, E 121/5/7/14, entry 559. Emerson served as an officer agitator in the autumn of 1647: Clarke Papers i, p. 438.

150 TNA, SP 28/31, fo. 281; ibid, E 121/5/7/unnumbered, entry 599.

151 Ibid, E 121/5/7/unnumbered, entry 597. He was quartermaster in 8/45: ibid, WO55/1647, unfol.

152 Ibid, E 121/5/7/14, entry 642.

153 Ibid, SP 28/44, fo. 349. Thompson had transferred to the 10th regiment of horse by 8/47: ibid, SP 28/47, fo. 113.

154 Ibid, SP 28/39, fo. 229.

155 Disher was lieutenant to Berry's troop in Manchester's army and in the New Model: ibid, SP 28/33, fo. 35; ibid, E 315/5, fo. 61.

156 Ibid, SP 28/41, fo. 555 and ibid, SP 28/45, fo. 330 place Joyce in the 1st regiment of horse. He claimed to be cornet of Fairfax's lifeguard. If so his appointment was later than 4/47: LJ ix, p. 238.

157 TNA, SP 28/39, fo. 5.

158 Ibid, E 121/5/7/unnumbered, entry 186.

159 Ibid, SP 28/140/7, fos. 288-9.

2nd Regiment	Lieutenant	Cornet	Quartermaster
John Butler	Joseph Mullineaux	**Thomas Aske**[160] Clement Arnold[161]	
Thomas Horton	William Forster[162]		**Robert Collingwood**[163]
Benjamin Burgess	Thomas Ellis[164]	Richard Essex[165]	
Samuel Gardiner	William Jayce[166]	John Phelps[167]	**Anthony Palmer**[168]
Walter Bethell	John Godfrey[169]	William Parry[170]	
Thomas Pennyfather	Arthur Manwood[171]	**William Millward**[172]	
Unplaced			Elias Green[173]

160 Ibid, E 121/1/6/66, entry 67.
161 Ibid, SP 28/38, fo. 19. Arnold's name also appears amongst the signatures to the Vindication but without a rank: BL, Thomason Tracts E 385 (19).
162 TNA, SP 28/31, fo. 259. Previously he was cornet to Sir Arthur Haselrig's troop in Waller's army: ibid: 121/4/1/53, entry 4.
163 Ibid, E 121/1/7/25, entry 23.
164 BL, Thomason Tracts E 390 (3).
165 Ibid, Thomason Tracts E 390 (26). Essex had previously been quartermaster: TNA, E 121/4/5/99A, entry 6.
166 Ibid, SP 28/33, fo. 622.
167 Ibid, E 121/3/4/77, entry 3. In May 1647 his regiment chose Cornet Phelps as an agitator: F. and D., p. 83.
168 TNA, E 121/4/1/75, entry 8.
169 Godfrey was lieutenant to Captain Bethell in 6/46 and fought at St. Fagans in 1648: ibid, SP 28/140/7, fo. 287.
170 Ibid, SP28/37, fo. 561. Parry was quartermaster to the troop in Waller's army: ibid, E121/5/5/15, entry 1.
171 Ibid, SP 28/36 fo. 604.
172 For both positions, see ibid, E 121/5/5/15, entry 1. Millward had been quartermaster of the troop Pennyfather commanded in Waller's army: ibid, E 121/4/7/48B, entry 21. He was probably wrongly entered as captain in the list of signatures to the Vindication: BL, Thomason Tracts E 385 (19).
173 Green was quartermaster in 10/46: TNA, SP 28/40, fo. 261.

3rd Regiment	Lieutenant	Cornet	Quartermaster
Thomas Sheffield	Richard Young *	Richard Comber *[174]	Robert Arthur *[175]
Richard Fincher	Henry Bartlett[176]	John Norcott[177]	John Tyley[178]
Arthur Evelyn	John Peck[179] Charles Whitehead	Charles Whitehead[180] John Kellett[181]	John Kennett[182] XXX Savage
Robert Robotham	Michael Hale *[183]	Thomas Partridge[184]	Henry Dethick *[185]
William Rainborough	Thomas Fitch/Fish [186]	Joseph Deane[187]	Thomas Savage[188]
Gabriel Martin	Robert Dawes *[189]	Charles Martin *[190]	Thomas Hey *

174 Ibid, SP 28/38, fo. 134.
175 He was quartermaster of the troop in 12/4/45: W.S. Library, SMS 463, unfol.
176 Ibid, SP 28/41, fo. 298; ibid, E 121/2/3/44, entry 94; ibid, SP 28/32, fo. 234.
177 Norcott was cornet of the troop in 1/47: ibid, SP 28/44, fo. 162; ibid, SP 28/56, fo. 594.
178 Ibid, SP 28/45, fo. 464. Both Bartley and Tyley were in Fincher's troop in Waller's army: Spring ii.
179 TNA, SP 28/39, fo. 356. The three junior officers had served as cornet, quartermaster and corporal in General Thomas Hammond's troop in Manchester's regiment of horse in the Eastern Association army: Spring i.
180 TNA, E 121/3/4/71, entries 1-2; BL, Thomason Tracts E 390 (3).
181 Kellett and Savage appear in the commissions' book as junior officers to Captain Evelyn, but he left the regiment in 6/47. They must therefore be amongst the few entries recording a commission issued earlier than the first Army coup: Worc. College, Clarke Ms 67, fo. 25. For Whitehead and Peck as junior officers see p. 93 above.
182 Ibid, Thomason Tracts E 390 (3), (26); TNA, E 121/5/7/16, entry 37.
183 This man had been lieutenant to Major John Hale's troop in James Sheffield's regiment in 4/49: ibid, SP 28/29, fo. 422. He may also have served in Oliver Cromwell's troop post 12/45: ibid, SP 28/41, fo. 42.
184 Ibid, E 121/2/11/unnumbered, entry 371. Partridge had been quartermaster of the troop in Essex's army: ibid, E 121/3/2/5B, entry 4. In 6/47 or very soon afterwards he was promoted to lieutenant and Quartermaster Dethick to cornet: Worc. College, Clarke Ms 67, fo. 25.
185 TNA, E 121/4/1/34, entry 31.
186 Ibid, SP 28/31, fo. 42; ibid, SP 28/45, fo. 462. Fish signed the attestation of loyalty to Parliament in late 5/47.

187 Deane was cornet in 12/46: ibid, SP 28/41, fo. 332.

188 Savage served between 6/45 and 5/47: ibid, SP 28/51, fo. 367.

189 The wording of Dawes'ss claim for pay arrears suggests very strongly that he was not in service after 5/47: ibid, E 121/1/6/117, fo. 38. He had been Martin's cornet in Essex's army in 3/45 and was lieutenant to Captain Martin by 10/45: ibid, SP 28/32, fo. 249; ibid, SP 28/28, fo. 394.

190 Ibid, E 121/5/7/unnumbered, entry 426.

4th Regiment	Lieutenant	Cornet	Quartermaster
Charles Fleetwood	Joseph Blissett[191]	Richard Webb[192]	William Williams[193]
Thomas Harrison	Griffith Lloyd[194]	John Spencer[195]	Robert Stannard?[196] Joseph Strange??[197]
William Coleman	James Lloyd/Flood[198]	Thomas Else[199]	Richard Smart[200]
Richard Zanchy	George Everard[201] William White[202]	William White George Tracey[203]	William White[204]
James Laughton	Stephen White [205]	Samuel Boalley[206]	Phillip Sismy[207] Nathaniel Phillips[208]
Thomas Howard	Gilman Taylor[209]	XXX William Buck[210]	William Buck George Craven?[211]

191 Ibid, SP 28/31, fo. 86; Worc. College, Clarke Ms 41, fo. 102.

192 BL, Thomason Tracts, E 390 (26); TNA, SP 28/45, fo. 246.

193 Ibid, SP 28/42, fo. 293; ibid, SP 28/45, fo. 427.

194 Ibid, SP 28/140/7, entries 283-5.

195 Ibid, E 121/3/4/entries 29-31; Thomason Tracts E390 (26).

196 Robert Stannard signed a petition of 3/47 as quartermaster, but he may not have been in the 4th regiment of horse at the time. He was probably commissioned as cornet in Lloyd's troop after 16/6/47 rather than as lieutenant given the order in which the names are written in the commissions' book: BL, Thomason Tracts E 390 (26); Worc. College, Clarke Ms 67, fo. 19.

197 Strange signed for Laughton's troop with no rank given in 12/45: TNA, SP 28/33, fo. 596. In 1/47 he was only a corporal: ibid, SP 28/44, fo. 145. However, he claimed to have served in Harrison's troop as a quartermaster. When Harrison became colonel of the 3rd regiment of horse in 6/47, he became cornet in his troop: Worc. College, Clarke Ms 67, fo. 25.

198 TNA, E 121/4/8/5, entry 7; BL, Thomason Tracts E 390 (26).

199 TNA, SP28/38, fo. 119. Else was not promoted to lieutenant until after 6/47 as his troop commander is described as Major Coleman. Before the first Army coup Coleman had been a captain: Worc. College, Clarke Ms 67, fo. 19.

200 Smart was quartermaster in 7/46: TNA, SP 28/57, fo. 512. He deserted the army in 6/47: CSPD 1625-49, p. 710.

201 Worc. College, Clarke Ms 41, fos. 103, 126.

202 White had been trumpeter and quartermaster in Le Hunt's troop in the Eastern Association Army and cornet and lieutenant in the New Model in Zanchey's troop: Spring i: TNA, E 121/4/6/8A, unnumbered; ibid, SP 28/32, fo. 237. He seems to have transferred to the 1st regiment of foot c. 6/47.

203 BL, Thomason Tracts E 390 (3); TNA, E 121/3/6/4, unnumbered.

204 White must have been quartermaster in the troop in the spring of 1647 according to the information given in his claim for pay arrears. For this see note 199 below.

205 TNA, SP28/31, fo. 73; BL, Thomason Tracts E 390 (26).

206 Ibid, Thomason Tracts, E 390 (3); TNA, SP 28/45, fo. 254.

207 Ibid, SP 28/39, fo. 58.

208 Ibid, E 121/3/4/9A, entry 34. Phillips was quartermaster in 3/47 after Sisme: BL, Thomason Tracts E 390 (26).

209 A lieutenant Taylor was described as of the troop late Captain Howard's in 13/6/47. As Gilman Taylor became captain soon afterwards, it is inconceivable that he was not the same man: TNA, SP 28/46, fol. 195.

210 Ibid, SP 28/31, fo. 10; Worc. College, Clarke Ms 41, fo. 102. In BL, Thomason Tracts E 390 (3) he appears as Cornet William Benck.

211 For Craven, see note 604 below.

5th Regiment[212]	Lieutenant	Cornet	Quartermaster
Edward Rossiter	Richard Curzon[213]	**William Morris**[214]	
Phillip Twistleton	John Byfield??[215]		Thomas Ward?[216]
Anthony Markham	Thomas Deane[217]	Thomas Mann/Munn	Joseph Stroud[218]
John Nelthorpe	John Sherman[219]	**William Ascott**[220]	Richard Ransom?[221]
Original Peart			**Joseph/John Holt**[222]
Henry Markham	Thomas Izod[223]	Gabriel Bellerby[224]	

212 Rossiter seems to have kept his officers from signing petitions in the spring of 1647: F. and D .These are the major source of information about junior officers at that time, but to make matters worse clerks, not officers, almost invariably signed receipts for the regiment's pay. However, cross-referencing between pay warrants, claims for arrears and other documents has enabled some identifications to be made.

213 See entries relating to Curzon in the company and troop commanders' section of this volume.

214 See note 614 below, though it is just possible that Morris was not in continuous service between 1645 and 1649.

215 Spring names Byfield as Twistleton's lieutenant in the Eastern Association army but does not provide a reference. Byfield need not have held that rank in the New Model, but the link with Rossiter's regiment in a letter dated late 3/47 cited by Gentles makes it a very strong possibility. See also Bodleian, Tanner Ms 58, fo. 18.

216 BL, Thomason Tracts E 390 (3) where his name appears as Wood, but at that time he was apparently in the 7th regiment of horse. Ward was quartermaster in the 5th regiment in 7/47: TNA, SP 28/47, fo. 411.

217 Deane and Munn were lieutenant and cornet in the troop in Manchester's army, and in what was later Captain Cambridge's troop: ibid, E 121/3/3/113B, entries 110-12; ibid, E 121/5/7/unnumbered, entries 203-4. For Deane, see also ibid, E 121/4/7/104, entry 1. Deane was lieutenant of the Belvoir Castle troop in 6/48: BL, Thomason Tracts E 451 (19).

218 Stroud was quartermaster of the troop on 28/6/47 before Anthony Markham had been replaced: TNA, SP 28/46, fo. 228. I have therefore assumed he was quartermaster earlier in the year as his name does not appear under the page dedicated to the regiment in the commissions' book: Worc. College, Clarke Ms 67, fo. 23.

219 Sherman had served in Leicestershire as cornet to Captain Meldrum's troop in Lord Grey of Groby's regiment and then as captain: TNA, E 121/3/3/113B, entries 204, 435. He was in the 5th regiment of horse in the autumn of 1647 as an officer agitator: Clarke Papers i, p. 439.

220 TNA, E 121/3/3/113B, entry 371.

221 Ransom was quartermaster in late 6/47: ibid, SP 28/46, fo. 231.

222 Ibid, E 121/3/3/113A, entry 391. Holt was quartermaster to Captain Peart's troop in late 6/47: ibid, SP 28/46, fo. 230. Spring claims that he served in the troop in Manchester's army but the reference cited does not say so.

223 Izod was lieutenant to Captain Henry Markham and to his successor Hezekiah Haynes: ibid, E 121/5/7/unnumbered, entries 264-6; Clarke Papers i, p. 439.

224 Bellerby was cornet of the troop in 6/47 before the new captain was in place. Although his promotion is not recorded in the commissions' book, it can be assumed that he later became lieutenant of the troop: TNA, SP 28/46, fo 228.

6th Regiment	Lieutenant	Cornet	Quartermaster
Oliver Cromwell	Joseph Wallington	John Fox[225]	**John Carness**[226]
Robert Huntington	Nathaniel Whight[227]	Thomas Barker[228]	
John Jenkins	John Hurdman[229]	William Cobbe[230]	Samuel Oliver[231]
John Blackwell	Thomas Sheares	Thomas Shoudhorne?[232]	Robert Markham?[233]
John Reynolds	Edward Scotton[234]	Richard Southwood[235]	Thomas Savage[236]
Henry Middleton	George Ensor[237]	Edward Winstanley[238]	James Goodwin[239]
Unplaced	John Byfield??[240]		Edward Warren

225 Ibid, SP 28/38, fo. 153.
226 Ibid, E 121/4/7/80B, entry 23; ibid, E 121/5/6/42A, entry 2.
227 Ibid, E121/4/1/59, entry 32; ibid, SP 28/45, fo. 236.
228 Ibid, SP 28/45, fo. 402.
229 Ibid, SP 28/45, fo. 406; ibid, E 121/4/1/59, entry 129.
230 Ibid, SP 28/46, fo. 235.
231 Ibid, SP 28/39, fo. 298; ibid, SP28/44, fo. 456 – 2/47.
232 Ibid, SP 28/31, fo. 185.
233 Ibid, SP 28/30, fo. 84.
234 Ibid, SP 28/38, fo. 70; ibid, SP 28/45, fo. 541.
235 Ibid, SP 28/36, fo. 122.
236 Ibid, SP 28/45, fo. 493.
237 Ibid, SP 28/44, fo. 408.
238 Ibid, E 121/3/4/41, entries, 4-5; BL, Thomason Tracts E 390 (3)..
239 TNA, SP 28/45, fo. 402.
240 Gentles, *New Model Army*, p. 151 citing Bodleian, Tanner Ms 58, fo. 18 places Byfield in Cromwell's regiment. I do not read the source in that way. Moreover, there was no space for him as lieutenant in the regiment in 3/47. However, he was certainly in the regiment in 1649: BL, Thomason Tracts E 557 (10) In my opinion Byfield either transferred into the 6th regiment of horse from the 5th after 6/47 or was not in the New Model Army until after the first Army coup.

7th Regiment[241]	Lieutenant	Cornet	Quartermaster
Nathaniel Rich	William Weare[242]	John Ledbrook[243]	John Ledbrook
John Alford	Henry Barton[244]	Francis Rawson *[245]	Richard Blunt?[246] Christopher Gold
Azariah Husbands	John Merriman[247]	John Clarke[248]	
Thomas Neville	Ralph Hooker *		**Roland Floyd**[249]
Thomas Ireton	Edward Lisle[250]	George Southwood[251]	Robert Sprigg[252]
Francis Hawes	George Elsmore	John Chapman[253]	Caleb Lee[254]

241 The claims for pay arrears for this regiment show that the following officers served in the same troop – Cornet John Clarke and Quartermaster Thomas Ward, Cornet Francis Rawson and Quartermaster Christopher Gold, Lieutenant George Elsmore and Cornet John Chapham, and Cornet George Southwood and Quartermaster Robert Sprigg: TNA, E 121/2/11/64, passim.

242 Ibid, E 121/4/5/81, entry 2; BL, Thomason Tracts E 390 (3).

243 Ledbrook signed one of the petitions of 3/47 as a cornet, but was apparently not commissioned until after mid 6/47. He was probably acting cornet to the colonel's troop in March: ibid, Thomason Tracts E 390 (26); Worc. College, Clarke Ms 67, fo. 21.

244 Barton also appears as Burton: TNA, SP 28/41, fo. 549.

245 Rawson was lieutenant to Captain Barton by 7/47: ibid. SP 28/47, fo. 386.

246 Richard Blunt was quartermaster in Major Alford's troop in 4/46: Ibid, WO 55/1646, unfol.

247 Ibid, E 121/2/11/unnumbered shows that Merriman was a lieutenant in the regiment before 6/47. He is not described as being in Husbands' troop, but all the other troops had lieutenants in place at the time.

248 Ibid, SP 28/31, fo. 313. Clarke was cornet from 16/6/45 to c. 6/47: ibid, SP 28/49, fo. 122.

249 Ibid, E 121/5/6/51, entry 17, but he was probably quartermaster in the troop in the earl of Manchester's army rather than the New Model.

250 Rushworth, *Historical Collections* vi, p. 465; TNA, SP 28/45, fo 307.

251 Ibid, E 121/2/11, entry 330; ibid, SP 28/39, fo. 8. I suspect that this man appears in BL, Thomason Tracts E 390 (3), (26) as John Southwood.

252 TNA, SP 28/39, fo. 9; ibid, SP 28/47, fo 331; ibid, E 121/2/10/49, entry 330.

253 Chapman appears in one of the 3/47 petitions as Cornet John Chyman: BL, Thomason Tracts E 390 (26).

254 Ibid, E 121/2/11/19, entry 228; BL, Thomason Tracts E 390 (26).

8th Regiment	Lieutenant	Cornet	Quartermaster
Sir Robert Pye	Edward Hamden[255]	Nathaniel Waterhouse[256]	Jeremy Hippersley[257]
Matthew Tomlinson	Robert Glyn[258]	William Raunce[259]	Thomas Walker?[260]
Ralph Knight	Thomas Johnson[261]		Edward Hayley?[262]
Ralph Margery	**John Pidgeon**[263]	Christopher Keymer[264]	Benjamin Pett[265]
Samuel Barry	Zouch Allen?[266]	Paul Bunting[267]	Samuel Saxon?[268] **John Wells**[269]
Thomas Rawlins	**Levitt Aldridge**[270]	Peter Willmot[271]	**John Baily**[272] Peter Major[273]
Unplaced	Thomas Aldrevy[274]	Thomas Symnell[275]	

255 BL, Thomason Tracts 669 f11 (15). This broadsheet contains more errors of transcription than most printed lists. Some mistakes in transcription can be corrected by consulting the New Model Army's copy of the petition, which also gives the officers' first names, but that too is a transcription and contains errors of its own: Worc. College, Clarke Ms 41, fo. 134.

256 TNA SP 28/36, fo. 105; BL, Thomason Tracts 669 f 11 (15); Worc. College, Clarke Ms 41, fo. 134.

257 TNA, E 121/5/7/109, entry 148; BL, Thomason Tracts 669 f11 (15). His name is also given as Ipsley: TNA, E 315/5, fo. 30.

258 Ibid, SP 28/31, fo. 7. Glyn became a captain soon after Tomlinson was promoted to colonel.

259 Ibid, SP 28/140/7, fos. 283-5. Raunce had been quartermaster in the Eastern Association army: ibid, E 121/1/6/117, fo. 374.

260 Ibid, SP 28/31, fo. 241; ibid, SP 28/140/7, fos. 278-9. Walker had held the same position in Manchester's army: ibid, E 121/4/3/ unnumbered, entry 2.

261 Spring i, p. 53; BL, Thomason Tracts E 390 (26); TNA, E 121/1/6, entry 292; ibid, E 121/1/1/unnumbered, entry 145.

262 Ibid, SP 28/36, fo. 108.

263 Ibid, E 121/1/1/unnumbered, entries 268-70 relate to Pigeon, Keymer and Pett.

264 BL, Thomason Tracts E 390 (26).

265 TNA, SP 28/45, fo. 392.

266 Ibid, E 121/1/1/unnumbered, entry 342; ibid, WO 55/1646, fo. 240; ibid, SP 28/36, fo. 136. He may be the lieutenant Ralph Allen whose name appears in the loyalty declaration of late 5/47: BL, Thomason Tracts 669 f11 (15); Worc. College, Clarke Ms 41, fo. 134.

267 Bunting was cornet in 4/45 and 1/3/47: TNA, WO 55/1646, fo. 57; ibid, SP 28/46, fo. 163.

268 Ibid, SP 28/32, fo. 166.

269 See below note 655.

270 TNA, E 121/1/1/unnumbered, entry 204; ibid, SP 28/140/7, fos. 283-5.

271 Ibid, SP 28/33, fo. 44.

272 Ibid, E 121/3/3/19/3B, entry 1.

273 Ibid, E 121/1/1/unnumbered, entry 203; BL, Thomason Tracts E 390 (26).

274 TNA, SP 28/36, fo. 136. Aldrevy and Aldridge are almost certainly the same man as Thomas Aldridge's name appears amongst the lieutenants of horse in one of the petitions of 3/47: BL, Thomason Tracts E 390 (26).

275 Symnell had served as quartermaster in Knight's troop in Manchester's army. He was a lieutenant in the regiment in 1654 at which time he took over Captain Margery's troop: ibid, E 121/5/6/51, entry 48; F. and D.

9th Regiment[276]	Lieutenant	Cornet	Quartermaster
Edward Whalley	Daniel Dale[277]	John Wright[278]	Phillip Rumsey[279]
John Pitchford	John Savage[280]	William Whittingham[281]	William Millner[282]
William Evanson	Edmund Chillington[283]	Anthony Lacon[284]	John Addis[285]
John Grove	Thomas Chamberlain	Abel Warren[286]	George Saunders
Robert Swallow	Solomon Camby[287]	Joseph Sabberton	Thomas Stewart
Henry Cannon	John Frank[288]	Henry Miles[289]	John Dewe[290]

276 All the junior officers signed at least one of the petitions from the army to Parliament in 3 and 4/47 a record not attained by any other regiment. Their names are also to be found in the book in which their claims for arrears of pay were collated, namely BL, Harleian Ms 427.

277 For Captain Lieutenant Dale, Lieutenant Chamberlain, Cornet Sabberton and Quartermaster Stewart, see BL, Harleian Ms 427, fos. 27-9.

278 TNA, SP 28/44, fo. 394.

279 Rumsey was in the regiment in 2/47: ibid, SP 28/44, fo. 395.

280 Savage was in the regiment by 2/47: ibid, SP 28/44, fo. 393.

281 BL, Harleian Ms 427, fo. 31; BL, Thomason Tracts E 390 (26).

282 BL, Harleian Ms 427, fo. 75.

283 TNA, SP 28/38, fo. 58. Chillington had formerly been cornet to Captain Dingley in Manchester's regiment of horse in the Eastern Association Army and before that a scout for the City of London brigade: BL, Harleian Ms 427, fo. 133.

284 Ibid, Harleian Ms 427, fos. 30, 41, 52.

285 TNA, SP 28/38, fo. 57; ibid, SP 28/45, fo. 394.

286 Ibid, SP 28/31, fo. 285; ibid, SP 28/140/7, fos. 281-2.

287 Ibid, WO 55/1646, fo. 263. Camby received supplies from the ordnance office in 12/45 accompanied by Sergeant William Lynley, later a commissioned officer in the regiment.

288 Ibid, SP 28/31, fo. 246; BL, Thomason Tracts, E 390 (26).

289 TNA, SP 28/44, fo. 124; ibid, E390 (3); ibid, E 121/2/11/15, entries 131-2. In his claim for pay arrears Miles alleged that he had been in Captain Groves's troop.

290 Ibid, SP 28/38, fo. 360; ibid, SP 28/44, fo. 386.

10th Regiment	Lieutenant	Cornet	Quartermaster
Richard Graves	Charles Holcroft[291]	Theophilus Farmer[292]	
Adrian Scroop	Richard Watson[293]	William Peverill[294]	Thomas Bayly[295] **Evan Lewis**[296]
Skippon's troop: Capt. Nicholas Bragg	Edward Lewis[297]	Edward Lewis[298] Richard Cornes[299]	**John Ayott**[300] Gilbert Taylor[301]
Christopher Fleming	John Everard[302]	John Everard Francis Pick[303]	Francis Pick?? Alexander Stewart[304]
William, Lord Caulfield	Thomas Goddard *[305]	John King *[306]	John Ray *[307]
Nathaniel Barton	Philip Prime[308]	William Watts?[309]	William Watts[310] Robert Agard[311]
Unplaced		Abraham Deane[312]	

291 BL, Thomason Tracts 669 f11 (15).

292 TNA, SP 28/33, fo. 569. Farmer opposed the army's petitioning Parliament in 3/47: Worc. College, Clarke Ms 41, fo. 126. In 1659 he commanded a troop in Major General Morgan's regiment of dragoons: F. and D.

293 TNA, E 121/3/5/47, unnumbered.

294 Ibid, E 121/3/5/47, unnumbered. Peverell was cornet and then lieutenant of Scroop's troop.

295 Ibid, SP 28/31, fo. 68. Bayly had been quartermaster to Scroop in Essex's army: ibid, E 121/3/4/9B, entry 41.

296 Ibid, E 121/3/3/78, entries 44-6. Lewis had been a trooper under Major Crosse and a corporal under Captaiin Scroop in Essex's army.

297 Ibid, SP 28/56, fos. 193-4; ibid, E 121/3/3/82, entry 5.

298 Ibid, SP 28/56, fos. 193-4. He held the position from 6/44 to 9/46.

299 Ibid, E 121/2/9/unnumbered, entry 412. He may be the Cornet Combes who signed the loyalist petition in late 5/47: BL, Thomason Tracts 669 f11 (15).

300 Ibid, E 121/2/9/32, unnumbered.

301 Taylor was in post in 11/46 and in London in 6/47 having left the regiment: TNA, SP 28/41, fo. 290; ibid, SP 28/124, fo. 332.

302 For Everard's two positions in the regiment, see ibid, E 121/4/8/25, entry 3. He was lieutenant by 12/45: ibid, SP 28/33, fo. 571. He had fled to London by 6/47: ibid, SP 28/124, fo. 332.

303 Pick was in the regiment in 2/47: TNA, SP 28/44, fo. 419; ibid, 28/61, fo. 38.

304 Ibid, SP 28/46, fo. 388; ibid, SP 28/124, fo. 332..

305 For Goddard's military career, see p. 108 above.

306 TNA, SP 28/140/7: fos 284-5; Ibid, SP 28/44, fo. 494 – 2/47. He opposed army petitioning in 3/47: Worc. College, Clarke Ms 41, fo. 103.

307 TNA, E 121/3/4/77, entries 8-9. Ray was quartermaster in 3/46: ibid, SP/38, fo. 630.

308 Ibid, SP 28/36, fo. 580; ibid, SP 28/45, fo. 430; BL, Thomason Tracts E 390 (26).

309 TNA, SP28/37, fo. 270.

310 W.S. Library, SMS 463, unfol. 23/4/46.

311 TNA, SP 28/41, fo. 296; ibid, E 121/4/6/101B, entry 9; Worc. College, Clarke Ms 41, fo. 126; BL, Thomason Tracts E 390 (3).

312 TNA, SP 28/124, fo. 332.

11th Regiment	Lieutenant	Cornet	Quartermaster
Henry Ireton	Robert Kirkby[313]	James Wilson[314]	Robert Browne[315]
George Sedacue	Henry Collier[316]	William Bush[317]	William Walkerton[318]
Robert Gibbon	Henry Johnson[319]	William Raunce/Rance[320]	
Anthony Morgan	Benjamin Gifford[321]	Jervaise Jeffrys[322]	Thomas Wolsall[323]
Henry Pretty	Samson Twogood[324]		Henry Ward[325]
William Cecil	William Hill[326]	James Jennings[327]	Richard Hunt[328]

313 Kirkby was captain lieutenant by early 7/45: TNA, SP 28/31, fo. 66.

314 Ibid, SP 28/38, fo. 41; ibid, SP 28/45, fo. 349; BL, Thomason Tracts E 390 (3).

315 TNA, SP28/44, fo. 117; Worc. College, Clarke Ms 67, fo. 17.

316 TNA, SP28/32, fo. 210; ibid, SP 28/45, fo. 390.

317 Ibid, SP 28/44, fo. 115.

318 Ibid, SP 28/140/7, fos. 282-3; ibid, SP 28/44, fo. 372.

319 Ibid, SP 28/31, fo. 98.

320 Ibid, SP 28/33, fo. 123; BL, Thomason Tracts E 468 (18). There seems to have been two officers with the name William Raunce or Rance in the New Model Army, one in the 8th regiment of horse and the other in the 11th.

321 Ibid, SP 28/45, fo. 231.

322 Ibid, E 121/4/6/16A, entry 4; ibid, SP 28/44, fo. 37; Worc. College, Clarke Ms 67, fo. 17.

323 TNA, SP 28/38, fo. 34; BL, Thomason Tracts E 390 (26).

324 TNA, SP28/38, fo. 46. When Pretty left for Ireland in Oliver Cromwell's new regiment of horse, Twogood was still his lieutenant: ibid, SP 28/61, fo. 382.

325 Ward signed for horses for Pretty's and Sedacue's troops: ibid, SP 140/7, fo. 281.

326 Ibid, SP 28/31, fo. 95; ibid, SP 28/45, fo. 391.

327 Ibid, E 121/5/7/unnumbered, entry 865; ibid, SP 28/44, fo. 374.

328 Ibid, E 121/4/1/16, unnumbered. He was quartermaster in 2/47: ibid, SP 28/44, fos. 116, 373.

Lifeguard[329]	Lieutenant	Cornet	Quartermaster
Henry Hall	Andrew Goodhand *	Thomas Moore	William Brewerton

329 The officers of the troop in early June 1647 were Hall, Goodhand, Moore and William Brewerton: LJ ix, p. 282. Ingram may have been a corporal.

Junior Commissioned Officers June 1647 to 1650

Infantry

1st Regiment of Foot Company Commander	Lieutenant	Ensign
Sir Thomas Fairfax	Lewis Audley Robert Luson[330]	Robert Luson
William Cowell William Goffe	William Bird[331] Thomas Smith[332] Robert King	Thomas Smith Robert King Thomas Clarke[333]
Francis White	XXX William White[334]	William White **William Gore**[335]
Charles Bolton	**Robert Wild**[336]	
James Priest	**Matthew Garrett**	**John Jackson**[337]
James Pitson	XXX **John Cope**[338]	**John Cope** John Hammond/Hancock[339]
Clement Keene	XXX? **John Miller**[340]	**John Miller** **Richard Webster**[341]
William Leigh	Stephen Baldwin[342]	
William Farley	Robert Scrope[343]	XXX Robson Zachary Shepherd[344] **Samuel Leverington**[345]
George Baldwin	George Hadfield[346]	Thomas Wright
Unplaced	XXX Streader[347] XXX Wilkinson[348]	

330 TNA, E 121/2/9/unnumbered, entry 65. Luson specifically states that he was ensign and lieutenant in His Excellency's own company. He cannot have been ensign earlier that 6/47. For this see p. 113 above. Luson is recorded as Robert Lawford in the commissions' book: Worc. College, Clarke Ms 67, fo. 3.

331 Ibid, E 121/2/9/69, entry 222. He or a man of the same name had previously served in the 3rd regiment of foot. For this see p. 114 above.

332 Ibid, E 121/2/9/69, entry 102. He and King were commissioned in 4/49: Worc. College, Clarke Ms 67, fo. 3.

333 King and Clarke were commissioned in 2/50: ibid.

334 TNA, E 121/2/9/69, entry 337. The wording shows that White entered the regiment after 5/47. He seems previously to have been cornet and lieutenant in the 4th regiment of horse: ibid, E 121/4/6/8A, unnumbered.

335 ibid, E 121/3/1/unnumbered, entry 6.

336 Ibid, E 121/3/1/unnumbered, entries 4-5. Wild, who had been ensign in the company, probably became lieutenant in 6/47. It is not recorded in the commissions' book, but George Watson, lieutenant in the spring of 1647, had probably left the army after signing the loyalty petition: BL, Thomason Tracts 669 f11 (15).

337 Ibid, E 121/2/9/69, entry 40. He had previously been sergeant in the company.

338 Ibid, E 121/2/9/69, entry 171.

339 Ibid, SP 28/59, fo. 59.

340 Ibid, E 121/2/9/unnumbered, entry 181. Miller claimed to have served as both ensign and lieutenant to Captain Keene. He had probably been a commissioned officer in the regiment before 6/47: Rushworth, *Historical Collections* vi, p. 465.

341 Ibid, E 121/2/9/69, entry 290.

342 Ibid, E 121/3/4/1A, entry 3; Worc. College, Clarke Ms 67, fo. 3.

343 TNA, E 121/2/9/69, entry 463; Worc. College, Clarke Ms 67, fo. 3.

344 Ibid. Shepherd was later ensign to Captain Hadfield: TNA, E 121/2/9/unnumbered, entry 374.

345 Ibid, E 121/2/9/unnumbered, entry 269.

346 For Hadfield and Wright, see ibid, E 121/2/9/46, entry 126-7. Hadfield succeeded Baldwin as captain and must have been his lieutenant. For this see p. 97 above and the lack of gaps in the regimental list.

347 Worc. College, Clarke Ms 66, fo. 17.

348 Ibid, Clarke MS 67, fo. 3.

2nd Regiment		
Phillip Skippon Alban Cox	Samuel Clarke[349] XXX Heyrick[350]	John West[351] Thomas Powell
Richard Ashfield	James Mayer[352]	William Fitch[353]
John Cobbett	Bezahell? Etherington[354] John Milbourne[355]	John Milbourne[356] Willliam Davies[357]
John Rogers John Barber	Nicholas Copeland[358]	Henry Sutton[359]
Edward Streater Arthur Helsham	**John Streater**[360] XXX John Williamson[361]	John Williamson[362] John Giles
James Harrison	Arthur Helsham[363]	John Hardwick[364]
John Clarke	John Dove[365]	Richard Wynn[366]
Maurice Bowen	Thomas Jubbs[367] Thomas Coppinger William Slade[368]	John Hardwick William Slade[369]
Thomas Butler James Symcock	James Symcock[370] Richard Hatton[371]	Jacob Barthomley[372] John Tinke
William Symonds	John Stoddard[373] Francis Mercer[374]	James Whitfield[375] William Engler[376]

349 TNA, E 121/5/7/35, entry 2. He became a full captain in 11/49: Worc. College, Clarke Ms 67, fo. 4.

350 For Captain Lieutenant Heyrick, Ensigns Tinke and Powell and all Lingwood's and Baynes's officers, see ibid.

351 TNA, SP 28/125, fo. 316. Powell at the time was a sergeant.

352 In 8/48: ibid, SP 28/133/1, fos. 55-6. He was a full captain in 6/49: Worc. College, Clarke Ms 67, fo. 4.

353 TNA, E 121/5/7/35, entry 124; ibid, SP 28/126, fo. 227.

354 For Etherington and his ensign Milbourne, see SP 28/125, fo. 437.

355 Ibid, SP 28/125, fo. 187

356 Ibid, SP 28/133/1, fos. 55-9.

357 Ibid, SP 28/125, fo. 187.

358 For Coppinger and his ensign Sutton, see ibid, fo. 256.

359 Worc. College, Clarke Ms 67, fo. 4.

360 TNA, E 121/1/5/57A, unnumbered.

361 Ibid, E 121/3/3/129, entry 30. For Williamson and his ensign Giles, see ibid, SP 28/126, fo. 420.

362 Ibid, E 121/3/3/129, entry 30.

363 Ibid, E 121/5/7/35, entry 63; W.S. Library, SMS 463, unfol. 21/4/45.

364 Ibid, E 121/5/7/35, entry 65.

365 For Dove and Wynn, see ibid, SP28/125, fo. 183.

366 Ibid, E 121/5/7/35, entry 3.

367 For Jubbs and Hardwick, see ibid, SP 28/125, fo. 243.

368 CSPD 1650, p. 534.

369 For Coppinger and Slade, see TNA, SP 28/125, fo. 428.

370 Ibid, E 121/1/7/49, entry 1.

371 Worc. College, Clarke Ms 67, fo. 4.

372 TNA, SP 28/133/1, fos. 55-9. For Symcock and Barthomley, see ibid, SP 28/125, fo. 430.

373 Ibid, SP 28/56, fo. 426; ibid, SP 28/133/1, fos. 55-9. Stoddard was killed in 1648: ibid, SP 28/58, fo. 426.

374 Mercer's commission was issued in 2/50: Worc. College, Clarke Ms 67, fo. 4.

375 Ibid, E 121/5/7/35, entry 200.

376 See ibid, E 121/5/7/35, entries 200, 201 for Whitfield and Engler. Engler was ensign in 1648 when Stoddard was lieutenant: ibid, SP 28/125, fo. 322.

Additional Companies raised for service in Scotland[i]

Lionel Lingwood	William Hooper	Richard Everard
Robert Baynes	John Rudlee	XXX Jefferson

3rd Regiment		
Sir Hardress Waller	Ralph Wilson[377]	
Edward Salmon		Richard Waller[378]
Thomas Smith		Samuel Chase/Case[379]
Phillip Ebzery	John Filkins[380]	Daniel Hincksman[381]
Richard Hodden		Robert Mason[382]
Amor Stoddard		
Richard Aske		Thomas Tandy[383]
Ex XXX Howard		
John Clarke	Robert Smyth[384]	John Hardier
Nathaniel Chase[385]		Edward Allen[386] **Ralph Carde[387]**
Unplaced	Brian Smith[388]	**William Seymour[389]** Richard Kingdom?[390]

377 For Wilson, Tandy and Aske, see TNA, E 121/1/6/30, entries 161-8.
378 Worc. College, Clarke Ms 67, fo. 5.
379 TNA, E 121/1/6/30, entries 1-6; Worc. College, Clarke Ms 67, fo. 5.
380 For Filkins, see ibid, E 121/1/6/30, entry 105; Worc. College, Clarke Ms 67, fo. 5.
381 TNA, E 121/4/7/50, entry 6. He had transferred to the 12th regiment of foot by 11/47: BL, Thomason Tracts E 417 (6).
382 For Mason, see TNA, E 121/1/6/66, entry 299.
383 Worc. College, Clarke Ms 67, fo. 5; TNA, E 121/1/6/30, entry 161.
384 For Smith and Hardier, see ibid, E 121/1/6/ 30, entries 307-8; Worc. College, Clarke Ms 67, fo. 5.
385 Chase and his lieutenant Carde were serving in the Weymouth garrison in 1/49: BL, Thomason Tracts 669f13 (71).
386 TNA, E 121/1/6/30, entry 4.
387 Ibid, entry 1.
388 Smith was successively lieutenant and captain in the regiment: ibid, E 121/1/6/unnumbered, entry 17.
389 Ibid, E 121/4/8/1, unnumbered.
390 Kingdom was stationed in Exeter in 1649 as were some companies of the 3rd regiment: Worc. College, Clarke Ms 69, unfol. 10/7/4.

Additional Companies authorised in 1650[ii]

Robert Smith	John Blackburn	XXX Jeffries
XXX Hooper	XXX Woram	Thomas Cooper
XXX Davison	XXX Goodwin	David Bowen
Henry Davies	Stephen Combe	William Powell
Maurice Bowen	XXX Growte	Matthew Thorowgood

4th Regiment[391]		
Robert Hammond		Henry Duck[392]
Isaac Ewer	William Ewer	
Robert Saunders	Edward Singleton[393]	**William Oram[394]**
Edmund Rolfe	Robert Cuppage[395]	**William Cooper**
Israel Smith		Henry Harridge

i   All the officers' names are given in Worc. College, Clarke Ms 67, fo. 4.
ii   All the officers' names in the five new companies are given in ibid, Clarke Ms 67, fo. 5.

4th Regiment[391]		
Francis Wheeler	James? Hutchinson	John Bennett[396]
William Disney		Edmund Overs[397]
Edward Humphries	Thomas Turner	
John Puckle	John Friend[398]	
William Stratton	Downhill Gregory	John Gregory

391 The commissions of Lieutenants Ewer, Cuppage, Hutchinson, Turner and Gregory and Ensigns Duck, Harridge, Bennett and Gregory are recorded in the commissions' book: ibid, Clarke Ms 67, fo. 6.

392 TNA, E 121/3/6/4, unnumbered. Duck was on the Isle of Wight in 1/49: BL, Thomason Tracts 669f13 (71).

393 Singleton served in the regiment under both Hammond and Ewer: TNA, E 121/3/4/69B, entry 2; BL, Thomason Tracts, E 390 (26).

394 TNA, E121/1/6/63, entry 141. Oram served in Ewer's regiment under Lieutenant Colonel Saunders.

395 For Cuppage/Coppage and Cooper, see ibid, E 121/2/2/16, entries 11-13; Worc. College, Clarke Ms 67, fo. 6.

396 This man was major in the regiment under Colonel Lawrence in Ireland in 8/59: Dunlop, *Ireland under the Commonwealth* ii, p. 711, 715.

397 Overs served as ensign when Disney was major of the regiment: TNA, E 121/4/8/6, entry 1.

398 Friend served under Colonels Hammond and Ewer as lieutenant: ibid, E 121/1/1/26B, entry 3. He subsequently fought in the dragoons. In 4/56 and in 7/59 a Captain John Friend was in the army of occupation in Ireland and probably in Henry Cromwell's, later Peter Wallis's, regiment of horse: Dunlop, *Ireland under the Commonwealth* ii, p. 90: CSP Ireland 1647-1660, p. 700.

5th Regiment[399]		
John Barkstead	Thomas Buckner[400] William Bayly[401] Roger Jones	John Hatten[402] XXX Benjamin Larken[403]
Ralph Cobbett	Richard Hatt	**Francis Beachamp**[404] Nicholas Cordy[405]
Robert Cobbett John Biscoe	Jeremiah Campfield[406]	
Arthur Young	**Edward Jones**[407]	Richard Owen[408] Richard Richbell
John Cox William Read	Matthew Martell Matthew Martell[409]	XXX Clarke[410] Humphrey Hughes[411]
Richard Pooley	William Read[412] Thomas Baxter[413]	Thomas Baxter XXX
John Denison Thomas Buckner	William Bayly[414] Richard Owen	Blennerhasset Fuller
John Miller	XXX Samuel Wise[415]	Samuel Wise John Styles[416] XXX Baxter
John Groome	William Broadhurst[417]	Nicholas Tews[418]
Henry Dorney	William Jones	Walter Kemis

399 The following commissions are noted in the commissions' book: Captain Lieutenants Buckner, Bayly and Roger Jones; Lieutenants Campfield, Wise, Owen and William Jones; Ensigns Larken, Richbell, Hughes, Thomas Baxter, Fuller, Styles, Baxter and Kemis: Worc. College, Clarke Ms 67, fo. 8.

400 Buckner became a full captain well before 1650, his replacements being first William Bayly, lieutenant to Capt. Denison in 4/47, and then Roger Jones, lieutenant to Capt. Whitton in 4/47: ibid, Clarke Ms 67, fo. 8; TNA, E 121/2//11/17A, entries, 235, 240.

401 Bayly helped suppress a riot in London in 5/48: BL, Thomason Tracts E 443 (5).

402 TNA, E 121/2/11/17A, entry 108.

403 Larken was previously in the garrison at Windsor Castle: ibid, E 121/2/11/unnumbered, entry 196.

404 Ibid, E 121/2/11/17B, entry 208.

405 Cordy was successively corporal, sergeant and ensign in Cobbett's company: ibid, E 121/2/11/17A, entry 39. Before that he had served in the regiment in Essex's army commanded by Colonels Bulstrode, Cunningham and Fortescue: ibid, E 121/2/11/17B, entry 82.

406 Ibid, E 121/2/11/17A, entry 40. See earlier under the 12th regiment of foot.

407 Ibid, E 121/2/11/17A, entry 76.

408 Read and Owen helped put down riots in the capital in 5/48: BL, Thomason Tracts, E 443 (5).

409 Martell was first ensign and then lieutenant to Captain Cox after Lieutenant Luke: TNA, E 121/2/11/17A, entry 266, 268. He was also lieutenant to Captain Read: ibid, E 121/2/11/unnumbered, unnumbered.

410 Worc. College, Clarke Ms 69, unfol. 2/2/50.

411 Ibid, Clarke Ms 69, unfol. 25/3/50.

412 TNA, E 121/2/11/17A, entry 84.

413 Worc. College, Clarke Ms 69, unfol. 1/2/1650. He was already a lieutenant in the spring of 1648 when he helped to put down riots in the capital: BL, Thomason Tracts E 443 (5).

414 For Bayly and Bush, see TNA, E121/2/11/17A, entries 37-40.

415 Wise claimed to have served as an ensign and a lieutenant in Backhouse's regiment: ibid, E 121/2/11/17A, entry 151.

416 Ibid, E 121/2/11/17A, entry 181.

417 Ibid, SP 28/61, fo. 78.

418 Ibid. E 121/2/11/17, entry 253.

6th Regiment[419]		
Richard Ingoldsby	Abraham Davies[420] Consolation Fox	Edward Nutt[421] **John Scott[422]**
Thomas Kelsey	William Duckett	
John Mill		**George Hopkins Alexander Newland[423]**
Francis Allen	Benjamin Southwood	**William Manners[424]**
John Grime	**Thomas Smith[425]**	Thomas Brookes
Edward? Stephens Francis Messervy	John Chamberlain[426] **Richard Barker[427]**	XXX Francis
Thomas Ingoldsby William Duckett	**Francis Andrews[428] Stephen West[429]**	**Francis Andrews** Benjamin Southwood[430] XXX Francis
Richard Wagstaffe	Thomas Banks **John Scudamore[431]**	**John King[432]**
John Shrimpton XXX Davies	John Davies[433]	XXX Moore
John Hunt	Samuel Fisher	**Samuel Fisher** XXX Brookes
Unplaced	XXX Matthews[434]	

419 Captain Lieutenants Abraham Davies and Fox, Lieutenants Fisher, Duckett, Southwood, Chamberlain, Banks and John Davies, and Ensigns Nutt, Southwood, Francis, Moore and Brookes are recorded in the commissions' book: Worc. College, Clarke Ms 67, fo. 13.

420 TNA, E 121/3/3/31, entry 2. Davies was succeeded by Lt. Consolation Fox before 5/50. Either he or John Davies, Shrimpton's lieutenant, was a full captain in the regiment by 6/50 at the latest, probably in succession to Thomas Ingoldsby: Worc. College, Clarke Ms 67, fo. 13.

421 TNA, E 121/5/7/45, entry 94.

422 Scott and Captain Shrimpton were dismissed in the autumn of 1649 for not assisting their colonel in suppressing a mutiny: F. and D. Scott's first name and his company are supplied by ibid, E 121/5/7/45, entry 95.

423 Ibid, E 121/2/10/49, entry 627.

424 Ibid, E 121/5/7/45, entry 208.

425 For Smith and Brookes, see ibid, E 121/5/7/45, entries 281, 298.

426 Ibid, E 121/3/3/31, entry 7.

427 Ibid, E 121/3/3/31, entry 3.

428 Ibid, E 121/4/1/100, entries 10, 11.

429 Ibid, E 121/5/7/45, entry 184.

430 Ibid, E 121/5/7/45, entry 183.

431 A man of this name had been ensign to Major Urry and lieutenant to Captain Penn's company in Lord Robartes' regiment in Essex's army in 4/45. He was not discharged and so probably joined the New Model Army: ibid, SP 28/29, fo. 334; ibid, E 121/3/3/115, entries 146, 159; Worc College, Clarke Ms 41, fos. 102-3.

432 TNA, E 121/5/7/45, entry 150.

433 Ibid, E 121/5/7/45, entry 333. Ensign John Davies signed the Vindication and one of the army's petitions in the spring of 1647: BL, Thomason Tracts E 385 (19).

434 Matthews is mentioned in an entry in Chequers Ms 782, fo. 66. He was probably the Lieutenant Christopher Matthews who was serving in the regiment before June 1647. For this see p. 116 above.

7th Regiment[435]		
Thomas Rainborough Richard Deane	XXX George Townshend	
Henry Bowen		
John Edwards		Humphrey Maddox
George Drury		Robert Spencer[436]
Thomas Dancer		John Adams
Thomas Creamer	**John Townshend**[437]	
John Browne Thomas Segrave	**John Cobbe**[438] James Knight[439]	**John Herwick**[440] John Wakeham
Henry Flower	John Quelch[441]	**John Ellis**[442] Henry Gill
Thomas Walker	XXX **William Hoyes**[443]	**William Hoyes** Richard Barber[444]
Henry Whittle		
Unplaced		**William Audley?**[445]
		John King

435 For Captain Lieutenant Townsend and Ensigns Maddox, King, Adams and Gill, see Worc. College, Clarke Ms 67, fo. 9. Maddox's and King's commissions were issued before 2/48, Townshend's, Adams's and Gill's between 4 and 7/48.

436 TNA, E 121/1/6/117, fo. 209.

437 Ibid, E 121/1/6/27B, entry 23.

438 Ibid, E 121/2/11/47A, entry 7.

439 Worc. College, Clarke Ms 67, unfol. section.

440 TNA, E 121/2/11/11B, entry 6.

441 Ibid, E 121/4/2/40, entry 48; BL, Harleian Ms 427, fo. 60.

442 TNA, E 121/1/6/117, fo. 161.

443 Hoyes was successively sergeant, ensign and lieutenant under Captain Walker: Ibid, E 121/4/7/80B, entry 12.

444 Ibid, E 121/1/6/1, unnumbered.

445 Audley was ensign in the regiment in Ireland in 1649: ibid, SP 28/62, fo. 103.

8th Regiment[446]		
Robert Lilburne Sir Arthur Haselrig	William Bray XXX Henry Goodyear[447]	Robert Hurlston[448] Timothy Leving[449]
Henry Lilburne Paul Hobson	Henry Goodyear[450] James Mayer[451] John Turner[452]	Nathaniel Strange
Paul Hobson	William Woodcock[453]	George Lower
Jeremiah Tolhurst	Ralph Baldwin	Oliver Blisse[454] John Mudge[455]
Abraham Holmes	Edward Boone[456] Bartholomew Davies	Bartholomew Davies Ralph Walton[457]
John Topping	John Blinkinstone[458] William Bramston	XXX Everfield George Jones John Turner[459]
William Mitchell James Hart	James Hart[460] Edward Boone[461]	Michael King[462]
Robert Hutton	John Mason	Nicholas Clarke Edward Toll[463]

8th Regiment[446]		
Richard Deane	Francis Nicholls[464]	Jacob Swallow John Gardner[465]
XXX Haynes?? Gabriel Earwood	John Rosse[466]	Herbert Field **Thomas Knowles**[467] John Simpson
Ethelbert Morgan	William Elmes[468] Thomas Cartwright	William Dike[469] William Indigo
Unplaced	Nathaniel Strange	John Bramston[470] William Endicott Henry James Peter Bush

446 The commissions' book contains evidence of the appointment of many officers in the regiment, namely Captain Lieutenant Bray; Lieutenants Woodcock, Baldwin, Hart, Mason, Nicholls and Elmes; and Ensigns Lower, Bliss, Davies, Everfield, Jones, Clarke, Swallow and Field: Worc. College, Clarke Ms 67, fo. 10.

447 For Goodyear and Turner as officers in these companies in late 1648: TNA, SP 28/125, fos. 28, 148.

448 Ibid, E 121/2/11/24A, unnumbered. For Goodyear and Hurlston, see ibid, SP 28/125, fo. 148.

449 Leving was an ensign in late 1648 and 2/50 and captain in 7/59: ibid, SP 28/133/4, fos. 30-77.

450 He was lieutenant when Tynemouth Castle was betrayed but remained loyal.: Perfect Occurences, issue 142, 9/49. He may then have been raised to captain lieutenant as his reward: BL, Thomason Tracts E 450 (22).

451 For Mayer and Strange, see TNA, SP 28/133/1, fos. 55-6.

452 Ibid, E 121/4/8/12, entry 257. For Turner and Stringer, see ibid, SP 28/125, fo. 28.

453 Ibid, E 121/5/1/13A, entry 4.

454 Ibid, SP 28/124, fo. 270.

455 Ibid, SP 28/125, fo. 18

456 Ibid, SP 28/133/1, fos. 59-60; ibid, SP 28/133/2, fo. 11.

457 For Davies and Walton, see ibid, SP 28/125, fo. 226.

458 Ibid, SP 28/124, fo. 268.

459 Ibid, SP 28/125, fo. 11. His lieutenant was William Bramston.

460 Ibid, E 121/3/2/106, entry 2.

461 See ibid, SP 28/125, fo. 17 for Lieutenant Boone and Ensign James.

462 Ibid, SP 28/125, fo. 347.

463 Ibid, SP 28/125, fo. 26 for Mason.

464 Ibid, SP 28/133/1, fos. 59-60.

465 Ibid, SP 28/125, fo. 18 for Nicholls and Gardner.

466 For Rosse and Simpson, see ibid, SP 28/125, fo.104.

467 Ibid, E 121/5/6/60, entry 52.

468 Ibid, SP 28/133/4, fos. 59-60.

469 See Worc. College, Clarke Ms 67, fo. 7 for Cartwright and Indigo and TNA, SP 28/125, fo. 30, 35 for Indigo and Dike. Dike was almost certainly in Hart's or Topping's company: ibid, SP 28/133/2, fo. 11; ibid,SP 28/133/4, fos. 71-80 passim. He was also concerned with constructing additional fortifications at Tynemouth Castle in 1649: ibid, SP 28/57, fo. 861

470 The officers' names in the unplaced section come from a remonstrance of 11/47 from the 8th regiment of foot which includes the names of nine lieutenants and seven ensigns. For this see Thomason Tracts E 471 (15).

9th Regiment[471]		
Thomas Pride	William Galhampton[472]	Nicholas Certen/Crispe[473]
William Goffe Waldine Lagoe	XXX Nathaniel Bateman[474]	Nathaniel Bateman[475] XXX
George Gregson John Mason	**John Clarke**	**John Pimm**[476]
John Ferguson Richard Mosse	Thomas Pride	Ralph Prentice
Thomas Parsons		**William Hume**[477]

9th Regiment[471]		
John Hawes	John Ward	John Pearson William Newnham
Roger Alsop	John Dirdo[478] **John Dixon**	William Goodwin **John Dixon**[479]
Joseph Salkeld	Nicholas Mitchell	George Barnett/Burnett[480]
John Pearson	Nicholas Andrews	Edward Kates
Richard Kemp		
Unplaced	Thomas Mason[481]	

471 The names of Captain Lieutenant Galhampton; Lieutenants Andrews, Mitchell, Dirdo, Pride and Ward; and Ensigns Certen, Bateman, Kates, Burnett, Newnham, Goodwin and Pearson appear in the commissions' book: Worc. College, Clarke Ms 67, fo. 12.

472 Galhampton was commissioned in 8/47 and may have served in the regiment until 1660 when he was a captain, but he could have left at any time in between and returned later.

473 Chequers Ms 782, fo. 12.

474 TNA, E 121/3/1/unnumbered, entries 12-13. Bateman's promotion took place on 5/11/48: Worc. College, Clarke Ms 67, fo.12.

475 TNA, E 121/3/1/unnumbered, entries 12-13.

476 For Clarke and Pimm, see ibid, E 121/4/8/40B, entries 235, 263.

477 Hume was sergeant and ensign to Captain Parsons: ibid, E 121/3/3/88, entry 7.

478 Ibid, E 121/3/1/unnumbered, entries 1-2.

479 Dixon was sergeant, ensign and possibly lieutenant in Alsop's company: Ibid, E 121/5/6/unnumbered, entries 195-6.

480 Ibid, E 121/3/4/61B, entry 60.

481 A garbled entry in the commissions' book gives Mason as lieutenant colonel.

10th Regiment[482]	Name	
John Lambert Sir William Constable	Samuel Ross William Eure??[483]	
Mark Grime		Robert Baldwin[484]
Wroth Rogers	John Thomas	Richard Oliver[485]
John Biscoe John Nicholas	John Nicholas John Madder[486]	Richard Phillips
Lawrence Nunney	John/James Clarke[487]	Richard Cleaver[488] John Jones/**John Johns**
Thomas Disney	William Meredith[489]	**Jeremiah Hand**[490]
Giles Saunders		
William Style	XXX **John Hedworth**[491]	**John Hedworth** Richard Oliver
Matthew Cadwell		Rice Thomas[492]
Francis Blethin Roger Lewis	Roger Lewis Thomas Lewis[493]	William James[494]
Unplaced	Henry Hedworth	Thomas Bannister

482 The names of Lieutenants Thomas, Clarke and Hedworth, and Ensigns Phillips, Cleaver, Johns and Bannister appear in the commissions' book: Worc. College, Clarke Ms 67, fo. 7.

483 TNA, E 121/2/11/17B, entry 119. The identification with the 10th regiment is shown as unlikely as a William Ewer had a well-documented career in the 4th regiment of foot.

484 Worc. College, Clarke Ms 17, fo. 83.

485 TNA, E 121/5/7/21, entry 331; Worc. College, Clarke Ms 17, fo. 83.

486 TNA, E 121/5/7/52, entry 81. Madder was commissioned as lieutenant to Nicholas in 12/47 on the same day as Nicholas was commissioned as captain: Worc. College, Clarke Ms 67, fo. 7.

487 For Clarke and Johns see TNA, E 121/5/7/21, entries 99-100. Both signed the regiment's petition of 10/48: Worc. College, Clarke Ms 17, fo. 83.

488 Ibid, Clarke Ms 69, fo. 83.

489 Meredith was discharged from Wallingford garrison in late 7/49 for sympathising with the Burford mutiny: Perfect Occurences, issue 135, 27/7-3/8/49.

490 Hand was sergeant in the company before becoming ensign: TNA, E 121/3/5/25, fos. 79-80.

491 Worc. College, Clarke Ms 17, fo. 83. For Hedworth and Oliver see ibid, E 121/5/7/21, entries 191, 195.

492 Ibid, E 121/5/7/21, entry 48; Worc. College, Clarke Ms 18, fo. 83.

493 For the two officers named Lewis see TNA, E 121/5/7/21, entry 127. Thomas Lewis had been ensign in the 12th regiment of foot: ibid, E 121/5/7/21, entry 262. Both were in the 10th regiment of foot in 11/48: Worc. College, Clarke Ms 17, fo. 83.

494 TNA, E 121/5/7/21, entry 264. He had been sergeant to Captain Price in the 10th regiment of foot.

11th Regiment[495]		
Robert Overton George Fenwick[496]	XXX Kingston??[497] William Collingwood[498] Matthew Fann/Fenn	**William Jackson**[499] George Parker
Thomas Read	Richard Clifton[500]	Humphrey Hughes **Samuel Martin**[501]
John Wade	Randle Warner	Richard Bourne[502]
John Spooner XXX Andrews	William Jones John Morris	Abraham Spooner[503] Thomas Cassinghurst[504]
Edward Orpin	John Thorpe	Francis Farmer[505] John Barnes
Robert Anderson	**John Patten**[506]	
Robert Read		John Thorpe Humphrey Hughes Edward Evans[507]
William Knowles	**Andrew Edwards**[508]	Thomas Russell Thomas Ellis
William Gough	Thomas Hunt	**John Miller**[509]
Thomas Hughes	John Timberlake	Richard Burrell[510]
Unplaced	Anthony Belcham	John Wheeler
	Henry Collingwood	Joseph Nicholls

495 The following commissions in the regiment are recorded in the commissions' book: Lieutenant Morris, Thorpe, Hunt and Timberlake, and Ensigns Parker, Barnes, Thorpe, Hughes, Russell, Ellis, and Burrell: Worc. College, Clarke Ms 67, fo. 11.

496 Fenwick's regiment, quartered in the far north of England, nevertheless made its solidarity with the other regiments known via a petition dated 11/48. The signatories included Lieutenants Fenn, Clifton, Thorpe, Hunt, Belcham and Henry Collingwood and Ensigns Jackson, Martin, Bourne, Russell, Wheeler and Nicholls: ibid, Clarke Ms 16, fo. 9.

497 A Captain Lieutenant Kingston was associated with Lieutenant Colonel Read in an entry in Fairfax's order book dated 1/5/1649: ibid, Clarke Ms 69, unfol.

498 Collingwood held that position in the regiment in 9/48: TNA, SP 28/133/3, fo. 36.

499 For Fann and Jackson, see ibid, E 121/5/7/unnumbered, entries 113, 115.

500 Ibid, E 121/5/5/5, entry 14.

501 Ibid, E 121/5/7/18, entry 121.

502 For Warner and Bourne, see ibid, E 121/5/7/unnumbered, entry 84.

503 Ibid, E 121/5/7/18, entry 212.

504 For Andrews and his officers, see ibid, E 121/5/7/18, entries 42, 73. 75. Cassinghurst had apparently been demoted from lieutenant to ensign. For this see note 109 above.

505 For Farmer and Thorpe, see ibid, E 121/5/7/18, entries 1-2. Farmer had been ensign in Captain Wingfield's company in Holbourne's regiment in Essex's army from 3/11/42 to 4/45: ibid, E 315/5, fo. 26.

506 Ibid, E 121/5/7/unnumbered, entry 33.

507 Ibid, E 121/5/6/60, entry 42.

508 Ibid, E 121/5/7/unnumbered, entry 3.

509 Ibid, E 121/5/7/18, entry 117.

510 Ibid, E 121/5/7/18, entry 177.

12th Regiment[511]		
John Hewson	William Arnop *XXX Ramsey*	Henry Williams[512]
John Jubbs *George Smith*	Martin Jubbs[513]	Joseph Growna[505] *XXX Fletcher*
Daniel Axtell	John Webb	Edward Hoare *XXX Walker*
John Carter	Jenkin Bevan	*XXX Hurlett*
Thomas Price *George Jenkins*	George Jenkins	**Thomas Lewis**[506] *XXX Jones*
John Toppendene *Ralph Gayle*	William Hill[507] *Edward Garne*	Edward Garne[508] *William Rosse*
Samuel Grime	Thomas Baker *Edward Hoare*[518]	John Davies[519]
Alexander Brayfield	George Smith[520]	Thomas Newnham[512] *XXX Cooke*
Henry Davies *Samuel Axtell*	Ralph Gayle[513] *Thomas Rawlins*	
Thomas Atkinson	Samuel Axtell[514] *Edward Granway*	*XXX Wood*
Unplaced	Robert Mullins[524]	Morgan Porter Thomas Rawlins Daniel Hincksman

511 The officers' names in italics were listed for Ireland in the spring of 1649: Worc. College, Clarke Ms 67, fo. 44.

512 Williams left between 12/47 and 4/49: TNA, SP 28/59, fo. 256.

513 BL, Thomason Tracts E 413 (6). See note 112 above for Jubbs's company. He may have left the regiment at the same time as the lieutenant colonel for the same reason. However, he may have been promoted to captain in the summer of 1649. For this and his subsequent career in Ireland, see volume two.

514 TNA, E 121/4/7/50, entry14.

515 Ibid, E 121/5/7/21, entry 262.

516 Ibid, E 121/4/7/50, entry 85; BL, Thomason Tracts, E 413 (6).

517 TNA, E 121/4/7/50, entry 80.

518 Hoare had been ensign in Major Axtell's company in 3/47: ibid, E 121/4/7/50, entry 46; BL, Thomason Tracts E 390 (26).

519 TNA, E 121/4/1/38, entry 73; BL, Thomason Tracts E 390 (26); ibid, Thomason Tracts E 413 (6). Davies was formerly sergeant in Captain Toppendene's company: ibid, E 121/4/7/50, entry 86.

520 Ibid, E 121/2/1/18, entry 11.

521 BL, Thomason Tracts E 413 (6); Spring i, p. 87.

522 TNA, E 121/4/7/50, entry 24.

523 Ibid, E 121/2/1/18, entry 15.

524 The unplaced officers' names appear in a declarartion signed in 11/47: BL, Thomason Tracts E 413 (6).

Dragoons[iii]

Troop Commander	Lieutenant	Cornet	Quartermaster
John Okey	*XXX Baldwin*[525] Richard Nicholetts	*James Pope*[526] John Sharpe[527]	Henry Crosse
Daniel Abbott	*Henry Crewkerne*[528]	*Thomas Joyner*	*John Parker*
Tobias Bridge	John Barrow[529]	Samuel Adey	
Christopher Mercer	John Rosse Thomas Okey?	Andrew Casse	
William Neale	*Charles Thompson*[530] William Cheese		
Francis Barrington	*William Hixt*[531]	*Stephen Elmes* **Stephen Clement**[532]	
Francis Bolton	*Charles Cary*[533]	*Robert Young*[535] William Dives[535]	
Henry Fulcher	*John Scrooby*	*John Gibbs*	
Francis Freeman	Joseph Gilmore Peter Evans[536]	*Richard Colton*[537]	XXX Gilmore[538]
John Garland John Daborne	*John Daborne*	**William Tinge**[539] Robert Line[540] Richard Pierce	
Unplaced		XXX Okey[541]	John Maynestree

525 Baldwin was soon succeeded by Nicholetts who commanded Okey's troop at the battle of St. Fagans in 5/48. Nicholetts took service in Ireland in Henry Cromwell's regiment and was killed in 9/51: F. and D.

526 TNA, E 121/1/1/26B, entry 247.

527 Worc. College, Clarke Ms 67, fo. 26. Sharpe and Crosse were commissioned in 1649.

528 Crewkerne was in post in 5/49: TNA, SP 28/60, fo. 681.

529 The officers in Captains Bridges, Mercer and Garlands' troops in 12/47 are given in Rushworth, *Historical Collections* vii, p. 931. Barrow and Adey applied for arrears in 1650: TNA, E 121/1/1/26B, entry 37-8.

530 Ibid, E 121/1/1/26B, entry 120; ibid, SP 28/48, fo. 117 (11/47).

531 Ibid, SP 28/48, fo.12; ibid, SP 28/47, fo. 154; ibid, E 121/1/1/26B, entry 209.

532 Ibid, E 121/1/1/26B, entry 127.

533 Cary and Young were commissioned in 6/47 or very soon afterwards. They were both in post in 11/47: BL, Thomason Tracts, E 413 (6).

534 TNA, E 121/5/7/9, entry 13.

535 Dives was in post in 4/49: ibid, SP 28/59, fo. 346.

536 Ibid, E 121/1/1/26B, entry 125.

537 Ibid, E 121/1/1/26B, entry 210.

538 BL, Thomason Tracts, E 615 (7).

539 TNA, E 121/3/4/61B, entry 37.

540 Ibid, E 121/4/1/16, unnumbered. Line was cornet by 11/47: Rushworth, *Historical Collections* vii, p. 931.

541 Okey was at the battle of St. Fagans in 5/48: BL, Thomason Tracts, E 441 (36).

Cavalry

1st Regiment[542] Troop Commander	Lieutenant	Cornet	Quartermaster
Thomas Fairfax	John Gladman	Peter Wallis[543]	
John Disbrow William Covell	William Covell Cox Tooke	Cox Tooke[544] Elias Whalley[545]	

iii The numbers of troops of dragoons in the New Model Army oscillated so markedly in the period 1649 to 1651 as did their regimental identity. I have therefore not recorded changes amongst the junior officers which took place after Oliver Cromwell's expeditionary force left for Ireland in 8/49. Officers whose names are in italics were almost certainly commissioned in 6/47 or very soon afterwards to replace the twelve or so who left or were expelled during the first Army coup: Worc. College, Clarke Ms 67, fo. 26.

1st Regiment[542] Troop Commander	Lieutenant	Cornet	Quartermaster
John Browne	Thomas Emerson[546]	William Barrington[547] William Malin[548]	
Adam Lawrence Richard Merest	Richard Merest	**James Thompson**[549]	**William Sharpe**
William Packer	Samuel Packer?[550]		
William Disher	William Malin	William Newman **Roland Gittins**[551]	William Newman[552] John Stockdell
Unplaced		Anthony Spinage[553]	

542 The commissions of Lieutenant William Malin, Cornets John Newman and Elias Whalley, and Quartermaster John Stockdell are recorded in the commissions' book: Worc. College, Clarke Ms 67, fo. 15.

543 Wallis was in post on 28/11/47: TNA, SP 28/48, fo. 420.

544 Ibid, E 121/5/7/14, entry 313.

545 Worc. College, Clarke Ms 69, unfol. 24/4/50.

546 Emerson distinguished himself at the battle of Dunbar in 9/50 and was appointed captain of a troop of horse in Hacker's regiment: F. and D.

547 TNA, E 121/5/7/unnumbered, entry 599; BL, Thomason Tracts E 390 (3). Barrington and Malin appear to have been serving as cornets in Browne's troop at the same time in the spring of 1647 if Malin's claims for arrears were correctly written down. My hunch is that Malin, who signs none of the petitions and declarations of that time, was brought in from another troop to serve as lieutenant to captain Disher in 6/47 or soon afterwards.

548 TNA, E 121/5/7/14, entry 229.

549 For Thompson and Sharpe, see ibid, E 121/5/7/unnumbered, entries 733, 751.

550 A cavalry officer named Packer was commissioned as lieutenant in mid-January 1650: Worc. College, Clarke Ms 69, unfol.

551 TNA, E 121/2/3/31B, entry 21.

552 Ibid, E 121/5/7/unnumbered, entry 270.

553 Spinage was cornet in 6/49: H. Reese, *The Army in Cromwellian England* (Oxford, 2012), p. 146.

2nd Regiment[554]			
Thomas Horton	William Forster	XXX Thomas Bull	Thomas Bull[555] Edward Lydiard[556]
Walter Bethell	John Godfrey[557]		
Samuel Gardiner	Clement Arnold[558] Robert Evans[559]	**Samuel Gardiner jun.**[560]	**Thomas Gibson**[561]
Thomas Pennyfather	**William Millward**[562] XXX Humphrey	John Pynner	Humphrey Wray[563]
Benjamin Burgess	Thomas Ellis[564]	Richard Essex[565]	**William Cartledge**[566]
Joseph Mullineaux	Elias Green	Robert Collingwood Thomas Aske[567]	Robert Clemerson Robert Clarke[568]

554 The names of Lieutenant Green, Cornets Collingwood and Pynner and Quartermaster Clemerson appear in the commissions' book: Worc. College, Clarke Ms 67, fo. 22.

555 Bull claimed to have served in Colonel Horton's troop as corporal, quartermaster and cornet: TNA, E 121/5/5/22, entry 58.

556 Lydiard was corporal and then quartermaster in Horton's own troop: ibid, E 121/3/3/92, entry 9.

557 Godfrey fought at the battle of St. Fagans in 5/48 as a lieutenant: Phillips, *Wales and the Marches* ii, p. 366.

558 TNA, E 121/1/6/27B, entry 7. Arnold appears to have moved from the colonel's troop to Gardiner's. For this see p. 122 above. He was an officer in 4/47 but did not give his rank: BL, Thomason Tracts E385 (19).

559 TNA, E 121/4/9/63, entry 8, in which Evans claimed to have been in Harrison's regiment. His second claim, however, was for service in Horton's regiment: ibid, E 121/5/6/unnumbered, entry 82.

560 Ibid, E 121/5/7/44B, entry 45.

561 Ibid, E 121/4/1/59, entry 117.

562 Ibid, E 121/5/5/15, entry 1.

563 Ibid, E 121/2/3/unnumbered, entry 27.

564 Ibid, SP 28/56, fo. 209.

565 Essex claimed to have been cornet in Horton's regiment and so presumably continued to hold that rank after 6/47. By 1650 he was a captain in the regiment: ibid, SP 28/69, fo. 438.

566 Ibid, E 121/5/1/2A, unnumbered. Cartledge had been corporal to Captain Foley: WO 55/1647, unfol. (10/09/45).

567 Ibid, E 121/1/6/30, entry 108.

568 Ibid, E 121/4/8/13, entry 15.

3rd Regiment[569]			
Thomas Harrison	John Spencer[570] Joseph Deane[571]	John Spencer[572] Joseph Strange[573]	Joseph Strange XXX
William Rainborough John Barker[574]	Joseph Deane[575] John Barker William Gough[576]	Joseph Deane Wentworth/Winter Day William Gough Thomas Knowles	Thomas Savage William Young[577] Thomas Knowles John Lediard
Stephen Winthrop	Thomas Partridge[578] Andrew Ashton (capt.) **Edmund Tapp**[579]	Henry Dethick[580]	Middleton Rogers[581] Benjamin Oakshott
Henry Cromwell William Boteler[582]	John Norcroft[583] Thomas Kenning	Henry Glover[584] John Key	Boteler Nock
John Peck	John Dawes[585]	John Monckton	XXX West John Neast[586]
Arthur Evelyn Charles Whitehead	XXX Kennett	**XXX Savage**[587]	Edward Starre[588]
Unplaced	Robert Evans??[589] Nicholas Wallis??[590]	Nicholas Wallis??	

569 The following names appear in the commissions' book: Captain Lieutenant Spencer; Lieutenants Partridge, Kenning, Ashton and Kennett; Cornets Strange, Day, Dethick, Glover, Monckton and Kennett; and Quartermasters Young, Rogers, Oakshott, Neast, West, Savage and Starre: Worc. College, Clarke Ms 67, fo.25.

570 Spencer was in post in 6/47: TNA, SP 28/46, fo. 240.

571 ibid, SP 28/57, fos. 507-11.

572 Ibid, E 121/3/4/unnumbered, entries 29-30.

573 Ibid, E 121/3/4/unnumbered, entries 33-4.

574 Ibid, E 121/3/4/unnumbered, entries 1-4 give the names of Lieutenant later Captain Barker; Cornet later Lieutenant Gough; Quartermaster later Cornet Knowles; and Quartermaster Lediard. None of these names occur in the commissions' book. It can be inferred that Barker was Rainborough's lieutenant as there is no other place for him in the regiment.

575 Ibid, E 121/4/1/10, entry 16.

576 Gough was lieutenant in 5/49: ibid, SP 28/60, fo. 690.

577 Lieutenants Partridge and Dawes, Cornet Glover and Quartermaster Young were officers in the regiment in 4/48: ibid, SP 28/53, fo. 332. Young was not in the regiment when the pay arrears were submitted: ibid, E 121/3/4/unnumbered, entry 101.

578 Ibid, E 121/5/7/44A, entry 42.

579 Ibid, E 121/4/5/64B, entry 1. He had been serving in the Lifeguard in 1/48: Perfect Occurences, issue 61 11-18/3/48.

580 Ibid, E 121/4/1/34, entry 31.

581 A man of this name had been quartermaster in Captain Abercromby's troop in the earl of Essex's regiment of horse and was apparently dismissed in 4/45: ibid, SP 28/29, fo. 419.

582 Butler and his three junior officers were commissioned on 26/5/49: Worc. College, Clarke Ms 67, fo. 25.

583 TNA, SP 28/56, fo. 594. Cromwell's lieutenant was killed in Lambert's brigade in 7/48 during the Scottish invasion: HMC, Portland Mss i, p. 488. However, it was probably not Norcroft who seems to have left the regiment in 12/47: TNA, SP 28/58, fo. 594.

584 Ibid, SP 28/53, fo. 332.

585 Ibid.

586 Ibid, E 121/4/1/unnumbered, entry 97.

587 Kennett and Starre received their commissions in 6/47 or very soon after: Worc. College, Clarke Ms 67, fo. 25. There is no mention of Savage becoming cornet, but this may have been an omission on the clerk's part.

588 Ibid, E 121/3/4/71, entry 8.

589 See p. 139 above.

590 Spring alleges that Wallis was cornet and then lieutenant in Evelyn's troop in Colonel Harrison's regiment in the New Model Army: Spring i, p. 54. I have found no evidence of this.

4th Regiment[591]			
Charles Fleetwood	Joseph Blissett Thomas Else	Thomas Williams[592]	Thomas Charlton[593]
William Coleman Joseph Blissett	XXX Thomas Else Richard Ashby[594]	**Thomas Essex**[595] Richard Ashby[596] William Darby	John Chapman[597] William Darby
Richard Zanchey	John Buckenham[598]	George Tracey[599] Nathaniel Charlton[600]	XXX Thomas Cheyney
Gilman Taylor	William Buck[601] Richard Webb[602]	William Buck George Craven?[603]	George Craven XXX Tiller
Griffith Lloyd	Robert Stannard Thomas Bayly[604]	Nathaniel Charlton	Thomas Beasley[605]
Stephen White		**Phillip Sisme**[606] **Nathaniel Phillips**[607]	**William Marshall**[608]
Unplaced		William Williams[609]	XXX Hellier

591 Captain Lieutenant Else; Lieutenants Else, Buckenham, Buck, Stannard, Ashby and Bayly; Cornets Ashby, Darby, and Charlton; and Quartermasters Chapman, Darby, Cheyney, Tiller, Beasley and Hellier are named in the commissions' book: Worc. College, Clarke Ms 67, fo.19.

592 TNA, E 121/3/4/9B, entry 62.

593 Ibid, E 121/5/1/2A, unnumbered;..

594 Ashby's commission was issued in 10/49. It is therefore highly likely that he was in fact Cornet Richard Ashby promoted as a result of Else becoming captain lieutenant. The latter's commission was also dated 10/49 as was William Darby's: Worc. College, Clarke Ms 67, fo. 19.

595 TNA, E 121/3/4/9A, unnumbered.

596 Ashby had been clerk to the troop: ibid, SP28/33, fol. 57; ibid, SP 28/44, fo. 432. He was commissioned as cornet in 3/49: Worc. College, Clarke Ms 67, fo. 19.

597 TNA, E 121/5/7/unnumbered, unnumbered. He was wounded at Colchester: ibid, SP 28/57, fo. 402.

598 Worc. College, Clarke Ms 69, unfol.

599 Tracey served as an officer in Ireland during the 1650s: TNA, SP 28/68, fos. 394, 488.

600 Charlton's commission and Cheyney's were dated 7/49: Worc. College, Clarke Ms 67, fo. 19.

601 TNA, SP 28/61, fo. 59. Buck had also been quartermaster and cornet in the troop; ibid, E 121/5/7/unnumbered, unnumbered.

602 Webb was lieutenant in 11/48: ibid, SP 28/56, fo. 290.

603 Ibid, SP 28/46, fo. 195; ibid, SP 28/58, fo. 606; ibid, E 121/5/7/unnumbered, unnumbered. Buck and Tiller were commissioned as lieutenant and quartermaster seemingly in the summer of 1647. Craven must have been quartermaster prior to that, and so is likely to have been the missing cornet, but his promotion is not recorded in the commissions' book: Worc. College, Clarke Ms 67, fo. 19. Buck and Craven were supposedly cornet and quartermaster in the engagement at Willoughby Field in 7/48, but it seems more likely that they were lieutenant and cornet: TNA, SP 28/58, fo. 606. He was still cornet in 11/48: BL, Thomason Tracts E 468 (32).

604 Bayly's commission was dated 25/4/50: Worc. College, Clarke Ms 69, unfol.

605 Beasley died before 9/47: TNA, SP 28/59, fo. 41.

606 Ibid, E 121/5/7/unnumbered, unnumbered.

607 Ibid, E 121/3/4/9B, entry 34.

608 Ibid, E 121/5/7/unnumbered, unnumbered.

609 BL, Thomason Tracts, E 468 (32).

5th Regiment[610]			
Phillip Twistleton	Richard Franklin[611]	Richard Over??[612]	Thomas Ward[613]
James Berry	John Vernon[614] Charles Norwood	William Morris[615]	
John Nelthorpe	John Sherman[616]	William Ascott[617]	Richard Ransom[618] Percival Robinson[619]
Original Peart	John Gardiner[620]	Robert Marsh	John Hoult
Hezekiah Haynes	Thomas Izod[621]	Gabriel Bellerby	John Chapman
Owen Cambridge	Thomas Deane[622] Edward Tapp	Thomas Munns[623]	Joseph Stroud[624]

5th Regiment[610]			
Unplaced XXX Taylor			Thomas Spencer Robert Sheilds[625]

610 The commissions' book only contains the names of the following officers: Captain Lieutenant Franklin, Lieutenants Tapp and Vernon, and Quartermaster Spencer.

611 TNA, E 121/3/3/113B, entry 415.

612 This man claimed to have served as a lieutenant in Rossiter's regiment of Lincolnshire horse: ibid 121/3/3/113B, entry 424. I doubt if he served in the New Model Army as Rossiter was commanding Lincolnshire horse in 1644 and in 1648. The latter seems the more likely as Manchester's army is not mentioned. If that was the case, Over had belonged to the scratch collection of local horse which the colonel used to defeat the East Midlands' royalists in an engagement at Willoughby in 7/48: F. and D.

613 Cornet Bellerby and Quartermasters Ward, Hould, Ransom and Stroud are associated with their respective troops in a document dating from late 6/47: TNA, SP 28/47, fos. 225-32.

614 Both names are given as receiving pay for Berry's troop in ibid, SP 28/47, fos. 412-13.

615 This man had served as a trooper in Edward Rossiter's troop in Lord Willoughby of Parham's regiment and then as quartermaster and cornet to Rossiter's troop in Manchester's army. He was subsequently cornet to Major Berry: ibid, E 121/3/3/93, entries 2-4; ibid, E 121/3/3/113B, entries 194-5.

616 Ibid, E 121/3/3/113A, entry 414. Sherman was in post in 11/47 and also in 12/51: ibid, SP 28/48, fo. 189; ibid, E 121/5/7/45, unnumbered docquet claiming arrears.

617 Ibid, E 121/5/7/113B, entry 371.

618 Ibid, E 121/3/3/113B, entry 371.

619 Ibid, E 121/4/2/73, entry 9.

620 For Peart's junior officers, see ibid, E 121/5/7/unnumbered, entries 55-7. Spring claims they also served under him in Manchester's army. Gardiner was certainly in post in 11/47: ibid, SP 28/48, fo. 188.

621 For Izod, Bellerby and Chapman holding these ranks in Haynes's troop, see ibid, E 121/5/7/unnumbered, entries 264-6. Izod and Sherman were officer agitators in the autumn of 1647: Clarke Papers i, pp. 438-9.

622 For Deane and Munns holding these commissions in Captain Cambridge's troop, see TNA, E 121/ 5/7/unnumbered, entries 203-4.

623 Ibid, SP 28/49, fo. 312

624 Ibid.

625 Ibid, E 121/3/3/113, entry 90. By 1/53 Sheilds was lieutenant to Captain Daniel Lisle's troop in Fleetwood's regiment in Ireland: ibid, SP 28/90, fo. 322.

6th Regiment[626]			
Oliver Cromwell John Disbrowe	Joseph Wallington * XXX	*John Fox** Charles Phelps[627]	Charles Phelps Richard Winsmore
Robert Huntington *John Blackmore*	Nathaniel Whight[628]		
John Jenkins	*John Hardman ** William Cobbe	*William Cobbe **[629] Samuel Bridgen	William Tatton *
John Reynolds *Edward Scotton*	Edward Scotton *Richard Southwood**	Richard Southwood *Thomas Savage**	Thomas Savage[630] Moses Scotton
Henry Middleton George Ensor	George Ensor[631] *James Goodwin **[632]	Edward Matthews[633]	
John Blackwell	Thomas Shears[634]		
Unplaced	*John Byfield**	*Theophilus Barnard**	Thomas Bernard[635]
		William Stafford *	*Henry Huntington **[636]
		Thomas Barker *	*Henry Hall**
		Samuel Whiting[637]	*Samuel Whiting**
			*Edward Warren**
			*Francis Browne**

*	indicates the junior officers who signed a pledge of loyalty to their general in mid-May 1649. [iv] Their ranks are given in the printed document but not the troops in which they were serving.

	The names in italics are the officers in the regiment who signed a letter to Oliver Cromwell in 11/48. It is impossible to tell their ranks from the position of their names on the page.[v]

626 The following junior officers' names appear in the commissions' book: Lieutenant William Cobbe, Cornets Samuel Bridgen and Charles Phelps, and Quartermasters William Tatton, Charles Phelps, Richard Winsmore and Moses Scotten: Worc. College, Clarke Ms 67, fo. 16.

627 Phelps's and Winsome's commissions in Disbrow's troop were issued on 9/3/50: ibid, Clarke Ms. 69, unfol. Phelps was not in the regiment in 5/49 but Winsome was a corporal: BL, Thomason Tracts, E 557 (10).

628 TNA, SP 28/47, fo. 466.

629 Cobbe was lieutenant by August 1647: ibid, SP 28/47, fo. 287.

630 Savage was still a quartermaster in 7/47: ibid, SP28/47, fo. 465.

631 Ibid, E 121/4/5/93A, entry 1; ibid, SP 28/44, fo. 408.

632 Goodwin's commission is dated 12/49: Worc. College, Clarke Ms. 16, unfol.

633 Matthews was in post in 6/47: TNA, SP 28/46, fo. 245.

634 Sheares took charge of pay for the 6th regiment of horse in 4/48: ibid, SP 28/54, fo. 404. He appears to have been captured by the Scottish army at Appleby in 7/48: HMC, Portland Mss i, p. 488. I have placed him in Blackwell's troop as it is the only one whose lieutenant's name is not known. He was still a lieutenant in 12/48: ibid, SP 28/57, fo. 433.

635 Worc. College, Clarke Ms, microfilm 16, part 3, unfol.

636 This man had been corporal in Major Huntington's troop in 4/45: ibid, SP 28/29, fo. 55.

637 Whiting was commissioned in 9/49 after Disbrowe had become colonel: ibid, SP 28/62, fo. 464.

7th Regiment[638]			
Nathaniel Rich	William Weare[639] Thomas French	John Ledbrook	Edward Rash[640]
Azariah Husbands	John Clarke[641]	Thomas Ward	Thomas Warren
Thomas Ireton	Edward Lisle[642]		Robert Sprigg[643]
Francis Hawes George Elmore	George Elsmore[644]		Caleb Lea[645]
Henry Barton	Francis Rawson[646]	Christopher Gold	Richard Williams
John Merriman	John Hawkridge[647]	John Braman[648]	John Toomes[649]

638 The commissions' book gives the following names: Captain Lieutenant French; Lieutenants Hawkridge, Clarke and Rawson; cornets Ward, Gold, Braman and Ledbrook; and Quartermasters Warren and Williams: Worc. College, Clarke Ms 67, fo. 21.

639 TNA, E 121/4/5/81, entry 2.

640 An Edward Rush was corporal in Rich's troop in 10/45: ibid, SP 28/32, fo. 398. Rash was killed fighting in Kent in 8/48: Perfect Occurences, issue 85, 11/18/8/48.

641 Clarke was wounded at Deal in 6/48 repelling an invasion force led by the Prince of Wales. He died soon afterwards: ibid, SP 28/49, fo. 122; ibid, SP28/56, fo. 39.

642 Lisle claimed to have served for a while in Captain Boreman's company on the Isle of Wight as ensign and lieutenant: ibid, E 121/2/11/19, entry 344. This was in addition to being lieutenant of Ireton's troop. It is known that a troop of Rich's regiment was part of the force defending the Isle of Wight in 1648 and 1649.

643 Ibid, SP 28/47, fo. 331.

644 Ibid, E 121/2/11/19, unnumbered gives Elsmore as lieutenant and Chapman as cornet. Elsmore was captain of the troop by 11/49: F. and D. However, I have no evidence that Chapman served beyond 3/47.

645 He was quartermaster in 12/47: TNA, SP 28/49, fo. 275

646 Ibid, SP 28/48, fo. 124.

647 Ibid, E 121/4/1/87, entry 5.

648 Ibid, E 121/2/11/64, entry 226/ ibid, SP 28/28/49, fo. 276.

649 Ibid, SP 28/46, fo. 140.

iv	BL, Thomason Tracts E 557 (10).

v	See note 1334 above.

8th Regiment			
Matthew Tomlinson	William Raunce[650]		Thomas Lee
Ralph Knight	XXX **John Ward**[651]	John Ward Thomas Symnell[652]	Thomas Symnell
Ralph Margery			Benjamin Pett[653]
Robert Glyn	**Richard Floyd**[654]	**John Wells**[655]	
Thomas Rawlins			
Thomas Johnson[656]	Paul Bunting[657] Richard White[658]	Richard White Richard Atkins(on)	Richard Atkinson John Smith
Unplaced			XXX Willmot[659]

650 For Raunce and Lee, see ibid, E 121/1/1/unnumbered, entries 357, 360.

651 The officers' names for this troop are given in ibid, E 121/1/6/117, fos. 129-133. For John Ward's service in the army of the Eastern Association where he began as quartermaster of Knight's troop, see ibid, E 121/1/6/117, fo. 326-7.

652 Ibid, E 121/1/6/117, entry 129.

653 Ibid, SP 28/46, fo. 170.

654 Ibid, E 121/2/11/51, entry 62.

655 Ibid, E 121/1/1/unnumbered, entries 57-63

656 The commissions' book entry for 23/9/48 only gives the names of White, Atkinson and Smith: Worc. College, Clarke Ms 67, fo. 24. A misplaced entry appertaining to this troop is to be found under the 4th regiment of horse. It names Cornet White and Quartermaster Atkinson: ibid, Clarke Ms 67, fo. 19.

657 TNA, E 121/1/1/unnumbered, entries 142-5; ibid, SP 28/140/7, fos. 282-3; ibid, SP 28/46, fo. 163.

658 White was killed or died in Scotland before 11/51: CJ vii, p. 38.

659 TNA, E 121/1/6/117, entry 1.

9th Regiment			
Edward Whalley[660]	Daniel Dale *John Wright*	John Wright *Phillip Rumsey*	Phillip Rumsey *James Horne*
Robert Swallow	*Joseph Sabberton*	*Thomas Stewart*	*Thomas Kendall*
William Evanson	Edmund Chillenden *Anthony Lacon*	Anthony Lacon *William Lynley*	William Linley *Cuthbert Reynoldson*
John Grove	*Thomas Chamberlain*	Abel Warren[652] *George Saunders*	George Saunders *Richard Ireland*
Henry Cannon Edmund Chillenden	*John Franks*[662] John Dew	*John Dew* William Russell	*Thomas Thompson* John Dew[663]
John Pitchford John Savage	John Savage Benjamin Bressie *Nathaniel Holt*	William Whittingham Nathaniel Holt *Timothy Thornborough*	Timothy Thornborough *James Watson*

660 The names given in bold are the junior officers in the regiment in April 1649: BL, Thomason Tracts E 555 (31). Those in italics held commands in 2/50: BL, Harleian Ms 427, fo. 52. Cuthbert Reynoldson and Richard Ireland had been senior corporals in the troops in which they were quartermasters in 1650, but Russell appears to have been merely the senior trooper in Evanson's troop. Possibly he had held a commission in another regiment previously. The promotions of John Dew and George Sanders and their successors are dated 6/49 and 5/50 in the commissions' book: Worc. College, Clarke Ms 67, fo. 20.

661 Warren took service in Ireland in c. 6/49: F. and D.

662 A Captain John Franks was serving in a regiment of horse in Ireland in 1651: TNA, SP 28/69, fo. 448.

663 Ibid, SP 28/46, fo. 127.

10th Regiment[664]			
Adrian Scroop	William Peverell[665] Thomas Bayly??[666]		
Nathaniel Barton			
Richard Watson	William Peverell Theophilus Farmer	Theophilus Farmer[667] James Thompson[668]	William Taylor Jacob Antrobus
Thomas Goddard	John Ray[669]	Henry Den[670]	John Emerson[671]

10th Regiment[664]			
Edward Wolfe	XXX Francis Pick[672]	Francis Pick Robert Salmon	George Finch[673]
Skippon's troop: William Peverill	John Lewis	Richard Combes	**John Ayott**[674]
Unplaced		Henry Porter[675]	

664 The following officers were noted in the commissions' book: Lieutenants Farmer and Lewis; Cornets Salmon, Thompson and Combes; and Quartermasters Finch, Emerson, Antrobus and Taylor: Worc. College, Clarke Ms 67, fo. 18.

665 TNA, E 121/3/5/47, unnumbered.

666 Bayly claimed to have been captain in Scroop's regiment but he cannot be easily placed. See p. 126 above.

667 Farmer's claim for pay arrears shows him as cornet and then lieutenant in the regiment: ibid, E 121/2/9/32, unnumbered.

668 Ibid, E 121/3/3/78, entry 73. Cornets Thompson and Den sided with the mutineers in the Leveller revolt that ended in the fracas at Burford in 5/49. Thompson was subsequently executed, Den spared at the last moment. Den may subsequently have become a commissary in the army of occupation in Ireland: ibid, TNA, SP 28/73, fo. 179.

669 Ibid, E 121/3/4/77, entries 8-9. His claim for pay arrears suggests that Ray went direct from quartermaster to lieutenant, though in the intervening period he could have been serving as cornet in another regiment.

670 Ibid, E 121/3/3/33, entries 3-7; F. and D.

671 Ibid, SP 28/48, fo. 130.

672 Ibid, SP 28/61, fo. 38; ibid, E 121/5/5/15, entry 5. Pick was lieutenant of the troop in 4/48: ibid, SP 28/53, fo. 418.

673 Ibid, E 121/3/3/81B, entry 7.

674 Ibid, E 121/2/9/34, entry 38.

675 Porter is mentioned in 4/48: ibid, SP 28/54, fo. 246.

11th Regiment[676]			
Henry Ireton	James Wilson[678] *Robert Browne*	Robert Browne *Jonathan Cokayne*[678]	Robert Browne *Richard Parnham*
Robert Gibbon	*Henry Johnson*[679]	*William Raunce/Raine*[680]	Alexander Weller[681]
William Cecil George Hutchinson	Richard/William Hill[682] James Jennings	James Jennings Thomas Shepherd	James Jeffries[683] *Richard Hunt*
Henry Pretty	*Sampson Twogood*	*William Lucas*	Henry Ward[684]
Anthony Morgan	Benjamin Gifford[685]	Anthony Nixon[686]	Thomas Wolsall[687] *XXX Walford*
Robert Kirkby	Jervaise Jeffrys[688]	*William Bush*	James Cockayne William Wallington/ Wilkinson[689]
Unplaced		Henry Clare jun.[690]	

676 The commissions' book records the following officers in the regiment: Lieutenants Twogood, Jennings and Jeffreys; Cornets Browne, Shepherd and Nixon; and Quartermasters Parnham and Cockayne: Worc. College, Clarke Ms 67, fo. 17. The officers whose names are in italics were in post at the time of the Leveller mutiny in 5/49: Worc. College, Clarke Ms 16, fos. 103-13; TNA, SP 28/61, fo. 382.

677 Wilson may not have directly succeeded Kirkby but he was certainly captain lieutenant in 11/47: ibid, SP 28/48, fo. 423. He was killed at the battle of Maidstone in 6/48: ibid, SP 28/56, fo. 355.

678 This man or somebody with an identical name was clerk of the 11th regiment of horse in early 1647: ibid, SP 28/46, fo. 179.

679 Ibid, E 121/4/9/23, entry 1.

680 Ibid, E 121/2/11/17A, entries 12-14.

681 Weller held the rank of quartermaster in 11/47: ibid, SP 28/48, fo. 428: ibid, E 121/2/11/17A, entry 11.

682 Ibid, E 121/2/6/42, entry 2. Jennings replaced Hill in 11/47: ibid, SP 28/48, fos. 8, 142.

683 Ibid, SP 28/30, fo. 334.

684 Ibid, E 121/5/7/14, entry 866; ibid, SP 28/59, fo. 265.

685 Gifford signed a warrant on 17/6/47: ibid, SP 28/46, fo. 166.

686 Ibid, E 121/4/5/94A, entry 15; ibid, SP 28/61, fo. 382.

687 Wolsall was quartermaster in 11/47: ibid, SP 28/48, fo. 422.

688 Ibid, E 121/4/6/16A, entry 4.

689 Ibid, E 121/4/6/16C, entry 4; ibid, SP 28/48, fo. 479.

690 Clare was an officer in the regiment in 11/48: BL, Thomason Tracts E 468 (18). He seems to have transferred to another regiment during 1649.

Lifeguard[691]			
Richard Cromwell	John Ingram[692] Andrew Ellis[693]	George Joyce[694] Edmund Tapp[695]	**Robert Herman**[696]

691 Fairfax's lifeguard was disbanded by a House of Commons decree of 19/2/48: F. and D.

692 Ingram was dismissed in 12/47 for Leveller opinions and replaced by Ellis: ibid.

693 Ellis was in post in 2/48: TNA, SP28/134, fo. 134.

694 Perfect Occurences, issue 23, 4/11/6/47.

695 See note 579 above.

696 TNA, E 121/2/6/42, entry 8.

Appendix I

The Earl of Essex's Army in Early April 1645

The principal sources of information have been the names of officers discharged in April 1645 in TNA, SP 28/28 and 29. A petition to Parliament in late December 1644 signed by most of Essex's company commanders in the House of Lords archives has also been of great value.[i] Its complement is the list of troop commanders discovered by Richard Symonds in the detritus left after Essex's army surrendered at Lostwithiel in early September 1644.[ii] As ever Alan Turton's monographs on the history of the Essex's infantry and cavalry from the autumn of 1642 have been of great assistance.

Columns 2, 3 and 4 in the tables below give the names of the commissioned officers known to have been in Essex's army in early April 1645. Officers whose names are bolded were chosen by Fairfax to serve in the New Model, those whose names are not bolded were not. Names in italics indicate officers who were brought into the New Model at a later date. In most cases this was as a result of resignations during April and May 1645 and of deaths during the siege of Taunton.

The fifth column indicates the New Model Army regiments in which officers from Essex's army found a new home.

Infantry

Lord General the Earl of Essex's Regiment

Col.	The Earl of Essex	Thomas Bushell	XXX Davenport Robert Eyre	
Lt. Col.	John Butler	XXX Bowen[1]	XXX Read	
Major	Christopher Matthews	XXX Blethen	XXX Higginson	
Capts.	Sir Anthony St. John	XXX Robinson		
	John Lloyd	XXX Ricroft		
	Arthur Ward			6th regt.
	Fulk Muskett			1st regt
	Isaac Turvey	Stephen Stansley	XXX Empson	
	Warwick Bamfield			6th regt.
	Lawrence Phipps	XXX Webb	XXX Meddows	
	Leicester Burdett	XXX Marbury	XXX Newman	
	John Horsey			7th regt.
	XXX?			

i   Ibid, Main Papers 177, fo.102. A slightly different version is given in the diary of Sir Simon D'Ewes: BL, Harleian Ms 166, fo.174.
ii   Symonds, Diaries of the Marches, p. 73.

1   In this regiment the junior commissioned officers are not assigned to company commanders in the TNA lists. I have placed them in the order in which they occur in ibid, SP 28/29, fo. 28 on the possibly false assumption that the commissioned officers in a company were discharged as a group they were in other regiments.

Major General Phillip Skippon's Regiment

Col.	Phillip Skippon			2nd regt.
Lt. Col.	John Francis			2nd regt.
Major	Richard Ashfield			2nd regt.
Capts.	Edward Streater			2nd regt.
	Maurice Bowen			2nd regt.
	James Harrison			2nd regt.
	John Clarke			2nd regt.
	Samuel Clarke			2nd regt.
	XXX			
	XXX			
Capt. Lt.	XXX			

Richard Ingoldsby's Regiment[iii]

Col.	Richard Ingoldsby	William Duckett[2]		6th regt.
Lt. Col.	Thomas Browne	John/Geo Chapman	Robert Warner	
Major	Robert Farrington			6th regt.
Capts.	Charles Duckett			6th regt.
	Henry Ingoldsby	John Deacon[3]		6th regt.
	Job Gibson			6th regt.
	John Blithe			
	Gabriel Cooke	Thomas Lee	Thomas Fisher	
	XXX			
	XXX			
Unidentified		Samuel Bayly		

2   Ibid, SP 28/28, fo. 107.
3   Deacon was ensign from 2/43 and lieutenant from 10/44. He was killed at the siege of Tiverton in 11/45: ibid, SP 28/59, fos. 218-20.

Richard Fortescue's Regiment

Col.	Richard Fortescue	Thomas Jennins		5th regt.
Lt. Col.	Thomas Bulstrode			5th regt.
Major	Jeffrey Richbell			5th regt.
Capts.	Edward Gittins			5th regt.
	Severus Dursey			5th regt.
	John Fowne			5th regt.
	XXX Curtis			.
	XXX			
	XXX			

iii   For Ingoldsby's company commanders in early 4/45, see TNA, SP 28/43, fos. 196-204.

	XXX			

Lord Robartes' Regiment

Col.	Lord Robartes	*William Hinder*		9th regt.
Lt. Col.	William Hunter	Thomas Hunter		
Major	Alexander Urry	*John Grime*[4]	*Thomas Day*	6th regt.
Capts.	**John Mill**			6th regt.
	John Penn			
	Henry Wansey	John Walters	Nicholas Awle	
	Mark Gryme	Robert Strate	Henry Green	
	John Spooner			11th regt.
	John Melvin	**William Gough**[5]		11th regt.
	XXX			

4   John Grime was commissioned as captain in late 1645. For this, see above p. 67. Day was ensign and then lieutenant: ibid, E 121/3/3/31, entry 9.
5   Ibid, SP 28/29, fo. 297.

Edward Aldridge's Regiment

Col.	**Edward Aldridge**	**Thomas Cooper**		11th regt.
Lt. Col.	**Walter Lloyd**			11th regt.
Major	Jonathan Newcomen	Daniel Worster	Nicholas Moore	
Capts.	**Phillip Gittins**			11th regt.
	James Forrett	Anthony Stamp[6]	William Harris	
	Richard Lundy			11th regt.
	Phillip Cooper	Nicholas James	John Norman	
	William Wilkes			11th regt.
	Thomas Gollidge?			5th regt.
	XXX			

6   Stamp served in the New Model Army, but possibly in the ranks: BL, Thomason Tracts E 397 (7). He was commissioned in William Herbert's regiment for service in Ireland in 1647. For this see p. 153 below.

William Davies's Regiment

Col.	William Davies	*Guy Philpot?*[7]		7th regt.?
Lt.Col.	George McKenzie			
Major	Archibald Waddell	Richard Aylett[8]		
Capts.	**Benjamin Wigfall/ Wingfield**[9]		**Francis Farmer**	11th regt.
	John Withers	Richard Aylett	Richard Jones/James	
	Daniel Carey	Richard Phillips	John Aylett	
	Thomas Read			11th regt.
	John Ferguson			9th regt.
	William Fowlis	Richard Thornhill	William Hall	
	XXX			

7   Philpot was in post in early 1645: Ibid, SP 28/27, fos. 444, 459. He may or may not have joined the New Model Army. For this see p. 68 above.
8   Ibid, SP 28/28, fo. 25.
9   For Wingfield and Farmer, see ibid, E 315/5, fo. 26; ibid, E 315/5, fo. 26.

Henry Barclay's Regiment

Col.	**Henry Barclay**	William Arnold[10]		9th regt.
Lt. Col.	**John Innes**			9th regt.
Major	*Thomas Pride*			9th regt.
Capts.	**William Goffe**			9th regt.
	George Ramsey			9th regt.
	George Gregson			9th regt.
	William Leete			9th regt.
	William Cowell			9th regt.
	George Sampson			9th regt.
	XXX			

10 This man was probably the Captain William Arnold whose company was sent to Ireland in 1649 as a recruit for Colonel Moore's regiment: ibid, E 121/3/4/122, unnumbered.

Dragoons[iv]

Cavalry

Lord General the Earl of Essex's Regiment (Colonel Sir Phillip Stapleton)

Col.	Sir Phillip Stapleton	**Charles Holcroft**		10th regt.
Lt. Col.	**Richard Graves**		**Robert Dawes**[11]	10th regt.
Major	Robert Hamilton	William Blair	John Warhope	
Capts.	**Gabriel Martin**[12]			3rd regt.
	Ex J. Abercromby[13]	John Platt	William Hall	
	Nathaniel Chute			10th regt.
	Nicholas Bragg[14]			10th regt.
	Nathaniel Draper			
	XXX			

11 Ibid, SP 28/28, fo. 68.
12 This was Captain Lionel Copley's troop until early 1645: Turton, *Chief Strength*, p. 26.
13 Abercromby had been killed on 9/3/45: TNA, SP 28/43, fo. 658.
14 This was Major General Skippon's troop of which Bragg was the captain lieutenant: ibid, E 315/5, fo. 7.

James Sheffield's Regiment

Col.	**James Sheffield**	Thomas Jewkes	Richard Mander	3rd regt
Major	John Hayle	**Michael Hale**	**Richard Young**	3rd regt
Capts.	**Thomas Sheffield**[15]			3rd regt.

---

iv   By 1645 Essex had only a single troop of dragoons. This was all that was left of Colonel James Wardlaw's regiment which had fought at Edgehill. Commanded by Jeremiah Abercromby, who also had a troop of cavalry, it was attached to Essex's own regiment of horse: TNA, SP 28/43, fo. 658.

	Edward Fiennes	Reynold Wenceslas	Peter Ashenhurst	
	Robert Robotham			3rd regt.
	Thomas Wogan	Lewis Wogan	Compton Wogan	
Unidentified		Richard Munder	James Phinne	

15   Ibid, SP 28/28, fo. 60.

Sir William Balfour's Regiment

Col.	William Balfour	Hans Steiger	John Rogers	
Major	William Balfour			
Capts.	Sir Samuel Luke		Henry Leigh	
	William Rainborough		James Fenn	3rd regt.
	Brice Semple			
	James Boswell	George Douglas	Josias Clapham	
	Walter Boswell	George Hume	Patrick Crowe	

Sir Robert Pye's Regiment[v]

Col.	**Sir Robert Pye**	**Edward Hamden**		8th regt.
Capts.	Adrian Scrope			10th regt.
	Seymour Pyle		George Combes[16]	
	Francis Ingoldsby?			
	Richard Grenville	John James		
	Thomas Tyrell?			

16   Ibid, SP 28/28, fo. 57.

Francis Behre's Regiment

Col.	Francis Behre			
Major	Samuel Boza			
Capts.	Anthony Buller			
	Christopher Fleming			10th regt.
	Ex John Carmichael[17]			
	Richard Stevens[18]	Edward Stevens	Thomas Allen	

17   Carmichael resigned in 2/45: Turton, *Chief Strength*, p. 24.
18   This troop had been seconded to Waller's army and did not serve in Cornwall: ibid, p. 64.

John Dalbier's Regiment

Col.	John Dalbier	John Hay		
Major	William Salkeld	Newman Humphreys[19]		
Capts.	Charles Pym			
	XXX Lukeman			
	Francis Thompson			

v   This regiment had formed part of Colonel Arthur Goodwin's regiment raised in Buckinghamshire. After Goodwin's death the last three troops were detached and remained in the county under Major General Richard Browne's command. The remainder fought in the Lostwithiel campaign: Turton, *Chief Strength*; Symonds, Marches of the Royal Armies, p. 73.

	William Frampton?			

19   Thomson, *Hertfordshire*, p. 29.

John Harvey's Regiment

Col.	John Harvey			
Major	XXX Manering			
Capts.	XXX Hacket			
	John Blackwell			6th regt.
	XXX Norwood			
	XXX Washburne			

Lifeguard

Capt.Lt.	**Charles Doyley**			10th regt.

Appendix II

Regiments for Service in Ireland in May 1647[i]

Names given in italics indicate officers who were serving in the New Model Army in early 1647 and are known to have resumed service in the New Model Army after June 1647.

Foot

1st Regiment	Name	Military career to date
Colonel Capt. Lt. Ens.	William Herbert William Matthews William Thomas	Col. 11th regt. F. N.M. army| Officer in the N.M. army
Lt. Col. Lt. Ens.	John Melvin Thomas Vaughan Matthew Manderson	Capt. Ditto Officer in the N.M. army
Major Lt. Ens.	Richard Lundy Walter Brough John Racke[1]	Capt. Ditto Lt. to Lundy[2]
Captain Lt. Ens.	Nathaniel Short William Hodkins William Hall	Capt. Ditto Lt. to Capt. Short ditto
Captain Lt. Ens.	Bartholomew Helby Peter Winchester William Easte	Lt. to Lt. Col. Read in ditto Officer in the N.M. army
Captain Lt. Ens.	John Dunklyn Richard Inyon/Onions Thomas Robbins	Lt. to Capt. Spooner in ditto Officer in the N.M. army
Captain Lt. Ens.	Anthony Stampe John Longe Thomas Haskins	Discharged from Aldridge's regt. as lt. in 4/45
Captain Lt. Ens.	Charles Awbry Edward Loe Richard Davies	Ens. to col's co. 11th regt. F. Officer in the N.M. army
Captain Lt. Ens.	Thomas Morgan Adam Pretty Robert Laine	Officer in the N.M. army
Captain Lt. Ens.	Henry Crofts *Blennerhasset Fuller*[3] John Shorte	

1   Captains Stamp and Dunklyn, lieutenants Onions and Rake. and Ensign John Stampe claimed to be due for pay arrears having served in Kempson's regiment: TNA, E 121/3/4/74, unnumbered.

2   Ibid, E121/2/11/67, entry 8.

i   LJ ix, p. 220.

3   He was ensign post 6/47: Worc. College, Clarke Ms 67, fo. 8.

2nd Regiment	Name	Military career
Colonel Capt. Lt. Ens.	James Gray James Knight	Lt. Col. 11th regt. F. to 6/46 N.M. army Capt. Lt. 3rd regt. F.
Lt. Col. Lt. Ens.	*Arthur Young* *Thomas Jones* *Richard Owen*	Capt. 5th regt. F. N.M. army Lt. Young's co. Ens. ditto
Major Lt. Ens.	*Richard Pooley* *William Read* *Richard Hatt*	Capt. ditto Lt. Pooley's co. Ens. ditto but Hart.
Captain Lt. Ens.	*John Denison* *William Bayly* George Forker	Capt. ditto Lt. Denison's co. Ens. ditto.
Captain Lt. Ens.	*John Locke (Cox)* *Nicholas Luke* *Matthew Marvell*	Capt. ditto Lt. Cox's co. Ens. Ditto
Captain Lt. Ens.	John Bushell John Ferror Richard/*Nicholas Cordy*	Capt. ditto Lt. Bushell's co. Ens. Ditto
Captain Lt. Ens.	XXX *Roger Jones* Francis Beauchamp	Lt. to Capt. Whitton's co. 5th regt. F. Ens. in same co.
Captain Lt. Ens.	Stephen Caine[4]	? Capt. 8th regt. F.
Captain Lt. Ens.	Daniel Thomas sen.[5] Walter Kirby Daniel Thomas jun.[6]	Capt. 3rd regt. F.
Captain Lt. Ens.	William Howard John Agey	Capt. 3rd regt. F.

4   For Caine, Kirby and Howard being in this regiment, see CSPD 1625-49, p. 707.

5   The two Thomases and Agey claimed for pay arrears for service in Herbert's regiment: TNA, E 121/6/7/9A, entries 4,6; ibid, E 121/6/7/9B, entry 1.

6   Daniel Thomas junior had served in Daniel Thomas senior's company in the 3rd regiment of foot as a foot soldier and drummer: ibid, E 315/5, fo. 16.

3rd Regiment[7]	Name	Military Career
Colonel Capt. Lt. Ens.	Nicholas Kempson Richard Hannaway Robert Roe	Lt. Col. in 8th regt. F. N.M. army
Lt. Col. Lt. Ens.	Christopher Peckham Robert Dormer John Maclellane	Capt. in ditto Officer in the NMA Corporal Weldon regt. W. Army
Major Lt. Ens.	Francis Dormer Evan Morris Thomas Gilbert	Capt. in ditto Ens. in Henry Lilburne's co. in ditto regt.
Captain Lt. Ens.	George Weldon Robert Gilbert Valentine Blee	Capt. in ditto Ens. in Capt. Lambe's co. in Weldon regt. W. Army

3rd Regiment[7]	Name	Military Career
Captain	Richard Fish	Capt. Lt. in col's co. 8th regt. F.
Lt.	Thomas Noone	Ens. in ditto.
Ens.	Robert Bates	Corporal Weldon regt. W. Army
Captain	George Master	Brother of Major William Master in 8th regt. F.
Lt.	George Hope	Ens. to Major Master
Ens.	Robert Choake	
Captain	Abraham Clarke/Cleare	Lt. to Major Master in ditto.
Lt.	David Holland	
Ens.		
Captain	Francis Wells	Lt. to Capt. Peckham in ditto
Lt.	John Pynce	
Ens.		
Captain	Livesey Sharpless	Ens. to Lt. Col. Kempson in ditto
Lt.	XXX Sydley	
Ens.	William Smith	
Unplaced		
Captain	Alexander Fry[8]	Lt. to Lt. Col. Kempston in ditto

7   Lieutenant Colonel Peckham; Captains Clarke, Wells, Weldon, Sharples and Master; Captain Lieutenant Richard Hannaway; Ensign Robert Roe; and Quarter Master Richard Chamberlain were in the regiment at the time of its disbandment late in 1647. They were quartered in villages in the Vale of Gloucester: ibid, SP 28/50, fo. 326.

8   Fry claimed arrears of pay together with Captain Fish ibid, E 121/4/8/54, entries 10-11.

4th Regiment	Name	Military career
Colonel	XXX O'Connelly	
Capt. Lt.		
Ens.		
Lt.Col.	Owen O'Connelly	
Lt.		
Ens.		
Major		
Lt.		
Ens.		
Captain	Charles O'Hara	Capt. 4th regt. F. N.M. army
Lt.	Bedingfield Creamer	Ens. to Capt. O'Hara
Ens.		
Captain	Richard Barnard	Lt. to Capt. William Stratton's co. 4th regt. F.
Lt.	Hercules Langford	
Ens.	George Wallis	
Captain	John Togwell	Lt. to Capt. John Boyce's co. ditto
Lt.	Richard Taylor	Quartermaster to the regt.
Ens.	William Pearce	
Captain	John Matthews[9]	Lt. to Capt. Isaac Smith's co. ditto
Lt.	Francis Bateman	Ensign N.M. army 5/47
Ens.	Robert Thomas	
Captain	John Thompson	Lt. to Major Robert Saunders's co. ditto
Lt.	Thomas Wood	Ens. to Major Saunders
Ens.	John Holsworth	
Captain	Joseph Slater[10]	Lt. to Capt. Edmund Rolfe's co. ditto
Lt.		
Ens.		

9   This company with the full complement of commissioned officers was stationed at Newport Pagnell in 6/47: ibid, SP 28/126, fo. 93.

10   Slater was in command of a company in 6/47: ibid, fo. 143.

A petition addressed to Sir Thomas Fairfax in June 1647 was signed by other officers who claimed to have served in the New Model Army but were not named in the list reproduced above. They may, of course, have been non-commissioned rather than commissioned officers.[ii]

Herbert's Regiment

| Lieutenants | XXX Caine
John Bissell
Jervis Murray
Timothy Clare | 8th regiment of foot[11]| |
| Ensigns | Robert Chaffe
Andrew Finch
Bryan Elton |

8th regiment of foot |

11   TNA, SP 16/539, fo. 349.

Kempson's Regiment

| Ensigns | James Short
James Stampe
James Williams | |

Appendix III

Major General Skippon's Bristol Regiment

From the autumn of 1645 until he resigned all his commands in the New Model army in early 1649, Skippon was colonel of a second regiment through his commission as governor of Bristol. It does not seem to have been ten companies strong.[i]

There appears to have been little or no overlap in officers between Skippon's Bristol regiment and his regiment in the field army. This is not surprising as the latter was for most of the time in garrison at Newcastle at the opposite end of the country. The names of the officers in Skippon's second regiment appear in the following places in addition to those given below: TNA, E 121/2/3/28A, entries 12, 27, 31; ibid, E 121/2/3/unnumbered, entry 44; and ibid, E121/3/5/81, unnumbered.

Claims for pay arrears give little indication of the time each officer spent in the regiment. However, Rolfe, Norris, Eaton and Harbottle were in post in July 1646 when their companies were withdrawn from Bristol to participate in the siege of Monmouthshire garrisons such as Raglan Castle which were still held by the king's forces.[ii]

Foot

Colonel	Phillip Skippon[1]	
Lt. Col.	William Rolfe[2]	
Major	Samuel Clarke[3]	
Captains	Abel Kelly[4]	? Capt. Lt.
	XXX Morris	Probably Thomas Norris
	Latimer Sampson[5]	
	XXX Beale[6]	
	Thomas Norris[7]	
	XXX Harbottle	
	XXX Eaton	
Capt. Lt.	XXX	

1   Skippon was governor of the fort and castle at Bristol: ibid, E 121/1/2/44B, entry 23.
2   Ibid, E 121/3/3/78, entry 4.
3   He and Captain Thomas Norris were at Bristol in 8/47: BL, Thomason Tracts, The Moderate, 8/47
4   TNA, E 121/3/3/78, entry 5; ibid, E 121/2/3/28A, entry 31.
5   Sampson was governor of the castle and fort at Bristol in 8/49: ibid, SP 28/62, fo. 341.
6   Ibid, SP 28/57, fo. 453; ibid, SP 28/61, fo. 590; Worc. College, Clarke Ms 69, unfol. 5/6/49.
7   TNA, E 121/4/5/94B, entry 12. Norris had served in Colonel Pickering's regiment of dragoons in the Eastern Association army: ibid, E 121/4/5/94A, entries 11-12.

---

i   There were four companies of foot in Bristol in 11/49: TNA, SP 28/64, fo. 134.
ii BL, Thomason Tracts E 506 (19).

Horse

Capt. Lt.	John Elliott[8]		

8   Ibid, E 121/3/6/357, entry 216.

Appendix IV

Regiments added to the New Model Army in 1647, 1648 and 1649

August 1647–April 1648

13th Regiment[1]	Name	Military Career
Colonel	Robert Tichbourne[2]	Capt., then col.? Yellow Regt. London Trained Bands| Replaced by Col. Simon Needham, ex of the N. Army, who was X at the siege of Colchester in 6/48|
Lt. Colonel	William Shambrook	Major, Tower Hamlets Auxiliary Regt., London Trained Bands|Col. of the regt. 6/48 in succession to Simon Needham. X at the siege of Colchester 7/48. Succeeded as col. by Col. Thomas Rainborough|
Major	Timothy Wilkes	London Trained Bands officer[3]|
Captains	William Billars	Officer of the ordnance[4]|
	Francis Massey/Maizy	London Trained Bands officer|
	XXX Gardiner[5]	XXX
Capt. Lt	Richard Stevens	XXX Succeeded by XXX Ferrialis by 4/48|

1. The New Model Army committee which recommended promotions wanted the regiment to be drawn largely from the ordnance wing of the army. The two companies of firelocks which guarded the train of artillery were to provide companies for the lieutenant colonel and major (not named) whilst two more were to be commanded by officials, Billars and Tomkins: Worc. College, Clarke Ms 66, fos. 26, 31. In the event Billars seems to have taken over from Robinson with Tomkins's company joining the regiment later. A full list of the company commanders when Tichbourne was colonel is given in Perfect Occurences, issue 35, 27/8-4/9/47.
2. Tichbourne, an alderman of the city of London, withdrew when it became apparent that the regiment was to be used in the field: F. and D. This was after 4/48: TNA, SP 28/53, fo. 465. All four ex-trained band officers had been expelled by the London Militia Committee in 6/47: Clarke Papers i, pp. 151-6.
3. For Wilkes's military background, see F. and D.
4. He was clerk of the deliveries in the office of the ordnance: Perfect Occurences, issue 31, 30/7-6/8/47.
5. Gardiner was described in late 1647 as captain lieutenant to the governor of the Tower: Worc. College, Clarke Ms 66, fo. 31.

New Companies[6]		
Captains	Edward Tomkins[7]	Artillery officer|
	Richard Stevens[8]	Capt. Lt. in 47, his co. was raised by 4/48|
	John Overstreet	XXX Capt. in the regt. in 6/48[9]
	XXX Watson	XXX Ditto[10]

6. Four companies under Major Wilkes were added to the original six companies in 29/4/48: TNA, SP 28/54, fos. 168, 224. The reason was serious rioting in London: F. and D
7. Tomkins was an ordinance officer who became commander of that branch of the army in Ireland. He held the post throughout the 1650s: CSPD 1649-50, p. 237; TNA, SP 28/112, fo. 231. One of his soldiers was killed during the siege of Colchester: ibid, SP28/58, fo. 602.
8. Clarke Papers i, pp. 153, 155.
9. Chequers Ms. 782, fo. 89.

10   Thoresby Society 11 (1904) pp. 170, 204.

September 1648

Colonel	Thomas Rainborough	X at Doncaster 10/48|
Lt. Colonel	George Cooke[11]	New England settler. Prob. appointed by Needham or Rainborough|Col. of this regt. 12/48. Gov. of Wexford 50. X by Irish guerrillas 4/52|
Major	Timothy Wilkes[12]	Lt. Col. of the regt. under Col. Cooke. Did not go to Ireland. Later lt. col. and col. of the 11th regt. F.|
Captains	John Overstreet	Later major in the regt.|
	William Billars[13]	
	Richard Stevens[14]	
	XXX Walters[15]	XXX
	Edward Tomkins	
	XXX Price[16]	XXX
	William Walker?[17]	XXX
Capt. Lt.	John Smith[18]	XXX
Possibles Captains	XXX Combie?[19]	XXX
	Henry Harbottle[20]	XXX

11   The regiment left for Ireland in 8/49 but ceased to exist as an independent unit c. 1652. See F. and D. pp. 581-2 for speculation about its fate.

12   Wilkes was lieutenant colonel in the regiment by 12/48: TNA, SP 28/57, fo. 472.

13   This is almost certainly the Captain Billars who sat on the council of war on 29/12/48 and was ordered to march from Sandwich to the Tower of London in 6/49: Worc. College, Clarke Ms 16, fo. 64; ibid, Clarke Ms 69, unfol. The company remained in England where it was attached to Colonel Robert Gibbon's regiment raised in the spring of 1650: CSPD 1650, p. 163. When that regiment was disbanded in 1651, it was transferred to the 6th regiment of foot: ibid, 1651, pp. 49, 188.

14   A man of this name was lieutenant colonel of foot in Ireland in Colonel Axtell's regiment by 1654: BL, Additional Ms 35102, fo. 49.

15   Walters's company was quartered in Surrey for part of 1648: TNA, SP 28/57, fo. 42.

16   This officer was named by Captain Lieutenant Smith as taking part in the siege of Colchester: BL, Thomason Tracts, E 472 (25).

17   Walker was captain by 6/49: Chequers Ms 782, fo. 95.

18   Ibid, Thomason Tracts E 472 (25).

19   Combie, Walker and Barrington were named as being in Colonel George Cooke's regiment prior to its being chosen for service in Ireland, but they may not have been in place until after Cooke had been commissioned: Worc. College, Clarke Ms 67, fo. 14. Combie may be the Captain Solomon Comby serving in Colonel Sadlier's regiment in Ireland in 1655 together with Lieutenant Colonel Overstreet and Major Walker: BL, Additional Ms 35102, fo. 34; Nickolls, Original Letters and Papers, p. 144.

20   Harbottle and Captains Thomas and William Walker were campaigning in Ireland in c. 1/50: Gilbert, Contemporary History iii, pp. 161-2. Harbottle may have originally been in the Bristol garrison. For this, see above p. 157.

September 1649

Colonel	George Cooke[21]	
Lt. Colonel	William Throckmorton[22]	Lt. Col. Edward Harley's Herefordshire regt. 44-5[23]|
Major	John Overstreet	Major by 9/49; Lt. Col. in Ireland in or before 1655[24]|
Captains	Edward Tomkins	
	William Walker	
	Henry Harbottle	
	XXX Combie[25]	
	Henry Cope/Cooper[26]	XXX
	Alexander Staples[27]	XXX
	XXX	

Capt. Lt.	Thomas Barrington[28]	XXX

21　Cooke was colonel by 1/49: TNA, SP 28/58, fo. 151.

22　Throckmorton signed a petition from officers engaged for Ireland in 7/49: BL, Thomason Tracts E 563 (13). His troops were discharged in c. 4/48 before they could be sent there. At the time he was lieutenant colonel He was lieutenant colonel in the 13th regt. F. by 11/49: Thoresby Society 11, p. 169; TNA, SP 28/64, fo. 26·

23　Spring ii; TNA, E 121/2/11/53, entry 17.

24　Ibid, SP 28/62, fo. 369; BL, Additional Ms 35102, fo. 34.

25　Perfect Occurences, issue 143, 8-9/49.

26　Cooper was captain in the regiment in 10/49: TNA, SP 28/63, fo. 267.

27　Staples was captain in the regiment in 11/49: ibid, SP 28/64, fo. 31.

28　Worc. College, Clarke Ms 67, second foliated section, fo. 14.

Former Northern Brigade Regiments

Infantry[i]

14th Regiment[29]	Name	Military career
Colonel	John Bright	Resigned in 6/50. Succeeded by John Lambert[30]|
Lt. Colonels	Simon Needham[31] William Goodrick[32]	Col. 13th regt. F. | In Lambert's brigade. Lt. Col. by 3/48|
Majors	Andrew Carter[33]	XXX|
Captains	Henry Pownall/Pennell	Capt. Lambert's brigade[34]|
	John Spencer	Ditto|
	John Greenleaf[35]	Ditto|
	Roger Coates[36]	Ditto|
	John Lambert[37]	Ditto|
	Thomas Davile[38]	Ditto|
	John Lawson[39]	Ditto|
	Christopher Skipper[40]	Ditto|
Capt. Lt.	Edward Bradshaw	Lt. to Capt. Godfrey Gimbert in Bright's regt. F.[41]|

Others: Captains John Hewley[ii], William Jackson[iii], Edward Gill[iv], Talbot, Legard and Challoner.[v]

29　A list of the regiment in 3/48 when it was added to the New Model Army payroll gives the names of Lieutenant Colonel Goodrick, Major Carter and Captains Pownall, Legard, Greenby, Daniel, Talbot, Challoner and Coates. Greenby is clearly Greenleaf and Daniel Davile: Perfect Occurences, issue 65, 24-31/3/48.

30　Bright had commanded a regiment in the Army of the North from 1643. He resigned just before the invasion of Scotland. A letter from his officers at York to Adam Baynes in London written in 5/50 suggests very strongly that he was in the process of leaving. The signatories in order were William Goodrich, Henry Pennell, John Greenleaf, John Spencer and John Lambert junior: BL, Additional Ms 21417, fo. 85. A slightly later letter on the same topic also includes the names of Andrew Carter and Christopher Skipper: ibid, fo. 72. This asked Baynes to confer with Captain Coates, who was presumably in London at the time.

31　TNA, E 121/4/8/unnumbered, entry 405. See p. 159 above for his death in action.

32　Ibid, E 121/4/1/30, entry 50. There were two William Goodricks, senior and junior. The former was an infantry officer and a lieutenant colonel in Poyntz's brigade under Colonel Legard, the other a cavalryman: ibid, E 121/1/7/54, entry 2. For Goodrick junior, see p. 163 below.

i　Although all three infantry colonels had commanded regiments in the Northern Army under Lord Fairfax and Sydenham Poyntz, the new Model Army regiments were the product of a drastic remodelling that took place under General Lambert's supervision between the late summer of 1647 and the spring of 1648. As the main principal source for the names of the company commanders is their claims for arrears in TNA, E 121, affixing dates to their time in service is difficult, but I have only included in the regimental listings men who had clearly served in Lambert's brigade in 1647/9 or in the New Model Army thereafter.

ii　Ibid, E 121/4/1/unnumbered, entry 174; ibid, E 121/4/8/30, entry 1.

iii　Jackson was lieutenant to Lieutenant Colonel Needham and then captain in Bright's regiment: ibid, E 121/4/8/unnumbered, entry 6. A Captain Jackson was one of the besiegers of Pontefract Castle in 12/48: Perfect Occurences, issue 103, 15-22/12/48.

iv　Ibid, E 121/4/1/30, entries 36, 409, 445.

v　See above note 29.

33　Carter's company garrisoned Clifford's Tower, York in 10/49: ibid, SP 28/63, fo. 226.

34　For Lieutenant Colonel Goodrick, Major Carter and the captains serving in Lambert's brigade, see ibid, E 121/4/8/30, entries 1, 12, 134, 162, 384; ibid, E121/4/8/B unnumbered, entries 41, 58, 68, 101, 136.

35　ibid, E 121/4/1/unnumbered, entry 64; ibid, E 121/4/8/30, entries 47-9.

36　Ibid, E 121/4/1/unnumbered, entry 489. Coates left the regiment in 3/50, but was still seen as willing to act on the regiment's behalf. See above and Worc. College, Clarke Ms 69, unfol.

37　Entry 46 in TNA, E 121/4/1/30 suggests that Lambert was captain lieutenant in the Army of the North, not in the New Model, but this is not so clear in ibid, E 121/5/5/28, entry 4.

38　Davile had been captain in Thornton's regiment in the Army of the North: ibid, E 121/4/1/30, entry 273.

39　Richard Rokeby succeeded to Captain Lawson's company on 1/5/50; Worc. College, Clarke Ms 69, unfol.

40　TNA, E 121/4/1/30, entry 108.

41　Gimbert's company served in the Scarborough garrison: ibid, E 121/4/1/30, entry 278.

15th Regiment	Name	Military career
Colonel	John Maleverer[42]	D 12/50. Succeeded by Major General Richard Deane|
Lt. Colonel	Thomas Oram[43] XXX Walters	Lt. Col. in 8/49[44]|
Major	XXX Linford[45] Thomas Oram	
Captains	John (Devis) Pepper[46]	Capt. Col. Boynton's regt. N. Army[47]|
	Richard Wisdom[48]	In this regt. in Lambert's brigade|
	William Siddall	Succeeded to William Mitchell's co. in c. 47. Later in Lambert's brigade[49]|
	William Walters[50]	XXX. Capt. 8/49. Major 56-9|
	Robert Walton	XXX
	Richard Webbe[51]	
	Henry Cleare	XXX
Capt. Lt.	XXX	

Others: Captains John Pye[vi], Edward Wingate[vii], John Northend[viii], XXX Richardson[ix], Timothy Scarth.

42　The origins of Maleverer's New Model Army regiment are obscure. He had a regiment in the Hull garrison in 1644. The names of the company commanders survive but only Captains Northend and Wingate were under his command in 1648: TNA, SP 28/301, fos. 703-82. Probably Richard Overton took over Maleverer's regiment when he became garrison commander at Hull in 1648 with Maleverer being given a new regiment recruited from stray companies in the north. It then took part in the siege of Pontefract, but it was not put on the New Model Army payroll until 2/49: CJ vi, p. 139.

43　Oram had been lieutenant colonel in Overton's regiment, presumably in Pontefract castle. He then became lieutenant colonel and major in Maleverer's field regiment apparently in that order: TNA, E 121/4/3/63, entry 8. A Lieutenant Colonel Gates's claim for pay arrears appears in ibid, E 121/4/1/16, unnumbered, but he served under Maleverer in Hull garrison not in the marching army: ibid, SP 28/301, fo. 752.

44　Ibid, SP 28/133/3, fo. 30.

45　Ibid, E 121/2/5/35B, entry 13.

46　Pepper and the other six captains appear in a listing of the regiment dating from 6/50 or earlier. It does not give the names of the field officers: Worc. College, Clarke Ms 67, fos. 28, 40.

47　TNA, E 121/4/8/30, entry 95.

48　Ibid, E 121/4/1/30, entry 34; ibid, E 121/3/1/57, entry 47. Wisdom was still captain in the regiment in 2/51: Akerman, *Letters of Roundhead Officers*, p. 9.

49　TNA, E 121/4/1/30, entries 36, 153. Siddall had command of the company previously commanded by Captains John Fitzwilliam and William Mitchell.

50　Ibid, SP 28/133/3, fo. 30.

51　Webbe is mentioned in the Newcastle garrison accounts from late 1648 onwards: ibid, SP 28/133/4, passim; ibid, SP 28/133/3, fo. 30.

---

vi　Ibid, E 121/3/3/90, entry 1. Pye was a captain in Hartlepool garrison in 8/49: ibid, SP 28/133/3, fo. 30.

vii　Ibid, E 121/3/3/90, entry 1. Wingate was in the regiment at Hull in 8/44: ibid, SP 28/301, fos. 73, 715, 732.

viii　Northend had served as lieutenant to Major Goodrich and captain in Maleverer and Overton's regiment in the Hull garrison: ibid, E 121/5/5/37, entry 2; ibid, E 121/3/4/unnumbered, entry 13.

ix　Like Scarth Richardson claimed arrears as captain in Overton's regiment: ibid, E 121/4/1/37, fos. 29, 31. If his first name was Michael, he was to have a long and distinguished career in the New Model Army: F. and D.

16th Regiment	Name	Military career
Colonel	Charles Fairfax[52]	
Lt. Colonel	William Crooke[53]	Major in Lord Fairfax's regt. N. army|
Major	Christopher Copperthwaite?[54]	Major in Lord Fairfax's and Col. Thornton's regts. N. army[55]|
Captains	John Pym?	In the regt. in 6/53|
	XXX Sutton?[56]	In Lambert's brigade and in the regt. in 12/50|
	XXX Wilkinson?	
	Samuel Poole?	In the regt. in 12/50|
	Robert Everard?	
	XXX Freeman?	
	XXX Sanders[57]	In Lambert's brigade|
Capt. Lt.	XXX	

Others: Captains Richard Dineley[x], William Fuggill[xi], XXX Blacker[xii]

52 Even less is known about Fairfax's regiment than Maleverer's. It was been raised in Yorkshire in the spring of 1648, and taken onto the New Model Army payroll in 2/49: BL, Additional Ms 21419, fo. 13; CJ vi, p. 139. This may explain why there are very few claims for pay arrears in the E 121 series. Like Maleverer's regiment it had taken part in the siege of Pontefract.

53 William Crook signed the terms for the surrender of Pontefract in 3/49: BL, Thomason Tracts, E 548 (25).

54 Copperthwaite was major in the regiment by 4/50: CCC i, p. 197.

55 TNA, E 121/4/1/unnumbered, entry 207.

56 Ibid, E 121/4/1/30, entry 160; ibid, SP 28/73, fo. 34.

57 Ibid, E 121/4/1/30, entry 54.

Cavalry[xiii]

12th Regiment[58]	Name	Military Career
Colonel	John Lambert	
Major	William Rooksby	Major Copley's regt. H. N. Army 5/47, then in Lambert's regt. in Lambert's brigade[59]|
Captains	William Goodrick	Capt. Sir William Constable's regt. H. N. army 4/45. In Lambert's brigade|
	Henry Westby	In Lambert's brigade in 12/48[60]|
	Adam Baynes	Capt. in Copley's regt. H. In Lambert's brigade in 12/48[61]|
	Amor Stoddard	Capt. Lt. in Lilburne's regt. H. N. army and then briefly capt. 3rd regt. F. N.M. Army. Served in Lambert's brigade[62]|
Capt. Lt.	John Pockley	Capt. Lt. in Lambert's brigade[63]|

58 Major Rooksby and Captains Westby, Goodrick, Bradford and Stoddard are listed in 3/48 when the regiment joined the New Model Army: Perfect Occurences, issue 65, 24-31/3/48.

59 TNA, E 121/4/1/30, entry 1.

60 Soldiers served under Westby in Lambeth's regiment in Lambeth's brigade. See, for example, ibid, E 121/4/1/30, entry 115; ibid, E 121/4/5/94b, entry 4. He is named as a captain in the regiment in 3/47: Perfect Occurences, issue 65.

61 Ibid, E 121/4/1/unnumbered, entry 1; ibid, E 121/4/1/30, entries 479-80. Baynes was in Lambert's regiment besieging Pontefract in 12/48: Perfect Occurences, issue 103, 15-22/12/48; York Minster Library (YML), Hailstone Mss BB 53, unfol. 4/12/48.

x Dineley had served as captain in Colonel Thornton's regiment in the Army of the North: ibid, E 121/4/3/66, entry 6; ibid, E 121/2/2/unnumbered, entries 15-16.

xi Fuggill had previously been captain in Colonel Legas's regiment in the Army of the North: ibid, E 121/4/1/37, entry 19; ibid, E 121/5/5/28, entry 90.

xii Perfect Occurences, issue 47, 19-26/11/47.

xiii As with the infantry, there had been considerable remodelling in the former Northern Army cavalry regiments in 1647 and 1648 with both Lambert and Lilburne becoming colonels of horse once again after serving briefly in the New Model Army as colonels of foot.

62 Stoddard was back in the north in time to serve under Lambert in 1648: ibid, E 121/3/1/57, entry 146; ibid, E 121/4/8/unnumbered, entry 406.

63 Ibid, E 121/4/8/30, entry 99; YML, Hailstone Mss BB 53, unfol. (resolution of officers in the Northern brigade, 12/48). Pockley was a full captain before 2/51. He may have become captain on Goodrick's promotion: TNA, E 121/4/1/unnumbered, entry 140 (Lieutenant Richard Purseglove's arrears). Purseglove served as cornet and lieutenant to Goodrick and then as lieutenant to Pockley.

13th Regiment[64]	Name	Military career
Colonel	Robert Lilburne	
Major	George Smithson	In Lambert's brigade[65]
Captains	John Sanderson	Major Col. Wrenn's regt. H. N. army| Died c.10/50.[66] George Watkinson prob. took over his troop|
	Thomas Lilburne	In Lambert's brigade[67]
	William Bradford[68]	Capt. in Copley's regt. H. N. army|
	Christopher Lister[69]	Ditto|
Capt. Lt.	XXX[70]	
Possible Captain	XXX Cholmley[71]	

64 The list in Perfect Occurences, issue 65 gives Major Smithson and Captains Sanderson and Lilburne, but also Captain Cholmley and a blank. Cholmley appears to be a mistake. A Major Cholmley operated with troops from Lilburne's regiment but was not necessarily of that regiment.

65 TNA, E 121/1/7/57, entry 26. Smithson had previously served as major in General Sydenham Poyntz's regiment in the Northern Army: ibid, E 121/2/11/1B, entry 5. He was major in Lilburne's regiment by 7/50: F. and D.

66 For Sanderson's death, see P. Hill and J. Watkinson, *Major Sanderson's War* (Stroud, 2008), p. 71.

67 TNA, E 121/1/7/57, entry 54.

68 Bradford fought in Robert Lilburne's regiment of horse in 1645 and later in Lambert's brigade: ibid SP 28/122, fos 390-410; ibid, E 121/4/1/unnumbered, entry 30; ibid, E 121/1/7/57, entry 7. He commanded a troop in the regiment in 1648 and in 12/50: Hill and Watkinson, *Major Sanderson's War*, pp. 85, 127; TNA, SP 28/73, fo. 24.

69 A list of the officers in three of the troops, those of Captains Lilburne, Bradford and Lister, with Wilkinson as lieutenant to Lister, occurs in ibid, E 121/3/3/23, entries 27-31.

70 Hill and Watkinson make quite a convincing case for Wilkinson as captain lieutenant: Major Sanderson's War, p.28. However the evidence cited under the previous footnote shows that this was not the case.

71 Perfect Occurences, issue 65, 24-31/3/47. Hill and Watkinson are of the opinion that Captain Cholmley did not fight in the regiment but acknowledge a second source which says that he did. Cholmley's troop was almost certainly the one in garrison at Greystoke Castle, Cumberland with Colonel Thomas Cholmley as the commander and John Cholmley junior as lieutenant. I am of the opinion that the Greystoke castle troop was attached to Lilburne's regiment for a time, but then returned home prior to the Preston campaign in which John Cholmley junior was killed. He was described as major because he held that rank in Thomas Cholmley's infantry regiment, but whether he was in command of his company or serving as a volunteer is not yet known: Major Sanderson's War, pp. 11, 166-7; J. Hodgson, *Memoirs* (1994 reprint), p. 16; TNA, SP 28/140, pt. 13.

14th Regiment[72]		
Colonel	Francis Thornhaugh	Col. Nottinghamshire regt. H.|X in the pursuit after the battle of Preston 8/48. Replaced by Saunders as col.|
Major	Thomas Saunders[73]	Capt. Derbyshire H.| Succeeded as major by Richard Creed by 12/48[74]|
Captains	Phillip Pendock	Capt. John Hutchinson's regt. H. Nottingham garr.|Left Thornhaugh's regt. c. 1/49[75]|
	George Palmer	XXX
	Richard Creed[76]	Capt. in Col. Coleman's Warwickshire regt. H.| Succeeded as major on Saunders's promotion|
	Richard Dolphin	Succeeded Capt. John Wright| Succeeded by Philip Prime[77]|
Capt. Lt.	John Pearson[78] Robert Hope[79]	XXX Capt. in the regt. by 54|

72 For a list of the troop commanders prior to Thornhaugh's death see Worc. College, Clarke Ms 67, fo. 47.

73 This man should not be confused with the Major Thomas Saunders who served in the southwest of England, first under Colonel Seeley at Lyme and then in the fort at Exmouth: TNA, E 121/1/7/42B, entry 4; ibid, E 121/1/7/46D, entry 5.

74 Ibid, SP 28/57, fo. 447.

75 Ibid, E 121/1/2/41, entry 3. For his previous regiment see ibid, E121/1/6/66, entry 37.

76 Ibid, E 121/3/4/unnumbered, entry 28; ibid, E 121/5/1/22, entries 2-3, 35.

77 Dolphin was a captain in the regiment in 3/49: Perfect Occurences, issue 114, 3/49.

78 Pearson was in post before Thornhaugh's death: Worc. College, Clarke Ms 67, fo. 47.

79 Hope had preceded Pearson but then left the regiment: TNA, E121/1/6/unnumbered, entry 9. He seems previously to have been in Sir John Gell's regiment: ibid, E 121/4/6/16B, entry 14.

15th Regiment	Name	Military Career
Colonel	Francis Hacker[80]	
Major	John Mayer[81]	Major in 11/49|
Captains	Richard Crackanthorpe[82]	
	John Fenwick[83]	Capt. in 11/49|
	John Wetwang[84]	Ditto|
	William Hobart/ Hubbart[85]	Ditto|
Capt. Lt.	XXX	

80 Hacker had held the rank of colonel as early as 10/44 when he commanded all the horse and foot in Leicestershire: Luke, Letter Books, p. 350. He also had a connection with the Leicester garrison: TNA, E 121/3/6/357, entries 100-1. In 6/48 he was described as colonel of the Leicestershire horse when he fought under Colonel Rossiter's command at Willoughby: BL, Thomason Tracts, E 451 (19). However, the names of his captains suggest very strongly that his New Model Army regiment came from the extreme north of England.

81 Mayer, Fenwick, Wetwang and Hobart were all troop commanders in Hacker's regiment in 10 and 11/49: CSPD 1649, pp. 366, 397. At the time the regiment was intended to serve in Ireland but it did not go there.

82 Crackanthorpe's commission was issued on 20/4/49: Worc. College, Clarke Ms 69, unfol. He was a militia officer in Westmorland.

83 Ibid, Clarke Ms 69, unfol. 7/5/50.

84 A John Wetwang was in the Northumberland horse in 10/48: BL, Thomason Tracts E 475 (13).

85 A listing of forces for the Irish expedition drawn up earlier in the year shows that Hubbard succeeded Captain Henry Ogle: Worc. College, Clarke Ms 67, fo. 46. Ogle too seems to have had connections with Northumberland: F. and D.

Appendix V

Junior Officers in Post between April 1645 and February 1647

Foot

Officer and regiment	Company or Troop Commander	Explanation
1st Regiment		
Capt. Lt. XXX Fortescue		Left c. 12/45[1]
Lt. Thomas Wolfe	Capt. XXX Maneste	Promoted to capt.
2nd Regiment		
Lt. XXX Norman	Lt. Col. John Francis	X at Naseby
Ens. XXX Green	Ditto	Ditto
Lt. William Symonds	Capt. Lt.	Promoted to capt.
Lt. Thomas Buxton		X at Sherborne siege 8/45[2]
3rd Regiment		
Lt. Robert Wilkinson[3]	Capt. Thomas Smith	
Ens. George Scale[4]	Ditto	
Lt. Phillip Ebzery		Promoted to capt.
Ens. Samuel Burgess[5]		
5th Regiment		
Lt. Richard Pooley		Promoted to capt.
Lt. Francis Jackson[6]	Capt. Edward Gittins	
Ens. William Batty[7]	Ditto	
6th Regiment		
Lt. John Deacon[8]	Capt. Henry Ingoldsby	X at Tiverton
7th Regiment		
Lt. Henry Whittle	Capt. John Crosse	Promoted to capt.
Capt. Lt. XXX Fleming		X at the siege of Sherborne
Lt. Joseph Crosse[9]	Capt. Henry Whittle	X at the siege of Woodstock
8th Regiment		
Trevor Oliver[10]		
9th Regiment		
Lt. Thomas Parsons[11]	Capt. George Gregson	Promoted to capt.

Officer and regiment	Company or Troop Commander	Explanation
11th Regiment		
Lt. Thomas Bourgh (sic)[12]	Lt. Col. Gray	
12th Regiment		
Lt. John Mowser[13]	Capt. John Jenkins	X at Faringdon 5/45
Lt. Samuel Grime	Capt. Silverwood	Promoted to capt.

1   See note XXX above.
2   TNA, SP28/ 49, fo. 490.
3   Ibid, E 121/1/6, entry 233.
4   Ibid, SP 28/41, fo. 364. Scale served between 7/45 and 7/46 and then retired because of his wounds: ibid, SP 28/49, fo. 224; ibid, SP 28/48, fo. 248.
5   Ibid, SP 28/41, fo. 365.
6   Ibid, E 121/2/9/64, entry 258.
7   Ibid, SP 28/265, fo. 427.
8   ibid, SP 28/59, fos. 218-20.
9   Crosse was killed in 4/46: ibid, SP 28/49, fo. 506.
10 Oliver lost a leg at the storming of Bristol in 9/45 and was discharged: ibid, SP 28/39, fo. 88.
11 Ibid, E 121/4/8/40, entry 592. Parsons began as lieutenant when Holborne was colonel.
12 Bourgh had served under Lord Fairfax and was killed at the storming of Bristol whilst in the 11th regiment of foot: ibid, SP 28/58, fo. 170.
13 Mowser and Jenkins his captain were killed at Faringdon in early May 1645: ibid, SP 28/30, fo. 59.

Horse

Dragoons		
Capt. Lt. William Hext[14]		
Lt. Henry Wayte[15]	Capt. Daniel Abbott	Gone by 3/47
Cavalry		
1st Regiment		
Cor. Thomas Moore	Fairfax's troop	Gone by 3/47[16]
Lt. Edmund Rolfe	Capt. Adam Lawrence	Capt. 8th regt. F. 8/45[17]
Cor. William Malin[18]	Ditto	
Cor. XXX Roberts[19]	Capt. William Packer	
QM Edward Cooke[20]		
2nd Regiment		
Lt. Benjamin Burgess	Capt. Edward Foley	Promoted to capt. 2nd regt. H.
Lt. Henry Pretty[21]	Ditto	Promoted to capt. 11th regt, H.
Lt. Thomas Sparling[22]	Capt. Thomas Pennyfather	X at Naseby
Cor. Thomas Clement[23]	Capt. Walter Parry	
QM Daniel Cleveland[24]	Major Thomas Horton	
3rd Regiment		
Capt. Lt. Thomas Jewkes[25]	Col. James Sheffield	
Cor. George Baldwin[26]	Capt. Gabriel Martin	Possibly in 1st regt. F. by 46
QM Francis Cony[27]	Capt. Robotham	
4th Regiment		
QM Paul Sismore[28]	Capt. James Laughton	
Cor. Richard Aske[29]	Capt. Thomas Howard	Promoted to capt.

6th Regiment		
Capt. Lt. Richard Curzon		Transferred to 5th regt. H.
Cor. John Chapman	Capt. John Jenkins	Transferred to 7th regt. H.
Lt. Edward Sharpe[30]	Capt. Henry Middleton	Wounded at Naseby
Lt. William Wyse	Capt. John Reynolds	Gone by 4/46[31]
Lt. Edward Johnson	Capt. Henry Middleton	Gone by 2/47[32]
Lt. Nathaniel Hale	Capt. John Jenkins	Gone post 12/45
QM Nicholas Morrell	Capt. John Jenkins	Gone by 12/46[33]
7th Regiment		
Capt. Lt. Francis Hawes		Promoted to capt.
Lt. Roger Hopkins	Major John Alford	Gone by 12/46[34]
Lt. George Wauton	Capt. Thomas Ireton	Gone before 3/47[35]
Lt. Seymour Altoffe[36]	Capt. Azariah Husbands	
9th Regiment		
Capt. Lt. William Evanson		Promoted to capt.
Lt. John Pitchford	Major Christopher Bethell	Promoted to capt.
Cor. Michael Thompson	Ditto	Left regt.
Cor. John Nix	Capt. Henry Cannon	Left regt.
10th Regiment		
Cor. Brinsley Lewis	Major General Phillip Skippon	D c. 9/45[37]
Capt. Lt. Edward Lewis	Ditto	Gone by late 46[38]
QM Gilbert Taylor	Ditto	Gone by early 47[39]
Lt. XXX Ellis[40]	Adj. Gen. Christopher Fleming	
11th Regiment		
Lt. Godfrey Pyard[41]		Last record 8/45

14 Hext had been a corporal in Okey's troop in Haselrig's regiment in the Eastern Association army and he received pay for Okey's troop as a lieutenant in 5/45: ibid, SP 28/31, fo. 293; ibid, E 121/1/1/26B, entry 259. However, in his claim for pay arrears he stated that he had served as cornet and lieutenant in Captain Barrington's troop, but Barrington was not a troop commander until c. 6/47. As Hext's commission as lieutenant to Barrington is recorded in the commission book, all I can surmise is either that Hext had resigned and been reappointed or that he should have been described as cornet in 5/45.

15 Wayte was lieutenant in 9/45: Ibid, SP 28/32, fo. 159. However, Francis Bolton was Abbott's lieutenant by 4/47. See p. 120 above.

16 Peter Wallis was lieutenant of the troop in 3/47: BL, Thomason Tracts E 390 (3).

17 See p. 67 above.

18 Malin was cornet in 10/45: TNA, SP 28/32, fo. 219. He was not in the regiment in the spring of 1647 but returned a little later as a lieutenant: Worc. College, Clarke Ms 67, fo. 15.

19 Roberts was wounded at Naseby: TNA, SP 28/44, fo. 189. Samuel Packer had replaced him by 3/47: BL, Thomason Tracts, E390 (3).

20 TNA, E 121/5/7/unnumbered, entry 144. He was cornet in 4/46: ibid, WO55/1646, unfol. section. George Hayes had replaced him by 4/47.

21 Ibid, SP 28/253/A/1, fo. 46.

22 Sparling died of wounds received at Naseby: ibid, SP 28/173/1, fo. 14.

23 Clement signed for Perry's troop in 4/45 and later: ibid, SP 28/29, fo. 103; ibid, SP 28/30, fo. 191.

24 Ibid, SP 28/33, fo. 113.

25 W.S. Library, SMS 463, unfol. 12/4/45.

26 TNA, E 121/4/1/61, entry 14.

27 W.S. Library, SMS 463, unfol. 12/4/45.

28 TNA, SP 28/31, fo. 218; ibid, SP 28/39, fo. 58. He was quartermaster in 7/45 and later cornet in the troop, but by 3/47 Samuel Boalley was cornet and Nathaniel Phillips quartermaster: BL, Thomason Tracts E 390 (3), (26).

29 Aske had previously been a gentleman in the Earl of Essex's Lifeguard: TNA, E 121/1/6/63, entries 67, 89. He had become captain of a company in the 3rd regiment of foot by 12/46: Sprigg, Anglia Rediviva, p. 329.

30   TNA, SP 28/173/1, fo. 11.

31   Ibid, SP 28/38, fo. 70.

32   W.S. Library, SMS 463, unfol. 19/4/45; TNA, SP 28/44, fo. 408.

33   For Hale and Morrell, see ibid, SP 28/41, fos. 42, 583.

34   Ibid, SP 28/41, fos. 2, 549.

35   Edward Lisle had replaced him as lieutenant of the troop by 3/47. For this see p. 143 above.

36   Altoffe had left before 3/47 when John Merriman was lieutenant of the troop.

37   Lewis died of wounds sustained at the battle of Langport: TNA, SP 28/55, fo. 63.

38   He held that command from 14/6/44 until 29/9/46: ibid, SP 28/56, fos. 193-4. See also ibid, E 121/3/3/82, entry 5.

39   Ibid, SP 28/41, fo. 290.

40   Ibid, SP 28/140/7, fos. 283-5.

41   Ibid, SP 28/31, fo. 96.

Bibliography

Principal Primary Sources in Manuscript
The National Archives: E 121, E 315, SP 16, SP 28, WO 55
British Library: Additional Mss 11132,21417, 35102; Harleian Mss 166, 427; Sloane Ms 1719
Bodleian Library, Oxford: Tanner Mss 57-60.
House of Lords Library: Main Papers
William Salt Library, Stafford
Worcester College Library, Oxford: Clarke Mss; Clarke Mss microfilms
York Minster Library: Hailstone Mss

Printed Primary and Selective Secondary Sources
Abbott, W.C., *The Writings and Speeches of Oliver Cromwell* (Cambridge MA: Harvard University Press, 1937, 4
    volumes)
Adair, J., *Cheriton 1644: the Campaign and the Battle* (Kineton: Roundwood Press, 1973)
Akerman, J. (ed.), *Letters of Roundhead Officers written from Scotland* (Edinburgh: Bannatyne Club, 1856)
Calendar of State Papers Domestic: HMSO
Carlyle, Thomas, *Oliver Cromwell's Letters and Speeches* (London: Chapman & Hall, 1849, 3rd ed., 3 volumes)
Davies, G. (ed.) 'The Army of the Eastern Association 1644-5', *English Historical Review* vol. 46 (1921)
Davies, G., 'The Quarters of the English Army in Scotland in 1656', *Scottish Historical Review* 10 (1923)
Dore, R.N., *The Letter Books of Sir William Brereton* (Record Society of Lancashire and Cheshire volumes 123 &
    128) (Gloucester: Printed for Lancashire and Cheshire Record Society by Alan Sutton, 1984, 1990, 2 volumes)
Dunlop, R., *Ireland under the Commonwealth* (Manchester: Manchester University Press, 1913, 2 volumes)
Firth, C.H. (ed.), *The Clarke papers: selections from the papers of William Clarke* (London, Camden Society 4th
    series, 1891-1901, 4 volumes)
Firth, C.H., *Cromwell's Army* (London: Methuen, 1962, 4th ed.)
Firth, C.H. & G. Davies, *Regimental History of Cromwell's Army* (Oxford: Oxford University Press, 1940, 2
    volumes)
Gentles, I., *The New Model Army 1645-53* (Cambridge: Cambridge University Press, 1992)
Gentles, I., 'The New Model Officer Corps in 1647: a collective portrait', *Social History* 22 (1997)
Gilbert, Sir John, *A Contemporary History of Affairs in Ireland 1641-1652* (Dublin: Irish Archaeological Society,
    1879-81, 3 volumes)
Green, Mary Anne Everett (ed.), *Calendar of proceedings of the Committee for Advance of Money, 1642-1656
    preserved in the State Paper Department of Her Majesty's Public Record Office* (London: For H.M.S.O. by Eyre
    and Spottiswoode, 1888, 3 volumes)
Green, Mary Anne Everett (ed.), *Calendar of the proceedings of the Committee for Compounding with Delinquents,
    1643-1660* (London: H.M.S.O., 1889-93, 5 volumes)
Hill, P.R. & J.M. Watkinson, *Major Sanderson's War* (Stroud: Spellmount, 2008)
Historical Manuscripts Commission, *Report on the manuscripts of His Grace the Duke of Portland, preserved*

at Welbeck Abbey. Appendix to the 13th Report, volume 1 (London: Printed for H.M.S.O., by Eyre and Spottiswoode, 1891-)

Holmes, C., *The Eastern Association in the English Civil War* (London: Cambridge University Press, 1973)

Hughes, A., *Politics, Society and the Civil Wars in Warwickshire 1620-1660* (Cambridge: Cambridge University Press, 1987)

Kishlansky, M., *The Rise of the New Model Army* (Cambridge: Cambridge University Press, 1979)

Journals of the House of Commons volumes IV-VII

Journal of the House of Lords Volumes VII-X.

Tibbutt, H. (ed.), *The Letter Books of Sir Samuel Luke* (Bedford: Bedfordshire Historical Record Society, 1963)

Nickolls, J., *Original Letters and Papers of State Addressed to Oliver Cromwell* (London: Printed by William Bowyer, and sold by John Whiston, 1743)

The Parliamentary or Constitutional History of England, being a faithful account of all the most remarkable transactions in Parliament from the earliest times (to the dissolution of the convention Parliament that restored king Charles II., together with an appendix). By several hands. (cited as *The Old Parliamentary History of England*) (London: Printed for J. and R. Tonson, and A. Millar and W. Sandby, 1761-63, 12 volumes)

Peachey, S. & A. Turton, *Old Robin's Foot: the equipping and campaigns of Essex's Infantry 1642-1645* (Leigh-on-Sea: Partizan Press, 1987)

Peacock, E., *The Army Lists of the Roundheads and the Cavaliers* (London: Chatto & Windus, 1874, 2nd ed.)

Phillips, J.R., *Memoirs of the Civil War in Wales and the Marches* (London: Longmans, Green & Co., 1874, 2 volumes)

Rushworth, J., *Historical Collections of Private Passages of State* (London: D. Browne, 1721, 7 volumes)

Sprigg, J., *Anglia Rediviva* (1647, 1854)

Spring, L., *The Regiments of the Eastern Association* (Bristol: Stuart Press, 1998)

Spring, L., *Waller's Army* (Farnham: Pike and Shot Society, 2007)

Symonds, R. (ed. C. Long), *Diaries of the Marches of the Royal Army during the Great Civil War*, (London: Camden Society LXXIV, 1859)

Temple, R., 'The Original Officer List of the New Model Army', *Bulletin of the Institute of Historical Research* LIX (1985)

Thomason Tracts (British Library) searchable online via www.jbooks.

Thomson, J., 'The Impact of the First Civil War on Hertfordshire', *Hertfordshire Record Publications 23* (2007)

Turton, A., *The Chief Strength of the Army: Essex's Horse 1642-45* (Leigh-on-Sea: Partizan Press, n.d. [c.1992])

Warmington, A.R., *Civil War, Interregnum and Restoration in Gloucestershire 1640-1672* (Woodbridge: Boydell Press for the Royal Historical Society, 1997)

Wanklyn, M.D.G., 'Choosing Officers for the New Model Army February to April 1645' *Journal of the Society for Army Historical Research* 92 (2014)

Index of Officers Serving in the New Model Army

Please note that the index does not include the names of officers serving in the earlier armies commanded by the earls of Essex and Manchester and Sir William Waller, who were not given commissions in the New Model Army in 1645.

In Part IV only the names of the lieutenants, cornets, ensigns and quartermasters are indexed. The captains lieutenant and above whose names appear in Part III are not indexed.

Baxter, Thomas   131
Baxter, XXX   131
Bayly, Thomas   108, 126, 141
Bayly, William   100, 115, 131, 154
Baynes, Adam   163
Baynes, Robert   130
Beachamp/Beauchamp, Francis   131, 154
Beale, Henry   117
Beale, XXX   157
Beamont/Beaman, Richard   43, 49, 55, 65
Beasley, Thomas   141
Belcham, Anthony   136
Bellerby, Gabriel   123-4, 141-2
Bennett, John   131
Bernard/Barnard, Richard   115, 155
Bernard, Thomas   142
Berry, James   50, 61, 72, 82, 94, 106-7
Bethell, Christopher   53, 63, 168
Bethell, Walter   29, 61, 72, 82, 93, 105
Bevan, Jenkin   119, 137
Billars, William   159-60
Bird, William   128
Birkham, Herbert   50
Biscoe, John   48, 58, 70, 77, 80, 87, 90, 99, 103
Bishop, John   115
Bissell, John   115, 156
Blackburn, John   130
Blacker, XXX   163
Blackmore, John   45, 107
Blackwell, John   73, 83, 94, 107, 152
Blagrave, John   48
Bland, Michael   55, 65, 76
Blethin, Francis   48, 58, 70, 80, 90-1
Blinkinstone, John,   133
Blisse, Oliver   133-4,
Blissett, Joseph   51-2, 61, 72, 82, 94, 106
Blunt, Richard   125
Boalley, Samuel   123, 168
Bolton, Charles   76, 85, 97, 113
Bolton, Francis   92, 104, 120, 168
Boone, Edward   133
Boteler, William   50
Bough, William   25, 52, 62-3
Bourgh, Thomas   167
Bourne, Richard   118, 136
Bowen, David   130
Bowen, Henry   46-7, 57, 68, 78, 88-9, 100
Bowen, Maurice   44, 55, 57, 65, 76, 85, 97-8, 148
Bowler, William   120
Boyce, John   45, 56, 77
Boyce, Vincent   43, 55, 65, 76, 85
Bradford, William   163-4
Bradshaw, Edward   161
Bragg, Nicholas   53, 63, 74, 84, 96, 105
Braman, John   143
Bramston, John   134
Bramston, William   133
Bray, William   89-90
Brayfield, Alexander   49, 60, 81, 91, 104
Bressie, Benjamin   144

Brewerton, William   127
Bridge, Tobias   50, 60, 71, 81, 92, 104
Bridgen, Samuel   142
Bright, Barnabas   120
Bright, John   161
Broadhurst, William   131
Brookes, Thomas   132
Brookes, XXX   132
Brough, Walter   118-19, 153
Browne, Francis   142
Browne, John I   50, 61, 72, 82, 92, 105
Browne, John II   68, 79, 88-9
Browne, Robert   109, 127, 145
Buck, William   123, 141
Buckenham, John   141
Buckner, Thomas   87-8, 99-100
Bulkham, XXX   50
Bull, Thomas   139
Bulstrode, Thomas   45, 148
Bunting, Paul   125-6
Burgess, Benjamin   82, 93, 105-6, 167
Burgess, Caleb   113
Burgess, Samuel   166
Burkett, XXX   50
Burnett, George   135
Burrell, Richard   136
Bury, John   64, 74
Bush, Peter   134
Bush, Thomas   52, 62, 73
Bush, William   127
Bushell, John   67, 78, 154
Bushy, Christopher   52, 62, 73
Butler, John   50, 61, 72, 82, 93
Butler, Nathaniel   50
Butler, Thomas   85, 98
Butler, XXX   50
Buxton, Thomas   166
Byfield, John   77, 124-5, 142

Cadwell, Matthew   70, 80, 90, 102
Caine, Stephen   47, 58, 69, 79, 154
Cambridge, Owen   94, 106
Camby, Solomon   126
Campfield, Jeremiah   119, 131
Cannon, Henry   44, 63, 74, 84, 95, 108, 168
Cannon, Peter   44
Carde, Ralph   130
Carness, John   124
Carr, Roger   120
Carter, Andrew   161-2
Carter, John   34, 49, 59, 71, 81, 91, 103
Cartledge, William   139
Cartwright, Thomas   103, 134
Cary, Charles   138
Case, Samuel   114, 130
Casse/Cosse, Adam /Andrew   120, 138
Cassinghurst, Thomas   118, 136
Caulfield, William Lord   53-4, 63, 74, 84, 96
Cecil, William   15, 34, 54, 64, 74, 84, 96, 109